HOME
FOOD

Enjoy!

OLIA HERCULES
HOME FOOD

Recipes to Comfort and Connect

Love,
Olia

Photography by Joe Woodhouse

BLOOMSBURY PUBLISHING
LONDON · OXFORD · NEW YORK · NEW DELHI · SYDNEY

Introduction

Someone once asked me to tell them what comfort food means to me.

It took some thought, but eventually it comes down to this: it is when you come home from school, feeling tired or a little low, hoping that your mum would make your favourite dish, and of course she is telepathic, so she makes exactly that thing. Your worries dissolve in a bowl of dumplings, and your neurons get wired and fixed in a way that makes dumpling dough forever a reminder of unconditional love and protection.

I will be honest, I wasn't entirely sure where this book was going to end up when I started writing it, but by the time I finished it was obvious: it is about the feeling of comfort, about the connections that we all make in life though our experiences and memories of meals shared with those we love. And that is what food, and choosing cooking as my livelihood, is all about for me.

I didn't cook as a child growing up in the South of Ukraine, but I ate very well because my mother Olga, my father Petro and my extended family were all so excellent at it. It was only when I left my family and ended up as a student in the UK that I was suddenly drawn to cooking. When phone conversations failed to satisfy my longing for comfort, home and love, cooking my mum's food succeeded. Suddenly, when I cooked, those early-wired neurons in my brain fired up very specific feelings; feelings of wellbeing.

In my last cookbook, I assumed the role of a travel food writer. I felt as though it was my mission to record recipes from the little-known and underrated food culture of Ukraine. I loved the anthropological and societal depth of the research and felt it was important to record recipes that may very soon become obsolete. During the coronavirus pandemic, when travel was no longer possible, I had an opportunity to write a different kind of cookbook. So much of the way that I see the world is shaped by the dishes that I taste, and I have been lucky enough to taste more than one cuisine and sample more than one culture.

 I emigrated twice, once to Cyprus at the age of twelve and once to the UK at the age of eighteen. I also studied Italian at university, so I got to experience life in Italy for a year and a summer. When I ended up in Italy, seeing friends who were my age cook with immense enthusiasm reinforced my interest in cooking.

Eventually, after two degrees, and the beginnings of a career as a journalist, I decided to turn cooking into my work, into my life. I wanted even the hardest physical graft to feel like fun. I was often exhausted and burnt out, but I loved cooking. The feeling of feeding many people at once was like a drug, it made me feel so good. With time, I also became an author and cookery teacher, often telling readers and pupils stories about my family and my childhood. That was an even bigger buzz.

I often wonder what it is that makes me feel this way. I can do no better at an answer than that it is a combination of sensory pleasure, story-telling, connection and the passing on of knowledge and skill.

This book, then, is a reflection of my life in food – from my grandmothers' stories to my own – which has been spent (so far at least) in Ukraine, Cyprus, Italy and the UK. It is a very personal book, but, as always, I love telling other people's stories, so you will find plenty of those within recipe introductions and in the short and poignant reminiscenses written by my friends – some in the food business, some not, but who all share a love of and fascination with food – scattered throughout the book.

All the recipes in this book had to pass two tests. The first was the test of universal deliciousness. I know it sounds obvious, but there are some recipes nestled in each of our lives that are a tad too esoteric to pass that scrutiny. (The sweet vermicelli dishes of Ukraine, or the 'salads' smothered in salad cream of 1970s UK come to mind.) The second important trial a recipe had to pass to get into this book was whether I wanted to get in the kitchen and make it again and again, aka 'the cooking enjoyment factor'.

Some of the recipes here are very easy everyday workhorses, others need a little more time. Some I have been cooking a lot in the past couple of years, others have been fetched back as happy and delicious memories from earlier times in my life. Almost all of them have been significant in the making of me as a person.

All of the dishes have also been cooked and tested many, many times by me, my friends and family, as well as by professional testers. They are 'lived-in' recipes, cooked by and for different people, for individuals, couples, whole families or a crowd. (And, in fact, it's always worth making a recipe that serves more people than you have to feed; it's an unusual soul who ever complains about leftovers…) I do find it difficult to estimate portion sizes, so you should know that all these dishes are intended to serve people who like to eat!

A lot of the recipes are canvases and are presented to you in their simplest form. But you can of course jazz them up, or substitute ingredients according to availability and seasonality. Just think: have you got some tired herbs at the back of the fridge that are not quite slimy and revolting yet, just very forlorn looking? Because they are already so soft and limp, consider blitzing them and adding to a stew, or stirring them through yogurt as a sauce or dip.

Perhaps a recipe calls for celeriac, which you don't have: could you swap in a potato or a parsnip or another starch? Another recipe may call for a specific vinegar or sugar, but unless I state that only this ingredient will work, you will likely be fine to use what you have at hand.

In this book, I am hoping to guide you, give you confidence and encourage you not to feel anxious in the kitchen. There are enough anxieties in life; cooking should be about trying to let go and relax. If something goes slightly wrong, more likely than not it can be fixed, overlooked or learned from!

For some of my favourite – but slightly more technical – recipes, I was keen for you to have me 'at your shoulder' as you cook. So we have created QR codes to take you straight to short videos, in which I guide you through how to roll dumplings, for instance, plait festive yeasted breads, or make delicious, nutty brown butter.

I was very keen to channel my grandmother Vera throughout the book, because she was the most frugal and mindful person: the Economising Queen. So please do look out for special sections I've placed within some of the recipes, with tips on using up leftovers and even transforming them into new meals, or how you can use a recipe with or within another. This accurately reflects the way I cook at home, and it felt natural to add these in for you too.

One of the stories I often tell is about the walnut tree that was right outside the summer kitchen at my other grandmother's house.

My maternal grandmother Lusia was an outstanding cook. She also had six children, so the extended family was huge and we got together often, especially in the summertime. Aunties, uncles, cousins, nephews and nieces would travel from many cities in Ukraine to feast under the walnut tree. (This joyful family scenario continues today, albeit these days under my mum's canopy of wild grapes instead of my grandmother's walnut tree.) We would sit and eat and drink and listen to stories. Some were laugh-out-loud funny, some were so sad we all cried. I often wondered how my grandparents managed to remain so kind and gentle, given all they had gone through.

But that was the answer. Those lunches under the walnut tree were akin to therapy. Cooking, eating, sharing food, stories and emotions. The overall feeling of wellbeing – and our much-missed togetherness – was genuine and true, and I always hoped to carry both with me to give to my children… and hopefully beyond.

Dear reader, I hope this book triggers similar feelings in you wherever you are in the world. We all have so much more in common than that which divides us, and good food and good stories are universal.

'Perhaps, like me, Sash will
only realise his childhood
apples tasted like onions
when he is thirty-six'

Those Things That Connect Us:
Onions and Apples

'Do you remember, when you were small, asking your mother to cut you some apple? And your mum would oblige, a little absent-mindedly, using a knife that she'd just cut an onion with. Or maybe there was a little bit of onion flavour soaked into the chopping board, or the blade of the knife itself. As a result, your slice of apple would taste a little bit of onion.

This happened to me in reverse the other day. It was an evening when winter dusk stretched its blue fingers across the kitchen floor. My youngest son Wilfred, exhausted after a day of festivities, was in his highchair, half-laughing-half-crying at the sound of my knife's rushed evening rhythms. To stave off the hunger of my eldest, Sasha, I cut him an apple, biting into a sliver before giving him the rest. The onion-tinged nostalgia of mum-cut apple washed over my tongue. This time, I was no longer the child, but the mother.

You'd think a child might say, "That's disgusting!" but Sasha did not complain that his apple was tainted by allium's sulphuric musk. Perhaps I do it all the time. Perhaps, like me, Sash will only realise his childhood apples tasted like onions when he is thirty-six.

I kept thinking about this and started asking friends if it happened to them, or, as I initially suspected, if it was a Ukrainian thing. More often than not, people knew what I was talking about. My best friend Caroline – who grew up in Shropshire – sent me this:

When I was around seven or eight, Mum would give me an apple to tide me over while she was prepping tea. It was always a Golden Delicious, and it was always tinged with onion because she used the same knife she was chopping with. I always wanted it peeled in one long swirl of apple skin, then cored and chopped into quarters, then into slices. She would put the lot into an empty margarine tub because I couldn't be trusted with a proper bowl!

Like you, I actually came to enjoy the flavour of the onion on the apple and I sometimes wonder if that is why I am someone who likes fruit in savoury dishes. Like you, it brings back really specific memories. Like when there was a space behind the sofa, where I set up a "café" and used the back of the sofa as my counter to serve people. I remember sitting in there with my teddies and eating my onion-y apple while I was on my "break"!

Caroline was brought up in Shropshire, I was born in Ukraine, Sasha was born in London. And yet we share a square in our patchwork of childhood memories. There are more stories like this from other friends with other nationalities, and, like Sasha, no one remembers complaining. Perhaps it just felt natural. Maybe, in the everyday fabric of things, it is fine for flavours to cross-pollinate this way. Apples and onions, laughter and tears.'

Home

How We Eat Now

Home

....

Not all good stories have to start at the beginning.

Just a couple of months before I met my husband Joe, I firmly decided that I was done with love and relationships. A solo parent, whose first cookbook had been published, I was working too hard and juggling too much to allow demanding new factors into my life and Sasha's. I was also the thinnest I'd ever been. At the time I attributed it to breastfeeding calorie burn, but I now realise it was because I was stressed, and, being a freelancer, worked non-stop, which made it easy to skip lunches.

So there I was, wiry, but for the first time in my life fully self-sufficient and confident. Within a couple of days of knowing Joe, I told him we couldn't be together in a meaningful and serious way. He agreed, invited me to dinner (whole roasted cauliflower and dill oil) and I asked him to marry me two months later. It was true love, all the songs and the 'if you know you know' comments finally made sense. In the following months Joe's love and skilful, creative cooking filled me out spiritually and physically. My anxieties retreated, I felt nourished and never skipped lunch again.

Six years later, we are now a family of four, after Wilfred was born in 2020. We are three omnivores (my kids and me) and one vegetarian (Joe) in our house. Joe has never been preachy or otherwise annoying about his vegetarianism. His cooking is so good that all four of us naturally started eating more of a vegetable- and pulse-rich diet.

We do cook with meat and fish, but not every day, and, when we do eat it, we buy high-welfare meat. Mostly, we buy cuts that need slower cooking, as I find they are the most flavoursome, and they are always cheaper.

When we first moved in with Joe five years ago, my older son Sasha objected to having so many vegetable dishes every day and not very much meat. Eventually, though, he got used to it. Now, if I say, 'Today, we are having a roast chicken,' he does a little dance. It is good to see him appreciate meat, rather than just expect it.

Of course, even the best 'eater' kids remain kids; being fussy over food is a way of practising independence and having control, so Sash has his moments. When he was younger I assumed quite a draconian attitude: 'No kid has ever voluntarily starved themselves,' I often said sternly,

and gave Sasha no choice but to eat what we cooked that day. It became harder as he grew older and we realised he had opinions that he expected us to respect. Eventually I softened, and now if we cook his detested barley, pumpkin or aubergines, he can sort himself out with 'bits and pieces': substantial chunks of freshly cut cabbage, cucumber, carrots, or other vegetables, some bread, cheese, boiled eggs or hummus. It works. He is nourished enough and we don't have to make separate dinners.

The only struggle that remains – and for which I have no solution – is his love of puddings. I feel powerless, because I also have a terrible sweet tooth. Along with screens, we have no desserts Monday to Friday, but then let rip over the weekend.

Wilfred, at the time of writing, is 20 months old and eats everything apart from mashed potatoes (too paste-y). He hasn't yet discovered the food-control-independence thing, so it's fairly easy. We never bothered with purées (life is too short, people!) so we cut whatever we cook for ourselves into small pieces and let him feed himself with his hands. I won't lie: I cannot see the day when I don't have to deal with the catastrophic splatters of The Mess.

Very often we make a big batch of something – either a complete but simple dish or a big pot of brown rice, barley (oi!) or beans – and use them in different ways, varying the garnishes each time or adding spices to make the meals taste different. (For this reason, some of the recipes in the book are deliberately placed near each other, so you can turn one recipe into another. I've also added lots of ideas about how you can use up leftovers, so nothing goes to waste.)

We love pasta, simple salads, roasts on a Sunday and cakes. I am also a custard obsessive, so you will encounter quite a few recipes involving custard and crème pâtissière in this book.

I cook a lot of Eastern European food for my family, as I want the kids to keep in touch with their roots. But I also cook dishes that have made a big impact on me, whether that is from when I lived in Cyprus and in Italy, or recipes I have collected while travelling and connecting with good cooks from all over the world. I'm sending them to your home now.

Carrots, Chickpeas and Sorrel

An easy midweek salad of sorts. Bright and acidic sorrel is sweet carrot's best friend. Feel free to add whatever spices you have at hand; cumin and coriander will work well. Whatever you do, if your carrots are excellent, which I'm sure they will be, go easy with the spices: just a whisper is all you need.

- 3 tbsp olive oil
- 250g carrots, cut on the bias if big, or left whole if young
- 1 small onion, finely sliced
- ½ tsp fennel seeds
- 1 tsp poppy seeds
- 400g can of chickpeas, well drained
- 50g sorrel, larger leaves torn, smaller leaves left whole
- sea salt

- Preheat the oven to 200°C fan. Pour the olive oil into a baking tray and put it in the oven to heat up.

- Put the carrots and onion into the hot oil with the fennel and poppy seeds (or a gentle sprinkling of other beloved spices, see recipe introduction) and tip in the chickpeas. Season generously with salt. Cook for 20–30 minutes. The idea is that the carrots just cook, still remaining a little firm, and maybe catch a little colour. The chickpeas may turn a little crispy (and that is a very good thing) if your baking tray is large enough and things are not too overcrowded. The onion, depending on how finely you sliced it, may also get a little colour, or just be soft and translucent: both outcomes are good.

- When ready, take the whole thing out of the oven. Place the sorrel leaves on a plate or small platter and top with the carrots, onion and chickpeas.

- You can always drizzle this with a tiny bit of your favourite vinegar for an extra-bright flavour, or serve it with a dollop of yogurt and some flatbreads or rice.

Joe's Beetroot, Cornichons, Feta and Potatoes

When we started weaning my younger son Wilf at six months, it turned out that he was crazy about beetroot. It may be his Ukrainian genes, or it may be the colour that excites him so much. We were so ecstatic about his beetroot obsession that we started boiling and grating it and adding it to all sorts of things. Wilf either ate simplified versions of our food, or we ate more complex versions of what he liked. Once, for lunch, my husband Joe threw this together from whatever we had lying around – the end of a bit of feta, some pickling liquid from a finished jar of cauliflower pickles, a gnarly potato – and it tasted wonderful. It tasted so much like home to me that I asked him for the recipe. I highly recommend serving the potatoes simply boiled, naked, unadorned. The flavoursome beets and feta will act as a kind of dressing for it when you scoop them all up on your fork. Serve this as a simple lunch, or as an accompaniment to grilled or smoked oily fish.

- 4 beetroots (total weight 400–500g)
- 4 potatoes, scrubbed but unpeeled
- 2 tbsp cider vinegar
- 1 tsp honey
- 50g cornichons, chopped
- 100g feta
- 4 tbsp yogurt
- sea salt

To serve (optional)

- a slick of good olive or sunflower oil
- soft herb leaves, if you like (dill is knocking on the door of this recipe)

- You can use ready-boiled beetroots here. But if you have fresh ones, put them into cold water to cover, bring to the boil and, depending on their size, boil them for about 1 hour, or until you can pierce them easily with a knife. If too much water boils off and exposes them, splash in some more. I peel them once they are boiled as I find it easier and couldn't care less if my fingers are stained pink.

- Separately boil the potatoes whole, with their skins on too, until they also can be easily pierced with a knife, then, keeping the skins on, cut each into 2–4 pieces, or leave whole if they are small.

- When the beetroots are done, wash them under a cold tap, peel and grate them on the coarse side of a grater. We mix a little bit of it with plain yogurt for our baby son. The rest we dress as follows: mix the vinegar with the honey and 1 tsp salt and then add ½ tbsp water to dilute it a little. Use this to dress the grated beetroot, then stir through the cornichons.

- Put the feta into a bowl, add the yogurt and crush them together with a fork. Serve the beetroot alongside the feta and the simple boiled potatoes, drizzling some oil over the whole thing, if you like. If this is too stark for you, carry on and embellish away with herbs, but sometimes I like the simplicity of it all.

Pasta with Confit Garlic, Goat's Cheese and Thyme

I don't normally find much pleasure in cooking for just me. Except when it's this dish. This is adapted from an old Nigel Slater recipe, a writer who inspired me and so many others to look beyond cookbook recipes and to cook more freely and creatively. I turn to this recipe time and again when I have some moments on my own. I have been cooking it for fourteen years, but have never made it for anyone but myself before testing it for this book. Now my family (especially my mum!) love it too. In the original, crumbled goat's cheese and confit garlic cloves are simply stirred through the pasta and it's delicious.

However, I have discovered that the confit garlic oil, goat's cheese and pasta water can create a very mellow and comforting sauce which is also brilliant eaten on, or rather mopped up with, lettuce leaves. So we always serve lettuce leaves alongside, it's almost the best bit! When we finish eating the pasta, we pile the leaves into our plates, add a sprinkling of salt and a touch of vinegar and mop at the remaining goat's cheese sauce with the leaves until the plates are sparkling clean. It's so delicious. I highly recommend you follow suit.

·· 2 small garlic bulbs (yes, that's correct, 1 per person)

·· 100ml good olive oil

·· leaves from 4 thyme sprigs

·· 200g spaghetti or linguine

·· 200g soft goat's cheese (logs are good)

To serve

·· lettuce leaves

·· good vinegar

·· sea salt

• I haven't yet found a garlic peeling hack that works. What I do is separate the cloves, then attempt to lightly bash on each with the heel of my hand and cut off the dry root end. The skins then slip off quite easily. If you accidentally squash some (or a lot, like I do, heavy-handedly) of the cloves, don't worry too much, they can still be used. Put the oil into the smallest saucepan or frying pan you have, heat it gently and spoon in the garlic. The cloves should be submerged in oil and cook very gently over the lowest heat possible. Sometimes I tilt the pan carefully, helping the cloves to submerge, and stand there holding the pan. But you can always use more oil. It won't go to waste, as the garlicky oil is so good in other recipes, or to dress boiled vegetables. The garlic will be spluttering away, its water escaping the oil. It has to soften, mellow and colour only ever so slightly. The whole process should take about 20 minutes, but use your judgement. When ready, the garlic will smell very sweet and the cloves can be easily pierced with a knife. Take it off the heat and add the thyme.

• Cook the pasta according to the packet instructions. Put the goat's cheese into a food processor. When there are 3 minutes to go before the pasta is done, ladle 200ml of the pasta water into a measuring jug. Blitz the goat's cheese with half of the measured pasta water and 2–3 tbsp of the garlic oil. You will have a smooth and rather liquid sauce, but do not worry, it will all be good. (If it is not quite liquid, I find the pasta eats too dry.)

• Drain the pasta and put it back into the pan in which it was cooking. Pour the sauce over the pasta and, using tongs, pick the pasta up and down, making sure to cover the pasta in the sauce. Keep agitating it like this for a minute. At this point I take a mouthful and check if it slips down smoothly. If it feels a bit dry rather than slippery, I add another splash of pasta water and swirl it around with tongs some more.

- Put the pasta into serving plates and pour over any goat's cheese sauce that remained behind in the pan. Serve with the confit garlic cloves scattered over the top and a drizzle of the garlic oil.

- When you finish the pasta, pile the lettuce leaves directly into the pasta plate and add a little vinegar and salt. The remainder of the goat's cheese sauce is so good with the leaves.

Thom Eagle, Chef, Writer and Fermenter

Blackberrying

'Try to forage for seaweed around the coasts of Britain, say, or mushrooms in the woods, and you will inevitably attract attention. "Do you have a foraging licence?" people ask, or "How do you know they're safe?" Forage for blackberries, on the other hand, and no one gives you a second glance, or, if they do, it will be a happy one, as they remember picking brambles themselves, with their parents or grandparents. I don't remember a specific trip to do so any more than I remember a specific ice cream I ate as a child. Blackberrying was simply a part of walks to or from my parents' allotment – or round the orchards behind – at the end of the summer holidays, or as school began in early autumn (though the season seems to creep forward every year). For every perfect berry you might get one stab with a thorn, one sour bite, and one caterpillar… but that is half the point, along with the stains on your fingers and clothes, and the dust you kick up in the September sun.'

Lamb Cutlets in
Kefir and Harissa Marinade

This is one of those no-brainer, easy and delicious recipes that I make both for me and my sons and also when people come over. We always have kefir in the house, as I love drinking it with a little pinch of salt, as if it was ayran. But you can use yogurt mixed with a little water instead. You can use a cheaper cut of lamb, such as scrag end, if you are serving it with flatbreads (the cooking times will be longer though). The lamb can be marinated for up to two days if left, covered, in the fridge, but sometimes I forget to do this and it still turns out delicious. Cooking times depend on how you like your lamb. Personally, I find rare lamb can lack flavour and be quite flabby, so prefer to cook it to medium... but I won't lie to you, even well-done lamb pleases me, so if you are in my camp don't stress about 'overcooking' it by a few minutes.

- ·· 100ml kefir or yogurt

- ·· 1½ tbsp rose harissa, or 1 tbsp Quick Fermented Chilli Sauce (see page 285)

- ·· 1 tsp ground coriander

- ·· 1 tsp ground cumin

- ·· 500g lamb cutlets, chops, or another steak-y cut

- ·· sea salt

Shown overleaf →

- Mix the kefir or yogurt in a bowl with the harissa or chilli sauce, spices and ½ tsp salt. Put the lamb cutlets into a medium baking tray and spoon over the marinade, turning the meat so it is well covered. Leave to marinate for up to 2 days in the fridge, or for at least 15 minutes.

- When ready to cook, if the meat was in the fridge and you have the time, return it to room temperature. Preheat the grill in your oven to its highest setting.

- What I do is this: put the lamb cutlets directly on a rack at the top of the oven and the baking tray with the marinade beneath them. I then cook the meat under the grill for about 5 minutes on each side. Meanwhile, the marinade should also reduce a bit (it will split, but that's not a problem).

- I like my lamb cutlets just well done, so I cook them – depending on thickness – for a further 2 minutes. You can always check yours by taking one of the cutlets out and cutting into it. Cook them for longer if you like them really well done. Put the cutlets into the now-hot marinade-sauce and serve.

- Eat them with Easy Flatbreads and either Easy Crunchy Vegetable Salad-Pickle or Radish and Pomegranate Salad (see pages 271, 129 and 68), or just with chopped cucumbers, chopped red or white cabbage and lots of soft herb leaves and yogurt. I sometimes add a bowl of chilli flakes, too.

Punched Potatoes and a Roast Chicken

I have had the pleasure to work with many excellent cooks throughout my career, and I watched a version of these potatoes being cooked over a giant fire-licked plancha by the Argentinian chef Francis Mallmann. I had travelled to Ballymaloe food festival with three other chefs and we came up with a cunning plan to wake up at 4am, turn up at Francis's prep station and offer to peel potatoes. He welcomed us and I ended up cooking with him the following year for Guy Ritchie and David Beckham (both very lovely; first time ever I name-dropped, but it felt OK). Now the important bit: the potatoes were boiled until very soft, cooled slightly, then hand-squashed into a flat patty and thrown on to a massive iron plate positioned over a fire. They were cooked for more than an hour with *tons* of butter (and I mean kilograms) chucked at them. The resulting potatoes developed very thick crispy bottoms but were fluffy on top. I raved to my mum about the dish and she developed this domestic oven version which works so well. She has been making them almost every Sunday, when the extended family comes over, for the past four years. The trick is to boil them sufficiently so you can squash them with your hand into a flat patty. Don't be all shy and sheepish about the squashing, you really must form them into a flat pancake. In this recipe we are throwing chicken with its fat into the action too, so you get the buttery, chickeny potatoes of dreams.

····

- ·· 6 medium floury potatoes (total weight 1.5kg), scrubbed but unpeeled
- ·· 2 tbsp olive oil
- ·· 1 small free-range chicken, about 1.7kg
- ·· 5 garlic cloves
- ·· 50g unsalted butter
- ·· 2 rosemary sprigs
- ·· sea salt

- Preheat the oven to 180°C fan.

- For the potatoes, put a pot of water on the hob, season the water well with salt and add the whole potatoes, skins and all. Boil them until they are very soft, but not completely disintegrated (20–30 minutes, depending on size). Drain them and leave to cool enough so you don't burn your hand. If I can, I will take them outside to speed up the cooling.

- Meanwhile, brush your largest baking tray with 1 tbsp of the oil. Rub the other 1 tbsp oil all over the chicken, especially where it will touch the tray so it doesn't stick, and season generously with salt. Put it on the baking tray breast side up and cook for 60–80 minutes, depending on size.

- Flatten the garlic, skins on, with a knife. If the cloves are little squashed, it's OK!

- QR CODE • *This might take a bit of practice. Put a potato on a work surface and cup it with your hand, then push down confidently, crushing it into a flat patty. My husband (unsavourily) calls these 'cowpat potatoes'. They need to be almost flat but still hold together in a rough oval. You can always tidy them up and stick back on any bits that detach from the edges. Repeat with the other potatoes.*

- *The chicken is ready when you pull at the leg and it gives quite easily. Take it out of the oven, tipping out its juices into the tray, and leave it to rest. Crank up the oven temperature to its highest setting and put the butter into the tray over a medium heat. Use a large spatula to scoop the potatoes gently into the tray. Throw in the garlic and rosemary, swirl the tray, transfer to the oven and roast for 30 minutes. If the potatoes are not sufficiently crispy after that time, cook them some more.*

- Carve the chicken and serve alongside the potatoes.

• TIP • In winter I serve this with simple, steamed kale or spring greens, or
Easy Honey and Caraway Kraut (see page 282) or kimchi, and in the summer
all you want alongside is a simple salad, such as Sweet Water Salad or Green
Bean Salad with Apples, Fennel and Nuts (see pages 71 and 34).

Brown Shrimp, Mayo, Egg and Pickles on Rye

This beautiful brunch dish plus *The Guardian* 'Weekend' section used to be my special Saturday morning treat. We had a local café called Tromsø run by two brilliant women, Hedvig and Lorna, situated in the arches by Forest Gate station. It was cosy and charming and their brunches, cakes and Norwegian waffles were a real joy. Eventually, because of Brexit and the rest of it, Hedvig moved back to Norway (and, like the café, 'Weekend' is no longer in existence. Sob). To commemorate beautiful Tromsø, I asked her to share this and her wonderful miso and walnut cake (see page 230) with me. This recipe is more of an assembly job, but if you want to make Hedvig's rye bread too, head to page 273.

·· 1 egg

·· 2 pieces of dark rye bread (for homemade, see page 273)

·· 100g mayonnaise (for homemade, see below)

·· 100g brown shrimps

·· a few dill sprigs

·· 1 pickled cucumber

For the mayonnaise (optional)

·· 1 tsp Dijon mustard

·· juice of ½ small lemon

·· 1 egg yolk

·· 150ml flavourless oil

·· sea salt

• I can make the most complicated dumplings, but I am rubbish at boiling eggs. I always forget what the timings are. So this method is for me as much as it is for you. I don't keep my eggs in the fridge, but if you do, try to remember to bring them to room temperature first, to reduce the risk of them cracking.

• Fill a medium saucepan with water and bring to a rolling boil. Gently lower in the egg and cook for 6 minutes. As soon as the timer goes off, drain the egg and run under cold water. Then peel and slice it.

• If you do want to make homemade mayo, put the mustard, lemon juice and egg yolk in a medium bowl with a generous pinch of salt. Pour the oil into a small jug. Now slowly start to trickle the oil into the bowl, whisking all the time, until it has all been incorporated. Taste it again, adding more salt if you like.

• Spread the bread with some mayo, top with shrimps and a generous sprinkling of dill and serve with the sliced egg and pickle. Serve with coffee and your favourite weekend newspaper supplement.

Sausages with Calvados Cream, Apples and Potatoes

Wilfred, my baby boy, never took to his bedside cot. He rolled and shimmied until he ended up under my armpit, where he stayed for two whole years. The bedside cot turned into a shelf, which was quickly filled with books, mostly his, but there were a couple of mine too that haven't moved since, as I loved dipping in and out of them during those two years. *Family Life* by Elisabeth Luard was one of them. She describes a scene where her large family, travelling in a van from Spain to France in the romantic gloom of autumn, were offered shelter in an orchard by a sympathetic French farmer. She writes:

'We set up our table under laden branches. I can taste the meal still: the succulent hoop of nutmeg-spiced *saucisse* slowly fried in butter, the apples crisp-fleshed, vanilla-scented, sliced and browned; the creamy mass of potatoes sauced with applejack and golden cream.' I fell in love with this passage and kept going back to it, dreaming of when I could recreate an approximation of this scene for my boys and our friends. It happened. I never looked back and I implore you to try it, especially while camping.

- ·· 5 potatoes, scrubbed but unpeeled, cut into chunks (total weight 500g)

- ·· 500g Cumberland sausage, or any sausages, the best quality you can get

- ·· 25g unsalted butter, plus more if needed

- ·· 2 firm apples, cored and each sliced into 8 wedges (total weight 200g)

- ·· 100ml Calvados, brandy, cider or apple juice

- ·· 1½ tbsp Dijon mustard

- ·· 100g crème fraîche or double cream

- ·· pinch of grated nutmeg

- ·· pinch of ground allspice

- ·· sea salt and black pepper

- Put the potatoes into a pan of cold, salted water and bring to a simmer. I usually cut them into 2cm cubes and they take 10 minutes to cook from the moment the water starts to boil. Drain them and let the steam roll off them in the colander while you do the rest.

- If you are using a sausage coil, prick it all over with the tip of a knife or a fork. Melt the butter in a deep frying pan or a heavy-based cast-iron pot. Add the coil and cook, loosely covered with a lid if you have one, for about 8 minutes or until the juices run clear. Now increase the heat, turn and let the coil colour a little on its other side. If you are using regular sausages, do not turn them too often, so they have time to develop a golden sheen on each side. Equally, watch that they don't get burnt, as you want to keep building on the pan flavours throughout. You can add a small splash of water to deglaze any time you feel the sausages might be getting scorched. When cooked, remove the sausages and keep them warm (I stick mine in a large bowl, cover with a plate and into a warm oven).

- Fry the potatoes in the sausage juices and butter (add more butter if needed) over a medium heat until they colour a little. Take them out. You may need to add a little water here to deglaze the bottom of the pan. If at any point you feel as though the residue in the pan is too burnt and crispy, wipe it out with kitchen paper.

- Add the apples (and more fat if needed) and cook them for 5–8 minutes, turning gently a couple of times. The fruit should just caramelise a little on the outside but remain firm inside. Now splash in your alcohol of choice, let it bubble and scrape at the crispy bits stuck to the pan if needed. Take the apples out and keep them warm with the potatoes while you do the sauce.

- After a minute or so, whisk the mustard and cream into the bubbling pan. Add the spices and season with salt and pepper. I pour a little bit of the sauce into each plate and pile the sausages, potatoes and apples on top. As Luard rightly implores us, 'Eat and lick your fingers so as not to miss anything.'

Green Bean Salad with Apples, Fennel and Nuts

I have a three-year experience of solo parenting, starting when my elder son Sasha was just over thirteen months old. With no family in London and a budding career as a professional cook, I don't know how I would have coped without my friends, especially Caroline, who lived a few streets away. I will never forget a bond-tightening meal in her flat in 2008. She made this salad from the *Riverford Farm Cook Book* (I bought the book immediately after), as well as Nigel Slater's taleggio focaccia (I was given a photocopy of a photocopied recipe to take with me) and

potatoes loaded with crème fraîche and smoked haddock (also Nigel). We have both made the salad many times ever since and this is what it morphed into. As always, you can play around with it, using runner beans or other crunchy vegetables, kohlrabi instead of fennel and any nuts that you have. In fact anything that you can toast so it brings crunch and flavour to this salad party. You can even scrounge around your cupboards and do a mixture of nuts and seeds, finishing all those forlorn-looking packets. Make this for your friends, old and new.

····

· 1 tsp sunflower oil

· 100g nuts or seeds, or both (I used chopped walnuts and pumpkin seeds)

· pinch of chilli flakes

· 300g green or runner beans

· 2 apples, cored and sliced

· 1 celery stick, finely sliced

· 1 fennel bulb, very finely sliced

· sea salt

····

For the dressing

· 1 garlic clove, finely grated

· 2 tsp Dijon mustard

· 2 tsp honey

· 3 tbsp sherry vinegar, or wine vinegar

· 3 tbsp unrefined sunflower or olive oil

• Preheat the oven to 180°C fan.

• Heat the sunflower oil in a pan and add the nuts and seeds. Cook over a medium-low heat for a few minutes until golden. Swirl in the chilli flakes, season with salt and cook for another 30 seconds or so. Tip them into a bowl, so they don't continue to cook and become burned.

• Cook the beans in boiling water for 5–7 minutes. I like them tender and not too squeaky, but if you are a squeak fan cook them for 3 minutes only. Plunge them into a bowl of cold water and ice, or run under a cold tap, to stop them cooking and preserve their colour.

• Whisk all the dressing ingredients together.

• Drain the beans and mix them with the apples, celery, fennel, dressing, nuts and seeds. Have a little taste and see if the salad needs more salt. This will happily sit for a bit, so you can make it in advance, just make sure to give it a fresh mix before serving.

Sumayya Usmani, Author and Intuitive Cook

The Scent of Life-Giving Pudding

'A delicate halo of lavender and cardamom always followed my Nani (maternal grandmother). She loved Yardley's English lavender scent and always used it as soaps or talcum powder. To me, her powdery fragrance was synonymous with comforting hugs and bottomless bowls of cardamom rice pudding called *kheer*. Growing up, I ran to her when I needed to find respite from fights at home. I'd burst through her back door to the kitchen and she'd be there, crouching over her white enamel gas cooker, stirring basmati rice and raw buffalo milk with cardamom.

The scent of cardamom filled the *kheer*, but I could also detect the lingering aroma of lavender within the bowl. It was as if a part of her was in it. If I closed my eyes, I could smell her… and that would mean all was well.

Many years after she passed away, I was going through a break-up and the only thing I craved was a way back to my Nani's kitchen. So I made myself some *kheer*. In the bowl, I could smell her soft lavender lingering within the warm cardamom rice milk. That life-giving moment filled each inhalation with hope and a way back to safety.'

Saffron Broth with Chickpea and Rice Balls

This was inspired by a broth from Azerbaijan called *kyufta bozbash*. The original has chickpeas and lamb meatballs stuffed with prunes or apricots. I love it, but wanted my vegetarian husband to enjoy a version of it too, so came up with this 'vegetarian ball' number. I find that chopping the dried fruit finely and mixing it through the chickpeas and rice is a good thing. As always, feel free to use any herbs you have in your fridge. Tarragon, basil, coriander or a mixture work beautifully. I often cook quite a lot of brown rice and then eat it in different dishes and this is a good recipe to use it up.

For the broth

· pinch of saffron threads

· 1 vegetable stock cube (optional)

· 1 leek

· 1 large onion

· 3 tbsp olive oil

· 1 large carrot, finely chopped

· 2 celery sticks, finely chopped

· 1 large potato, scrubbed but unpeeled, chopped into 5cm pieces (optional)

· 2 fat garlic cloves, finely chopped or grated

· handful (about 25g) of spinach, chard or sorrel leaves (optional)

· sea salt and black pepper

· herbs and yogurt, to serve (optional)

Continued →

• Put the saffron into a bowl and cover with 1.5 litres of hot, but not necessarily boiling, water. You can crumble in a vegetable stock cube if you have one lying around. Leave it be while you do the rest.

• Make sure you clean the leek really well as there is often some soil hiding under the first layer of the green part. I always only cut off the really dry edge of the green part, but use all the rest. Cut the leek lengthways in half, then lengthways in half again. Chop across into small pieces and set aside.

• Peel and chop the onion as finely as you can. Heat 2 tbsp of the oil in a pot (I use a cast-iron one but any soup-suitable pot will do) and add the onion and a generous pinch of salt. The salt helps draw moisture out of the onion and keeps it from burning so readily. Keep cooking and stirring over a medium heat. You want the onion to first soften, then start getting some colour. If the pan starts looking or sounding dry (you will hear it go muffled and quiet when there is no moisture), add small splashes of water and scrape at the base. This process will take 8–10 minutes, by which point the onion will look brown enough. Scrape into a bowl.

• Without wiping the pan, add the remaining 1 tbsp oil and then the leek, carrot and celery and cook over a medium heat, stirring occasionally. You want the vegetables to soften and get a little bit of colour. Just let them do their thing while you make the chickpea rice balls. As always, if the pan starts looking too dry, add small splashes of water and scrape at the base of the pan to deglaze.

• Drain the chickpeas, but not too intensely, you want a little bit of their water to cling to them to help the filling bind. Add them to the cooked onion and use a potato masher or the back of a fork to mash into a rough paste. Add the chopped dill stalks, spices, a generous pinch of sea salt and black pepper, the dried fruit and flour. Add the rice, mix it all well and maybe have another go with the potato masher to make sure the mixture is homogeneous. Now wet your hands and roll the mixture into fat golf ball-sized spheres. Keep wetting your hands if things get sticky. I normally get 16 balls. Leave them in the bowl for the time being.

Continued →

Continued...

For the balls

·· 400g can of chickpeas

·· bunch of dill, leaves and
stalks separated and chopped

·· ½ tsp ground cinnamon

·· 1 tsp ground coriander

·· 60g dried apricots or dried
sour cherries, finely chopped

·· 60g flour (any will work,
I tend to use spelt)

·· 300g cooked brown rice
(150g raw brown rice,
if cooking it for the dish)

• Pour the saffron water into the pot with the vegetables and season well with salt and pepper. Keep tasting; the soup should be well seasoned. Add the potato, if using, and cook for about 10 minutes or until the potato is soft.

• Finally, gently lower in the chickpea rice balls and cook for 5–8 minutes. They may be a little fragile, so take care to stir the soup gently. In fact, depending on what type of chickpeas you used, as a rule the more cooked they are (I find jarred varieties are more cooked and slushier) the better they hold together. The amount of flour in them should be sufficient to hold them together, but if they do fall apart, do not despair, the soup will still be delicious.

• At this point, add the garlic and spinach or chard too, if using. Cook the broth for 5 minutes or so and then switch off the heat. If you are using sorrel, add it only once the soup is off the heat. We often serve this with Easy Flatbreads (see page 271) and the reserved dill leaves, also some yogurt if you wish.

....

• TIP • This soup, like any soup, can have more than one life! The next day, you can crush the balls into the soup to thicken it. You can also bulk it up with half moons of roasted squash or other vegetables, more leftover rice or another grain, pieces of feta, a drizzle of chilli oil or a spoonful of harissa.

....

Squid Stew

I experimented with different foods when my oldest, Sasha, was still a baby. I remember him as a one-year-old loving this very dish the first time I made it, in fact Sasha is still obsessed with cephalopods, both eating them and admiring them. He now insists he doesn't like the cinnamon in this recipe, but I am sticking by it and adding a little piece because I love its welcome warm notes. You can also use cuttlefish if you have it (I actually prefer cuttlefish, but it's harder to come by). Make sure you have plain rice or fresh bread to dip into the rich maroon sauce, or it also serves as an excellent pasta sauce. The beauty of this is that you don't need masses of squid and you can use frozen, too, as the squid here is a flavouring rather than the main protagonist.

- 1 medium-sized squid or cuttlefish, cleaned (total weight 200g), or more if you like
- 3 tbsp olive oil
- 1 large onion, sliced
- 1 red pepper, cut into chunks
- 2 celery sticks, chopped
- 2 garlic cloves, chopped
- 2 tbsp tomato paste
- 50ml white or red wine (optional)
- 400g can of tomatoes
- 2 bay leaves
- small piece of cinnamon stick
- ½ tsp chilli flakes (optional)
- 400g can of chickpeas, drained (optional)
- sea salt and black pepper

- Slice the squid into 2cm rings and cut the tentacles in half. If you are using cuttlefish, cut its body into 4cm squares and cut through the tentacles too.

- Heat the oil in a cast-iron pan. Add the onion, pepper, celery and a pinch of salt and cook over a medium-low heat for about 5 minutes, just to soften it all a bit and gently colour it here and there.

- Add the garlic, then the tomato paste and cook for another 2 minutes or so, stirring often. Add the wine, if using, and cook it off for a few minutes. Now add the squid and canned tomatoes, bay and cinnamon. Fill the tomato can halfway with water and put that in too, swooshing the remaining tomato out of the can as you go.

- Season with salt and plenty of pepper, or chilli flakes if no kids are involved. If they are involved, you can add the chilli flakes later, to your own plate, as a finishing touch. Cook, covered, for 50 minutes over a low heat. Check if the squid is tender. If not, give it another 10 minutes; it should be soft enough to cut with a spoon. Stir the chickpeas, if using, through for the last 10 minutes of cooking.

- Serve with simple unadorned grains: plain rice is pretty good, or a huge hunk of fresh, crusty bread.

Butter Bean and Mushroom Soupy Stew

A recipe by brilliant chefs, a couple: Ola Aleksandra Schwarz, from Poland, and her Egyptian-Austrian partner Nadim Amin. They go by @centrala.vienna on Instagram and their posts always make me do a double-take. They spent a considerable time working in London kitchens and then returned to Austria. I have been admiring their work for a couple of years now and feel thrilled to include their recipe here. This is what Ola said about the dish:

'This is a very autumnal dish with all its ingredients readily available in the markets of Central and Eastern Europe from late summer on. That is also the time you can buy the most amazingly creamy, yet meaty white beans at the markets in Poland. They're dried but still quite fresh. If those are not at your disposal, white butter beans or dried judion beans will do just fine. We soak them overnight to make sure they are fully hydrated, strain them and just about cover them again with fresh cold water.'

- 250g dried butter beans
- 3 garlic cloves
- 2 fresh bay leaves
- 2 white onions, 1 halved
- 25g dried mushrooms
- 400g potatoes, scrubbed but unpeeled (Anya, Ratte or Pink Fir Apple work well)
- handful of kale, tough stalks removed, roughly chopped
- 100g cooked chestnuts, roughly chopped (optional)
- 1 medium-sized Kabocha squash/Delica pumpkin or butternut squash
- a little vegetable oil
- 2 tbsp extra virgin olive oil, plus more to serve
- 10g marjoram, oregano, thyme or tarragon leaves, chopped, plus more to serve
- sea salt and black pepper

- Soak the beans overnight in a large bowl covered with 2 litres of cold water. Or don't, it's actually not 100 per cent necessary, it just cuts cooking time.

- Put the beans into a large saucepan and add water to cover by 5cm (they absorb most of the soaking water). Add the garlic, bay leaves, halved onion and a couple of the dried mushrooms with a few pinches of salt and cover everything with baking parchment so it stays under water. Simmer over the lowest heat until the beans are soft and creamy but still keeping their shape; it will take 1–1½ hours. If you boil them too hard, they split and the skins come off. Do not drain; there should be a fair amount of bean water. Fish out and compost the onion halves.

- Add the potatoes, whole if they are little or in chunks if they are large, and a generous pinch of salt and cook for 10–15 minutes or until the potatoes are cooked through and crushable. Taste the liquid for salt: make sure it is properly seasoned, or the end dish will taste underwhelming. Add the kale and chestnuts and switch the heat off for the moment.

- Preheat the oven to 220°C fan.

- While all this is happening, rinse the squash of any dirt, cut it in half and scoop out its seeds, then cut into 3cm wedges. You want a manageable wedge, not too large. Sprinkle with a little vegetable oil and salt and bake in the hot oven until it's cooked but still firm and a little charred (roughly 25 minutes).

- Chop the remaining onion. Heat the 2 tbsp olive oil in a small frying pan and sweat the onion with a pinch of salt for about 10 minutes over a low heat.

- In a mortar and pestle, pound the rest of the dried mushrooms into a rough powder. I do this in batches. A tip – don't do a fast and furious bash-bash-bash – this will cause your mushrooms to jump out all over the place. I find a rhythm that works is more like: 'Confident bash. Pause. Bash. Pause. Bash. Pause'. Or just use a food processor. You don't want a powder, so don't overexert yourself. Add the crushed mushrooms to the onion and stir for 2–4 minutes. If the pan looks dry, add 4–5 tbsp of the bean-cooking water. Season generously with pepper.

·· something acidic, to serve, such as a good-quality wine vinegar, kraut or kraut brine, sour cream or crème fraîche

- Add the herbs of your choice to the bean pot.

- Stir the onion and mushroom mix (it will look sludgy) into the beans, check the seasoning and reheat. Add the pumpkin or squash and a pinch of fresh chopped herbs on top and serve. I drizzle good-quality olive oil on top like the Italians do and eat it with a little bit of Easy Honey and Caraway Kraut (see page 282) to cut the richness. My husband likes his with sour cream (I've trained him well). Whatever you do, this dish does benefit from a bit of acidity. You can always just put a tablespoonful of good vinegar into the main pot at the very end of cooking. Eat it with plenty of crusty bread.

Cauliflower Soup with Cashew Cream and Cashew Dukkah

There is a wonderful restaurant in Bristol called Root; head chef Robert Howell cooks with such sensitivity and lightness. We dropped in one drizzly October afternoon and ordered a dish which involved cauliflower couscous, roast cauliflower, cashew cream and a few delectable bits that we couldn't quite put our finger on. My husband and I fought for it. It was the best thing I ate that year. I asked Rob for the recipe and experimented a little bit over the winter months. This soup, with its ambrosial cashew dukkah and cashew cream (those two elements are Rob's)

will blow your mind. It is my go-to if we have a vegan friend for dinner… and to be honest it is just my go-to soup these days.

You will need a good blender to make the cashew cream, but you could always just use a little bit of yogurt instead. The dukkah is what really makes this. Once you make the dukkah, you can whip this soup up in a matter of an hour midweek without much effort. Use the leftover dukkah on *everything*. It's just incredible.

For the cashew cream (optional)

·· 200g cashew nuts

·· 100ml water, plus more if needed

·· 1 tbsp sherry vinegar

For the soup

·· 3 tbsp olive oil

·· 2 medium cauliflowers, leaves on (total weight 1.2kg)

·· 1 litre vegetable stock (made from a cube is fine!), or water

·· sea salt and black pepper

For the dukkah

·· 200g cashew nuts

·· 50g sunflower seeds

·· 50g pumpkin seeds

·· 10g coriander seeds

·· 10g cumin seeds

·· 20g sesame seeds

- If making the cashew cream, soak the cashews in plenty of water for at least 5 hours. When you drain and weigh them, you should find that they will now weigh roughly 240g.

- Preheat the oven to 210°C fan.

- Drizzle the oil over the cauliflowers and season with salt. Roast in the oven for 45–60 minutes, or even longer: you need to cook them until they are properly, completely soft and caramelised here and there. The leaves may become dark and crispy and they are my husband's favourite bit: keep them.

- For the cashew cream, drain the cashews, place in a blender and add the measured water, ½ tsp salt, cracked black pepper and the sherry vinegar. Blend on a high speed until you have a smooth, airy, creamy purée, splashing in more water if needed. Taste and adjust the seasoning. Place in a container and keep in the fridge for up to 5 days.

- For the dukkah, preheat the oven to 180°C fan. Put the cashews, sunflower and pumpkin seeds on a roasting tray. Cook in the oven for about 12 minutes, or until they turn golden and taste really good.

- I toast the coriander and cumin seeds in a small frying pan until fragrant (this takes 2 minutes or so), then I take them out and toast the sesame seeds in the same pan, until golden and tasty.

- The cashews should be lovely and golden. Keep a few of the whole nuts and seeds and pound the rest of them in a mortar and pestle until some are powdered and others are in coarse chunks. Pound or blitz the coriander and cumin seeds so they break, but stay coarse, not a powder. Leave the toasted sesame seeds whole.

- Mix all the toasted nuts, seeds and spices together, including the whole ones you reserved. This will make more dukkah than you need, but it can be kept in an airtight container for a month.

For the rehydrated dried fruit

·· 25g dried barberries
(or dried cranberries,
sour cherries or raisins)

·· 100ml water

·· 50ml white wine vinegar

·· 1 tbsp honey

- For the barberries or other dried fruit, simply put everything into a small saucepan, bring to a simmer and cook for 15 minutes. Then drain (don't throw the liquid away, it can be used instead of vinegar in dressings) and use that day.

- When the cauliflower is properly soft and charred, break it into smaller pieces, transfer to a large saucepan and add the stock or water. Use a hand blender to process until very smooth. Have a boiled kettle nearby, as you may need a bit more water to get the consistency that you like. Taste and adjust the seasoning.

- To serve the soup, reheat it very gently. Pour it into warmed bowls, swirl some cashew nut cream into each, sprinkle over a few rehydrated barberries and then some dukkah, which I also sprinkle over the crispy leaves when I serve those. Elegant and incredibly tasty.

Steamed Aubergines

This is one of my most favourite ways to eat aubergine. I first tried something similar in a Vietnamese restaurant in South London many years ago; I had never tried steamed aubergine before and it was a complete revelation. My husband Joe suggested I steam them whole; I did and have never looked back. You do literally just put whole aubergines on to steam and mix a couple of dressing ingredients together. You need to focus for two minutes only, while you are toasting sesame seeds. That's it. For the rest of it, you can relax, or put some rice on to boil, or maybe you have leftover brown rice… (then *really* just relax). You will come back to this dish again and again.

- 2 medium aubergines
- 1 tbsp honey, or to taste
- 3 tbsp rice vinegar, or to taste
- juice of ½ small lime, or to taste
- 2 tbsp soy sauce, or to taste
- small piece of ginger, unpeeled, finely grated (optional)
- ½ tbsp sesame oil
- ½ tbsp chilli oil (optional), or use more sesame oil
- handful of mint leaves (Vietnamese mint is great if you can find it, or I got all fancy for this photo and used Peruvian mint)
- 1 tbsp sesame seeds (white, black or both), toasted
- 2 spring onions, finely chopped

• Put your steamer on, or, if you don't have one, fashion one out of a large metal or enamel colander and a pot lid.

• Put the aubergines in the steamer whole. Depending on their size and age, they should take 30–40 minutes to become very soft. It's hard to overcook them, just make sure they are not undercooked: they should feel soft and squishy when you press or pierce them.

• Mix the honey with the vinegar and lime juice to dissolve. Then add the soy sauce and the ginger, if using, and taste; it will be more difficult to gauge salt-sweet-acid balance once you add the oil. The dressing should be almost a little overseasoned, as steamed aubergine is so neutral. When the mixture tastes punchy enough for you, whisk in the oil(s).

• You can either stir the mint leaves into the dressing or add them separately after.

• Cut into the soft aubergines gently and dress the creamy insides while still hot. Sprinkle over the sesame seeds, spring onions and mint (if you didn't add it to the dressing) and serve a half each with plain rice, or a whole aubergine if you are extra-hungry, with the dressing spooned over the rice too, if you like.

Serves 2

Spiced Aubergines with a Seed, Coconut and Peanut Crust

This is a simplified version of the brilliant Vivek Singh's recipe. I food-styled it at the dawn of my cooking career and it impressed me so much that I have been cooking it ever since. I reached out to Vivek to ask for permission to include this here and to ask for his inspiration behind the dish. He graciously gave me his blessing and explained the recipe's origins. 'Years ago it was inspired from the traditional Hyderabadi *baingan ka salan* curry, where aubergines and fat benign chillies are simmered in a rich nutty sauce. I used the same ingredients, but played with different textures.' If the Steamed Aubergines (see page 49) is a serene monk, this one is a strutting bejewelled diva. The flavour is incredible. You will not look back and it will enter your home-cooking repertoire. My friend Helena tried it with Cashew Cream (see page 46) and loved it. If you can't find tamarind, a plum paste such as the Georgian *tkemali* or a strained sour chutney work very well. And of course the spice crust granola-type mix keeps well in a container and is good on everything.

· 2 large aubergines, in wedges

· 3 tbsp tamarind paste

· 3 tbsp honey

· handful of watercress, to serve

....

For the marinade

· 4 tbsp vegetable oil

· 1 tsp each ground turmeric, fennel seeds, black onion seeds and sea salt

....

For the spice crust

· 2 tsp poppy seeds

· 2 tsp sesame seeds

· handful of coconut chips, or 1 tbsp desiccated coconut

· 2 tbsp peanuts

· 2 tbsp vegetable oil

· 5 garlic cloves, chopped

· ½ tsp chilli powder

· 1 tsp chaat masala, or curry powder

• Mix everything for the marinade in a small bowl. Score the flesh sides of the aubergine wedges lightly to make criss-cross marks, brush with the spiced oil, then set aside for 10–15 minutes.

• Meanwhile, make the spice crust. Toast the poppy seeds, sesame seeds and coconut chips separately in a dry frying pan over a medium heat for 1–2 minutes, until the aromas are released. Quickly tip them into a bowl and set aside.

• Now dry-fry the peanuts in the same pan over a medium heat, moving them around from time to time so they don't burn. When they are golden here and there, remove them from the pan and set aside to cool, then coarsely chop. Add them to the roasted seeds and coconut in the bowl.

• Heat the 2 tbsp oil in the pan. Add the garlic and cook, stirring, over a medium heat. When it is golden, remove it from the pan and allow to cool.

• Preheat the oven to 150°C fan. Now what you do next is not dissimilar to making granola. Mix the garlic with the toasted seeds and peanuts and the remaining ingredients for the spice crust, with 1 tbsp of the tamarind and 2 tbsp of the honey and mix together. Spread them on a baking tray to dry in the oven for about 10 minutes. They might still feel sticky when you take them out, but they should dry and set more as they cool.

• Increase the oven temperature to the highest your oven will go and roast the aubergines for 30–40 minutes, skin side down on a foil-lined roasting tin, until golden and tender all the way through. Meanwhile, mix the remaining 2 tbsp tamarind with the remaining 1 tbsp honey. Brush this on the aubergines and switch the oven off, but leave the aubergines in there for another 5 minutes.

• Place the aubergines on plates with the flesh sides facing upwards. Sprinkle generously with the spice crust and serve warm or at room temperature with a scattering of watercress. Serve any grain you like on the side, or offer it as part of a bigger feast. Make more spice mix granola because it is so good with any grilled vegetable, on top of a dhal, or on anything that needs a little texture and spice.

• TIP • The 'granola' can be used in a myriad of ways: sprinkle it on soup
(try Cauliflower Soup with Cashew Cream and Cashew Dukkah, or Dhal
(see pages 46 and 54), serve on roast sweet potatoes dressed with lemony,
garlicky yogurt… or just scatter on anything that needs a bit of crunch.

Serves 4 as a side dish, or 2 as a light lunch with rice

Steamed Cabbage with Sunflower Seed Dressing

I first tried something similar to this at a small restaurant called Peg in East London. The dressing, I figured, was based on a Japanese sesame seed preparation called *goma*, though its toasted seed flavour took me back home. I reimagined the recipe with an extra injection of Ukraine and used sunflower seeds instead of sesame. It is one of the most delicious dressings and would work on many other steamed or roasted vegetables, though this simply steamed recipe has an especially gentle effect. If you want that flavour to pack more of a punch, roast or fry the cabbage wedges after steaming. You can use any oil here, but something nutty will intensify the flavour.

····

- 100g sunflower seeds

- 2 tbsp mild vinegar (cider or rice vinegar is good), or to taste

- 1 tbsp honey, or to taste

- 1 tbsp soy sauce, or 1 tsp sea salt, or to taste

- 2 tbsp unrefined sunflower oil (or sesame, rapeseed, or another nutty oil)

- 1 pointed (Hispi) cabbage, or regular white cabbage

- Preheat the oven to 180°C fan. To make the dressing, put the sunflower seeds on a baking tray and roast in the oven for 6 minutes. They should become golden and very tasty. You may need to give them a little shake and put them back in for another 2 minutes; use your judgement here, as ovens vary.

- Blitz most of the sunflower seeds into a paste, reserving a handful for sprinkling over at the end. I use an old coffee grinder for this, but a spice grinder or a mortar and pestle should do the job. Put the seed paste into a bowl and add the vinegar, honey and soy or salt, then trickle in the nutty oil, combining it all into a smooth, thick dressing. Taste it and see if you fancy more vinegar or salt or sweetness and adjust the flavour to suit your palate. To make the dressing a little looser, add a small dash of hot water and whisk.

- For the cabbage, set a steamer (or a colander and a pan lid work too) over a pot of boiling water. Whatever cabbage you are using, cut off the dry end of the stalk. If using Hispi, quarter the cabbage lengthways through its core. If using a regular white cabbage, cut it into manageable wedges, again through the core. Steam for about 10 minutes until it looks rather relaxed and easy to cut through. White cabbage might take closer to 15 minutes.

- Let it cool down a bit and dress with the sunflower seed paste dressing (I use a brush and dab it on), putting the rest in a little bowl to spoon on extra at the table. Sprinkle the cabbage with the reserved sunflower seeds and serve.

Dhal

This recipe varies so much. It is not from any specific place or person, I just put ingredients I love together. I do love to mix up the lentils as well and I often have ends of packets at home, but you can use a single type, just adjust the cooking time accordingly. Sometimes I don't have fresh turmeric, so I substitute with ground. Sometimes I only have onion, ginger and spices. Since

Wilf started eating with us, I add chilli just to my plate. When it comes to ginger and turmeric roots, I often don't bother to peel them; the skin is just not detectable, trust me. But if you do want to peel it, scrape it off with a teaspoon, that's the easiest way. You do not have to do the blending bit if you don't have a machine, but if you do I think it's worth it, as it makes the sauce extra-silky.

- 2 tbsp coconut oil
  or
  1 tbsp flavourless oil,
  plus 10g unsalted butter
- 200g shallots, sliced
- 3 garlic cloves, finely grated
- 20g piece of ginger, finely grated
- 20g turmeric root, finely grated, or 1 tsp ground turmeric
- 400g can of chopped tomatoes
- 1 tsp ground cinnamon
- ¼ tsp chilli powder
- 1 tsp ground cumin
- 1 tsp ground coriander
- 400g can of coconut milk
- 150g Puy or brown lentils
- 150g red lentils
- sea salt

- Heat the 2 tbsp coconut oil, or the 1 tbsp oil flavourless oil and the butter, in a large pan, add the shallots and a generous pinch of salt and fry for 10 minutes over a medium heat, stirring from time to time, until golden brown. As always, if it feels like they are sticking, add a splash of water and scrape at the base of the pan. Now add the garlic, ginger and turmeric and cook for another 3–5 minutes.

- Blitz the contents of the pan with the chopped tomatoes (reserve the can) and all the spices until smooth in a food processor. Return it to the pan. Take the empty tomato can, add water to its brim and empty it into the pan, rinsing the can out in the process. Add the coconut milk, then fill this can, too, with water, and tip it into the pan.

- Bring to a simmer, then add the Puy or brown lentils, give them a good stir and cook for 20–30 minutes. Add the red lentils and cook for another 20–30 minutes or until all the lentils are nice and soft. The red lentils thicken the dish and the Puy provide a pleasant texture. If the dhal starts spitting furiously at any point but the lentils are still tough, I add more hot water, ½ cupful at a time, which makes it stop spitting.

- **TIP • Use this dhal as a canvas. Add your own creative flair! You can drop in a handful of spinach or chard the next day and warm through. Or serve with roasted squash, Crispy Pickled Shallots or savoury 'granola' spice crust (see pages 287 and 50). Or spoon it over some plain brown rice, or serve with Radish and Pomegranate Salad (see page 68), or just with some finely chopped raw red onion and loads of herbs.**

Bengali Chicken Roast

I have always pined for good neighbours. My Russian grandmother Vera found very good ones in her new home: Tashkent, Uzbekistan. They taught her so many recipes, which eventually entered our lives. But for years this situation refused to transpire for me. In my last house I had a neighbour to whom I brought cakes and made an effort… but was met with indignation, even hostility. Perhaps I did it all wrong. However, when we moved to our home three years ago, I finally lucked out. Our neighbours left, right and centre (literally) were the loveliest, friendliest people. It became obvious during lockdown. We had just had a baby, and were exhausted.

In came Fatima, as well as Emily and James with their incredible cakes, and, later on, Parvin, with a deep bowl of golden-hued Bengali chicken. I asked her for the recipe. She said, 'When we are allowed to meet, I will teach you.' I came with my notebook and enthusiasm. We cooked together, she fed me samosas and bhajis. I was blown away. I hope you make this and take it to your neighbour. Just watch out: it is very hot! Use milder curry blends if you or your neighbours can't take the heat. Sometimes, for Joe's veggie version, I make more sauce than in the recipe and mix half of it with roasted cauliflower or other vegetables.

- 7 generous tbsp vegetable oil
- 1 heaped tsp panch phoran
- 7cm piece of ginger, finely grated
- 20 garlic cloves, finely grated
- 5 medium onions, finely sliced
- 2 bay leaves
- 3 star anise
- 4 cardamom pods
- 3 cinnamon sticks
- 2 tsp chilli powder
- 2 tsp Rajah mixed curry powder (mixed masala)
- 3 bone-in whole chicken legs (drumstick and thigh pieces)
- 4 tsp hot curry powder (Parvin favours Bolst's, which has coriander, turmeric, mustard, chilli 12%, ginger, cumin and fenugreek)
- sea salt

• Start by making *moshla*, which often refers to a specific spice mix, but in this case is the onion sauce. Heat 5 generous tbsp of oil in a saucepan over a medium heat until it sizzles, then add the panch phoran and reduce the heat to its lowest. Add the grated ginger and garlic and cook for a further 2 minutes, stirring often.

• Now increase the heat again to medium, add the onions with a generous pinch of salt and cook for another 5 minutes, stirring from time to time. When the onions soften a bit, reduce the heat again and let them cook for a further 35–40 minutes with the lid on. You want the onions to soften properly and turn into a sauce (you can help them along by squashing with a potato masher). You do not want the onions to colour at any point.

• Now add the bay leaves and whole and ground spices (except the hot curry powder) and let them cook for a further 10 minutes with the lid on. It is important that the onions soften and become properly saucy, so they can cling to the chicken pieces later. If you feel at the end of the 50 minutes that your onions are not quite falling apart yet, give them a little longer.

• Meanwhile, preheat the oven to 200°C fan. Get a baking tray and some foil.

• Parvin washes and pats dry the chicken pieces, then makes slashes through the skin and flesh and rubs with ½ tsp salt and the hot curry powder.

• Heat the remaining 2 tbsp oil in a frying pan over a medium heat, then fry the chicken for 2–4 minutes on each side until properly browned. Do not overcrowd the pan. When golden, place the chicken into the tray. I then use the foil to create a kind of a 'tent', so it covers the tray without touching the chicken skin. Cook, covered, in the oven for 40 minutes, or until the juices run clear.

• Finally, add the chicken to the *moshla*, making sure to cover the pieces evenly with the sauce. Serve the chicken, with any remaining *moshla* in a bowl on the side for people to add extra at the table. If you can take really spicy food, add fresh green chillies. Scatter with coriander leaves, if you like, and serve with plain rice. I wanted to add yogurt, but Parvin was not a big fan of this idea!

Wedge Salad with Kefir and Blue Cheese Dressing and Bacon Crumbs

I love a wedge salad and get extremely excited when I see it on restaurant menus. When the restaurants were all shut in 2020, I decided to create my own homemade ultimate wedge salad. If you would like to keep it vegetarian, use Crispy Pickled Shallots (see page 287) instead of bacon crumbs. I know Iceberg lettuce gets a lot of grief, but personally I really love it, so if you can find it, use it! Otherwise, use any firm lettuce that you love and can make into wedges. You can use back bacon, but I love the crispy fat of streaky here.

- ·· 4 rashers of streaky bacon
- ·· 25g stale bread
- ·· 100g blue cheese
- ·· 150ml kefir
- ·· 1 tbsp sherry vinegar, or other good vinegar
- ·· a mixture of Little Gem and chicory (3–4 heads in total), or 1 Iceberg lettuce
- ·· sea salt and black pepper

- Preheat the oven to 180°C fan. Line a baking tray with some baking parchment and lay out the bacon on it. Cook in the hot oven for 20 minutes or until golden brown. If your oven is ferocious, check on your bacon before 20 minutes is up. Equally, if after 20 minutes it does not look quite as delicious as it could, give it another 3 minutes. The bacon may be a little floppy when you take it off the tray and put it on to some kitchen paper to drain, but it will crisp up as it cools. If you want to be cheffy, you can blitz the cooled bacon into crumbs. More often than not I can't be bothered to use and clean a food processor, so I just chop through it using a knife.

- Chop up the old pieces of bread small and bake it for 10 minutes, tossed in the bacon fat that remains in the tray, before blitzing it into crumbs. (Stir them around once halfway through.) Mix the bacon pieces with the crumbs.

- For the dressing, mash the blue cheese in a bowl with a fork to help break it up. Then add the kefir, vinegar and a good grind of black pepper and keep mushing it about until you have a homogeneous enough mass. You can always just blitz them together in a food processor or using a stick blender. Taste the sauce. Depending on how salty the cheese was, you may need to add a pinch of salt; remember your lettuce situation will be quite watery, so the dressing should pack a real punch.

- If you are serving this salad to a few people, put the lettuces on a platter and serve the dressing and bacon crumbs in separate bowls alongside so everyone can serve themselves.

- If you are plating it individually, put the lettuce or chicory on a plate, spoon over the dressing and sprinkle over the bacon. I find a wedge of lettuce enveloped in a dressing and eaten with a knife and fork really comforting.

Migrations

My Family, Interwoven Foods,
Cultures and Memories

Migrations

The skein of threads that bind the recipes in this chapter together create a sort of personal and family 'silk route': either telling of my family's historical migrations, or representing my own personal mini-relocations.

My Siberian grandmother Vera Paskova was an adventurer. She was a wanderer, both out of necessity and as a result of her strength of spirit. In 1956 she left her first husband, packed a suitcase and her eight-year-old daughter Valya and left Siberia's destitution for good. She took a train to Tashkent – the place they used to call 'the city of bread' – which is the capital of Uzbekistan. Apart from bread, the city promised work, friendship and markets filled with dried fruit, steaming dumplings and huge pans of *plov*.

On the train there, she met my Ukrainian grandfather Leonid, who charmed her with a card game he called a fancy English name: 'King'. Nine months later, he wrote her a heart-splitting love letter and immediately afterwards came to find her in Tashkent. They quickly married, and, after another nine months, my father Petro was born in the Tashkent general hospital. They were happy for a while. But, because the hot climate disturbed Leonid's head injury from the war, he eventually insisted they return to his homeland, Ukraine. She brought many a dish back with her, including rice *plov* and *manti* dumplings. When she couldn't find Central Asian ingredients, such as fat rump sheep fat, she adapted (Ukrainian butter). The marriage was a disaster – Vera and Leonid divorced acrimoniously – but my grandmother remained in Ukraine until she died in 2018.

This example of migration and adaptation made me think about what makes dishes our own. Can anyone ever own recipes and food? What *is* authenticity?

I often have people write to me along the lines of: 'I cooked your grandmother's recipe and I changed this ingredient,' or 'I altered the method slightly, I hope that's OK, I hope you approve.' And my thoughts are always the same: the minute you cook someone's recipe in your own home and fall in love with it deeply, while cherishing and acknowledging its source, you should feel free to consider the dish as your own. I always encourage and delight in adaptations made according to what's local to the cook, or what's in their fridge or cupboard that needs using up; it's healthy, it's good for the environment and it just makes sense! Little changes here and there are what move food forward, stopping it from stagnating. My California-based friend Adrian Chang and his husband Chris made my recipe for whole fermented watermelons (from my last book *Summer Kitchens*). They plonked a whole watermelon into a bucket, covered it with brine and let it ferment for 40 days. The way they used it? In a cocktail! I thought that was ingenious.

I guess my point is that I hope my grandmother's story inspires you and gives you licence (if you ever need it?) to play around with the recipes in this chapter – and indeed in the whole book – according to what you have and what you like to eat. Learn from the methods given, then tweak the recipe if you like, to weave your own story into mine. Most importantly, enjoy the process.

Butter Bean Dip with Garlic and Paprika Oil

This is based on a Balkan dish called *papula*. In the original recipe the beans are pounded quite roughly, but I do prefer a silky-smooth hummus texture. Pick whichever paprika you like best; I prefer mine sweet in this case as the garlic provides all the piquant notes I need, but if you are serving it with raw vegetables and enjoy spice, go with hot paprika. If you have fewer people to feed, it's still worth making the whole amount, as it keeps well in the fridge and will provide a quick lunch for a couple of days.

- 500g cooked butter beans, preferably those that come in a jar

- 3 tbsp olive oil

- juice of ½ lemon

- 1–2 tsp sweet or hot smoked paprika, as you prefer (see recipe introduction)

- 2 tbsp sunflower oil

- 4–6 garlic cloves, sliced

- sea salt (optional)

• Drain the beans over a bowl, but not too vigorously; it is good to retain some of the bean liquid as it makes the dip silkier. Keep a little bit of the drained bean water in the bowl, too, in case you want to make the mix looser later. Blitz the beans in a food processor and then add the olive oil in a steady stream. Add some of the lemon juice and taste it; the beans I get in jars are very well-seasoned, so I don't add extra salt, but you may need to if you used canned beans. Taste and add more lemon juice if you think it needs it. Check the texture: it definitely shouldn't be too dry, I like it to resemble silky hummus. If it does feel too dry, add a bit more of the bean water, or regular water if you've forgotten and chucked the bean water down the sink (done that before).

• Have a small bowl with the paprika at the ready. Put the sunflower oil into a small frying pan. Put the garlic into the cold oil, then heat it up over a low heat, swirling the pan gently. As soon as you see some of the garlic turning golden, reduce the heat or switch it off entirely, but keep swirling until most of the garlic looks pale gold. Do not let the garlic go too brown or it will taste acrid. As soon as the garlic colour is good, pour the oil and garlic over the paprika in the bowl.

• Spread the bean paste over a large plate, pour the red oil and garlic into the grooves and enjoy as you would a hummus, with some bread or raw vegetables such as carrots, fennel, broccoli… anything crunchy is great.

Central Asian *Plov*

This is the type of *plov* that my paternal grandma Vera and my mum Olga made when I was little. Vera's Uzbeki neighbours taught her, Vera taught Olga, Olga taught me, and I am delighted to pass this recipe to you. You might think the amount of meat is not sufficient for six, but here it's just a flavouring; this is all about the rice.

(If you feel you need more meat, add 200g extra.) It's a subtle *plov* that tastes of the ingredients themselves, though if you crave more spice, go ahead and add a little ground coriander or another favourite. But there is something very comforting about this dish and I tend to leave it exactly as it is.

- 400g basmati rice
- 1 garlic bulb (young garlic is best, but any will do)
- 400g carrots
- 100ml good-quality cooking oil (vegetable is fine)
- 400g lamb neck fillet, cut into 6 x 3cm chunks
- 300g onions, sliced
- 1 red chilli, fresh or dried
- 1½ tsp cumin seeds
- 1–2 tsp ground turmeric
- 1 tbsp chopped sour cherries, or other sour dried fruit such as barberries
- sea salt and black pepper

- Heat about 1.5 litres of water to 60°C, if you have a fancy kettle. Otherwise, boil the water, then pour into a large heatproof bowl and let it cool for 15 minutes or so. Put the rice into a heatproof bowl and pour this cooled hot water over. Add 2 tbsp salt. Leave to soak, uncovered, for at least 30 minutes, or up to 2 hours.

- If using regular garlic, cut the top off so you have a whole garlic bulb still in its skin but with an exposed top. If you have young, fresh 'wet' garlic, leave it whole.

- For the carrots, if they are organic, I rarely peel them. I scrub them, then cut them lengthways into 5mm slivers, then cut across to end up with thick-ish 6cm-long matchsticks.

- Heat the oil in a large pan for which you have a lid. I use the shallow cast-iron pan you see in the picture. Heat it until very hot, almost smoking.

- Add the meat and fry on all sides over a high heat until a golden crust appears. It will take about 7 minutes. Make sure not to move it too often, let it stay there to get properly caramelised. It will be quite intense, all high heat and spluttering, so take care not to burn your skin. Then add the onions and cook for 6–8 minutes, until golden, moving it all around from time to time. Now add the carrots and cook for another 5–7 minutes until they look softer. If you pick one up (carefully!) it should be floppy.

- Reduce the heat and pour in 800ml hot water with another 1 tbsp salt. Grind in plenty of black pepper, add the whole chilli and the garlic bulb. Gently stir through the cumin, turmeric and sour cherries. Reduce the heat to its lowest, cover with a lid and simmer for 30 minutes.

- Drain the rice in a sieve or a fine colander and put it back into its bowl. Wash it under a cold tap in the bowl. Just keep filling the bowl, stirring it, drain, then repeat gently. You may need to do this 5 times, until the water runs clear.

- Once the lamb looks softer, add the washed, drained rice and spread it in and around the meat. There should be 1cm of water above the rice. If there isn't, add some hot water until there is.

- Wrap the lid of the pan in a clean tea towel, making sure to secure the corners on top so it doesn't catch fire (a rubber band works well), and put the towelled lid on the pan. The towel is there to absorb the moisture coming off the rice, leaving the grains dry and separated.

- Cook it over a medium heat with the betowelled lid on for 30 minutes or until most of the liquid has been absorbed and the rice is soft. If it isn't soft after this time, make a hole in the middle, add 100ml boiling water and cook (covered) some more. When the rice is tender and the water has been absorbed, fluff the rice up well with a fork to let the steam escape.

- I put this whole pot of *plov* on a trivet in the middle of the table and serve with Sweet Water Salad, A Small Herb and Sour Cherry Salad, or Radish and Pomegranate Salad (see pages 71, 74 and 68), or all three.

Radish and Pomegranate Salad

This goes particularly well with Central Asian *Plov* (see previous page), but is also good with any grilled meat or vegetables. You can always prep the salad in advance, then dress it just before serving, though if it sits in its dressing that's no bad thing, as it pickles quite nicely. Daikon can be fairly normal sized or it can be humongous (*daikon* means 'big root' in Japanese), so I do provide grams here, which is roughly a small daikon.

- · seeds of 1 pomegranate
- · 300g radishes or daikon
- · 2 tbsp pomegranate molasses
- · 1 tbsp white wine vinegar, or lemon juice
- · 1 small mild white onion, finely sliced
- · handful of soft herb leaves, such as dill, coriander, mint, or Thai basil
- · pinch of sumac (optional)
- · sea salt

- Squeeze the juice from half the pomegranate seeds. The easiest way is to put the seeds into a sieve over a bowl and squeeze them with your hands so the juice flows into the bowl below and the pips remain in the sieve to be discarded. Reserve the whole seeds from the other half.

- If you are using regular radishes, cut them however you like: in halves, in quarters, or in slices. The thinner they are, the faster any leftover salad will pickle.

- If you are using daikon, I don't always peel it, especially if it is organic. To cut this bigger radish safely, slice a little 'cheek' off its side to create a stable platform; you don't want it rolling around while you slice it. If your daikon is huge, cut it across in half first, so it's easier to handle. Put it on its cut, stable side and slice it as finely as you can. Then cut each slice across, so you get thinnish matchsticks.

- Add the pomegranate molasses and vinegar or lemon juice to the bowl of pomegranate juice and season generously with salt.

- Put the radishes or daikon and onion in the bowl and mix them with the dressing. Leave to macerate for 15 minutes. Add the herbs, scatter with the reserved pomegranate seeds, sprinkle with sumac, if using, and serve.

Sweet Water Salad

There are many names for this tomato and onion salad in Central Asia, including *achik chuchuk* and *shakarob* (the latter translates as 'sweet water'), and it is traditional with *plov* (see page 66), though also good with grilled meats. This has such simple ingredients, but the method of letting all the tomato and onion juices leach out is very interesting. Please only attempt this recipe when tomatoes are in their prime: ripe, juicy and aromatic. I rarely insist you slice something in a particular way, but here I must: both tomatoes and onions have to be very finely sliced. You are looking for all those juices (the 'sweet water') to come out and cut through the richness of *plov*.

·· 2 medium onions (milder white varieties are best, but red onions work too)

·· 500–600g tomatoes (a mixture of large and cherry is nice)

·· soft herb leaves, such as coriander, dill, tarragon, or green or purple basil

·· 1 red chilli, sliced, or 1 tsp chilli flakes (optional)

·· sea salt

• This is a good opportunity to practise knife skills. Peel your onions, then cut in half through the roots. Now slice them as finely as you can along the grain: take your time, put a fun podcast on and slice away so they are translucent.

• If you managed to get hold of milder-tasting white-skinned onions or red onions, it's all good, proceed to the salting step. If your onions are quite strong and make you cry, plunge them into a bowl of iced water for 5 minutes or so, then drain them thoroughly, to take away a bit of the harshness.

• Put the onion slices into a bowl and mix them thoroughly with 1 tsp salt.

• Now cut the tomatoes in half, and, with a sharp knife (I use a small serrated knife), slice very finely, being careful to catch their juices. I just keep the onion bowl nearby and swoosh the juices off the board on top of the onions as I slice.

• Mix it all gently but thoroughly, and, if you have time, leave the salad for a while, before mixing again gently.

• Sprinkle over the herbs and the chilli, if you like, and serve. If you have lots of juices left over after you finish the salad, whisk 2 tbsp olive oil into them, keep in the fridge and use as a dressing for another salad the next day.

• **TIP • Any leftovers can be blitzed the next day into a kind of gazpacho; or leftover sweet water can be whisked with oil to become a dressing for a new salad. You can also squash any leftover tomatoes on to toast which has been rubbed with raw garlic, for a *pan con tomate*-type vibe.**

A Small Herb
and Sour Cherry Salad

During his parents' divorce, my dad Petro lived with his uncle Stepan and his Armenian wife Tamara in Baku, Azerbaijan's capital. My dad was 12 and he stayed a whole year! It must have been such an adventure. One of his brightest memories is how herbs were used as a salad rather than garnish. As a result I am always on the look-out for salads where herbs are the protagonists. The idea for this salad comes from *The Food and Art of Azerbaijan* by Khabiba Kashkay. If you cannot find fresh or frozen sour cherries, you can rehydrate dried sour cherries, cranberries or barberries in hot water, or raisins in hot vinegar, let them cool down, drain and then use. When I mention a large handful of herbs, it probably equates to the leaves from a 25g packet. So overall you will need 100g soft herbs that you love.

··

- ·· 100g fresh, frozen or dried sour cherries (or see recipe introduction)
- ·· large handful of mint leaves
- ·· large handful of purple or Thai basil leaves
- ·· large handful of coriander leaves
- ·· large handful of dill leaves
- ·· sea salt

- If you are using frozen sour cherries, put them in a bowl and let them defrost. If you are using dried sour cherries, put them in a heatproof bowl and pour enough hot water over them to cover, adding a pinch of salt. Let them cool; 15–30 minutes will do the job, otherwise just make sure they look plump! If you are using ripe fresh cherries, tear them right over the serving bowl to catch the juices (compost the stones). The juices that come out of frozen cherries can be saved and used as a dressing.

- Mix the herbs with the cherries, add a pinch more salt, if you used fresh or frozen cherries, and enjoy… it is so versatile, fresh and delicious.

··

- **TIP • Because this is so simple, it can be used in a hundred ways. Sprinkle over a lamb or vegetable stew, stuff it into a flatbread with some leftover roast chicken, pumpkin or sweet potato, or stir through pilau- and *plov*-style dishes. If you made lots but didn't finish it, chop through until finely shredded and whisk into a dressing, either for salads or to dress beans or roasted veg.**

··

Serves 4–6 (or 3 greedy people)

Chicken Pörkölt

Do not be fooled by the simplicity of this dish: the result is delicious, possibly one of the best chicken recipes I have ever tried. The idea for it comes from the doyenne of modern Hungarian cooking, Zsófia Mautner. Frying the chicken in goose fat is inspired, like all the best traditional cooking. Hungarians would serve this with spätzle-like pasta called *nokedli*, but you can use any short pasta. Whatever you choose, those russet paprika juices are best when soaked into something: rice, polenta, mashed potato or bread all do the job. Sometimes red pepper and tomato are added, but I like this simple version best. I implore you to give it a go and do not forget the goose fat. If you whisk in 1 tbsp crème fraîche at the end, Zsófia instructs us, you will have a chicken paprikás!

·· 2 chicken drumsticks

·· 2 chicken thighs

·· 2 chicken wings

·· 3 tbsp goose or duck fat

·· 2 large onions, sliced

·· 2 tbsp sweet paprika

·· 300ml water

·· sea salt and black pepper

• Season the chicken well with salt and pepper. Heat the goose or duck fat (or oil if you like, but it won't be as good) in a medium casserole pan. Fry the chicken pieces until golden brown on each side over a medium heat. You may need to do it in batches so as not to overcrowd the pan and make them sweat rather than brown. Don't be tempted to disturb and turn them too soon, a little bit of patience really helps the browning process! It may take up to 10 minutes.

• Now add the onions and reduce the heat ever so slightly. Mix it all well together; the onion should release its juices and you should be able to scrape at any chicken bits that got stuck to the pan. If there isn't enough onion juice, just add a small splash of water and scrape at the base of the pan as the water sizzles and helps release all the crispy bits.

• Cook, uncovered, over a medium-low heat, giving the onions and chicken pieces a little swoosh around occasionally, until the onions soften and start colouring a bit. No need to caramelise them too much, but do give this process, again, at least 10 minutes.

• Season well with salt, pepper and paprika. (If you are using hot or smoked paprika instead of sweet, perhaps go with 1 tbsp instead of 2, depending on how hot you like your food.) Now pour in the measured water; there's no need for the chicken to be fully covered, you just want the water for steam. Bring to a simmer, cover tightly with a lid and cook over the lowest heat for 1 hour. The chicken will be cooked through well before the time runs out, but cooking it for this long means it becomes very soft.

• This is, to me, the perfect dish. Chicken meat, essentially confited in goose and chicken fat, falling off the bone, juices gleaming with brick-red paprika. The chicken will be soft, and fresh bread is good for dipping into the juices. A little kraut or – to mix cultural metaphors – kimchi on the side would not go amiss.

'I can almost, sometimes,
feel my Mum's hand on
my shoulder, and, on
occasion, Granny's too'

Jeremy Lee, Chef-Proprietor of Quo Vadis

Lentil Soup for the Soul

'My Granny's tiny scullery in her flat in Dundee was a room I looked at in wonderment. It was so small, but everything in it fitted perfectly, just so, neat, orderly, spick and span. It reminded me of a galley in a boat in which you could reach for everything you needed from where you stood. From this miniature kitchen came forth pans of soup and other dishes, often simple and plain but warming and nourishing and always good.

The dish I loved best and craved most – and now make myself – is a pan of lentil soup. Mum made it at home, as indeed did a great many households in Scotland, for it is a national dish. When I was a schoolboy I ate lunch with my Granny every day, jumping on the bus to the Sinderins in the West End of Dundee and arriving in time for a bowl of the miraculous soup. I remember my nose catching a waft of the lentil soup in the air as it simmered and my body being lifted and carried after it to my stool in Granny's kitchen, awaiting a bowl.

It is a simple recipe: many carrots, a little onion and a small potato, coarsely chopped then lightly fried in a nut of lard, to which is added a smoked ham hock. Lentils are added and water enough to cover. These are then gently simmered for a fair few hours until the hock has imparted all it can and becomes a small cooked ham to be eaten with a dod of mustard in a soft white roll, or, as it is known in Scotland, a bap. The soup is ladled into bowls with a big scatter of chopped curly parsley and a grind or two of the pepper mill, and, of course, that ineffable ingredient, contentment. I can almost, sometimes, feel my Mum's hand on my shoulder, and, on occasion, Granny's too.'

Armenian Chard and Lentil Soup

I have been making *vospov-panjarov abour* broth from the brilliant *Armenian Cuisine* by Aline Kamakian and Barbara Drieskens for a couple of years. This is an approximation of their amazing recipe; I have reduced the amount of lemon to suit my palate. You can use chickpeas instead of lentils, or any pulse or grain you like really, just adapt the cooking times. The method of frying dried mint and garlic in butter is inspired; it adds so much flavour and extra buttery comfort. The original recipe instructs the reader to put the butter directly into the main pot, but I like to drizzle it into each bowl. Whatever you do, do *not* skip this step.

·· 500g chard

·· 2 tbsp olive oil

·· 1 onion, finely chopped

·· 2 tbsp tomato paste

·· 2 tbsp rose harissa

·· 200g brown or Puy lentils

·· 2 small potatoes, scrubbed but unpeeled, chopped into 2cm pieces

·· 1.5 litres water, or vegetable or chicken stock

·· 30g unsalted butter

·· 4 garlic cloves, finely chopped or grated

·· 1 tbsp dried mint

·· 1 lemon, quartered

·· sea salt

• Slice the chard stalks quite finely and roughly chop the leaves. It will feel like there is a lot of chard. But don't worry, it will wilt down, you may just need to use a large pot.

• Heat the olive oil in a large saucepan or cast-iron pot. Cook the onion and a pinch of salt over a medium-low heat until soft and translucent. Add the tomato paste and harissa and cook for a couple of minutes, stirring often. Add the lentils and potatoes, coat them in the pan juices and pour in the water or stock. Cook for about 20 minutes.

• When the lentils are soft and the potato is almost done, add the chard stalks, followed 5 minutes later by the leaves. Cook for about 10 minutes: the chard stalks will be cooked but still a little crunchy and the leaves will have wilted nicely. Taste and add a little more salt. Switch the heat off, you are almost ready to have lunch!

• Now, heat the butter in a small frying pan or saucepan and add the garlic, cooking for a minute over a low heat and swirling it around the pan. You don't want it to colour too much, just to mellow. As soon as it looks like it might start turning golden, add the dried mint and pour into a small bowl to be added immediately to each bowl for extra richness and flavour. If you are not using the butter immediately, simply reheat it when you are ready to serve.

• Squeeze lemon juice into each bowl and serve.

Serves 4 as a side dish (especially if eggs are involved)

Green Beans Cooked in Tomatoes

There is something so simple about this Armenian dish. Sometimes my aunt Nina just uses seasoned fresh grated tomatoes as a dressing, but sometimes the beans are cooked in onions and tomatoes. I love this version very much. Remember there is no harm in beans being cooked longer than we have been led to believe recently.

They do not need to be al dente in every dish, it is OK for them to be soft! In fact, I make this dish using frozen beans a lot in late winter, when I become particularly impatient for spring and summer. You can poach eggs in it, too, as with a shakshuka, to make a hearty breakfast or lunch dish.

···

- 300g frozen French beans, or fresh runner beans
- 20g unsalted butter
- 1 onion, chopped
- 400g can of chopped tomatoes, or 400g fresh ripe tomatoes, chopped
- 1 large garlic clove, chopped
- large handful of chopped herb leaves (dill, coriander, basil, tarragon, parsley or a combination all work)
- 2–4 eggs (optional)
- sea salt

- If you are using fresh runner beans, pinch the little stalk bit off with your fingertips and cut into 5cm pieces. Put a pot of boiling salted water on the stove. Add the beans and boil for about 5 minutes. Drain and set aside.

- Meanwhile, melt the butter in a pan and add the onion and a generous pinch of salt. Cook over a medium-low heat, stirring often, until the onion softens. Add the tomatoes (if I use a can, I also fill the can halfway with water, swirl it and add that too; if you didn't use a can, add about 200ml water) and let them start bubbling over a medium heat, reducing in volume ever so slightly. This will take about 10 minutes.

- Add the beans and stir to coat them in the sauce. If you are using fresh, boiled beans, cook for about 5 minutes. If you are using frozen, add them frozen into the bubbling sauce, cover and cook for 15 minutes.

- Finally, stir in the chopped garlic and cook for a minute. Finish with the fresh herbs and serve with fresh bread or flatbreads (for homemade, see page 271). If you want to poach eggs in it, make dips and crack your eggs in, then cook over a low heat (covered if you don't care about the white covering the yolks) until the whites have set sufficiently, but the yolks are still a little jiggly.

- **TIP • If you have leftover beans, or just their sauce, you can do what Armenian, Azerbaijani and the cooks of many other cuisines do: reheat the sauce in the pan and then whisk some beaten raw eggs through to make tomatoey scrambled eggs.**

Mother Taralezhkova's Potatoes

It has been wonderful to see more and more Eastern European cooks appear on the UK scene. One of them is the brilliant Aleksandar Taralezhkov from Bulgaria. His vegan kimchi rolls and other playful versions of Bulgarian classics have captured the imagination of the world wide web (and the residents of Margate). I was so excited to see he was opening a restaurant in Margate… and then lockdown 2.1 came crashing down on us all, delaying the opening. This is his mother Taralezhkova's recipe. Delicious jacket potatoes done in an unusual way, loaded with all the best things. If you want to just bake your potatoes whole, that's also cool, but do make the yogurt, feta and carrot topping, it is *so* good!

- 1kg medium potatoes (roasting potatoes are best), scrubbed but unpeeled

- 150g butter, salted or unsalted

- 300–400ml yogurt

- 150g feta, crumbled, or cottage cheese seasoned with salt

- 30g dill, finely chopped

- 30g parsley leaves, finely chopped

- 1 medium carrot, very finely chopped

- 3 spring onions, or 1 red onion, very finely chopped

- 1 small garlic clove, crushed

- sea salt

- Preheat the oven to 200°C fan.

- Cut the potatoes in half lengthways so you end up with potato boats and a wide surface for crisping up. So the potatoes are stable, you can always slice a little bit off the rounded side.

- Cut up the butter into as many chunks as there are potato halves, so each ends up with a generous amount to melt on top. Season with salt according to your butter, but don't be stingy if your butter is unsalted.

- Place on a baking tray sliced side up and cook in the oven for 25–35 minutes. Once well cooked, and they can be easily pierced with a knife, flip bottom side up so the crispy flat surfaces soak up all the nice buttery juices. Crisp up the bottoms for another 5 minutes. They should end up dark golden in colour. The butter will look dark at the end of cooking and you may think it will all taste rather burnt, but it won't.

- While the potatoes are roasting, prepare the topping.

- In a bowl, mix everything (do not skip the carrots!) with the yogurt and cheese. This should have plenty of greenery.

- Mother Taralezhkova says it's of paramount importance to only dish up and load the potato you are going to eat immediately, as otherwise you risk an awfully soggy situation, but personally I really rather like the soggy situation! So I actually slash the top of the crispy potatoes and then spoon the yogurt and feta topping over. Pick your own camp and enjoy, these really are wonderful and will lift you out of any baked-bean-and-cheese baked potato rut.

Pumpkin Stuffed with Sour Dried Fruit, Nuts and Rice

It may sound a little retro, but I cannot think of anything better than a pumpkin stuffed with buttery rice, perhaps served with garlic yogurt, whether you use a summer squash on a cool rainy evening or a sweet orange beauty during October. Use any nut or dried fruit you like, although in the Armenian recipe this was based on, walnuts and Cornelian cherries were used. These fruit of a perennial tree are mostly stone, but whatever flesh you do get off them tastes like sour cherries and cranberries, just a little bit more floral. Barberries, sour cherries and cranberries are best here, but dried apricots also work. A word of warning: all pumpkins are different in size and – importantly – texture, so you may need to use your judgement regarding how much filling your pumpkin will be able to take and how long it will need to cook.

....

·· 50g ghee or unsalted butter

·· 2 onions, finely chopped

·· ½ tsp ground cinnamon

·· 1 tsp ground coriander

·· 150g brown rice

·· 30g dried sour fruit (whole barberries or chopped sour cherries)

·· 500ml water

·· 1 x 1kg onion squash or pumpkin

·· 50g nuts, lightly toasted (see page 182)

·· vegetable oil

·· 1 small garlic clove, crushed

·· 100ml yogurt

·· sumac (optional)

·· sea salt

• Heat the ghee or butter in a heavy-based casserole. Add the onions, spices and a generous pinch of salt. Cook over a medium-low heat for about 15 minutes, stirring occasionally, until the onions become deep golden. If the pan becomes dry at any time, add little splashes of water and scrape at the base with a wooden spoon. Add the rice and dried fruit and pour in the measured water. Add 1 tsp salt and taste the water, it should be lightly salted. Cover with a lid and cook over the lowest heat for 25 minutes.

• Meanwhile, cut the top off the pumpkin (keep the top!) and scoop up the seeds with a spoon or with your hand (easier!). If it's an excellent pumpkin, you can always wash a handful of the seeds and dry them for a couple of weeks, then plant them out in spring, if you have a garden (the very pumpkin you see in the photo is the fruit of this kind of forethought).

• Preheat the oven to 180°C fan. The rice should be nearly cooked by now, the water gone. Stir the nuts through the rice mixture and fill the pumpkin. Replace the lid on top, drizzle some oil over the pumpkin's skin and cook it in the oven for about an hour. The pumpkin should look charred on the outside and the flesh should be easily pierce-able with the tip of a knife.

• Stir the garlic and a pinch of salt through the yogurt, scatter it with sumac, if you like, and serve in a bowl alongside the pumpkin. This is good with some pickles or fresh leaves.

'We ate them hot-juggled
in the mouth before they
even landed on the kitchen
paper meant to absorb
the extra oil, against all
dictates of common sense'

Yemisi Aribisala, Nigerian Author and Visual Artist

Fried Sweet Pastry Bows

'One of my earliest and fondest memories of home food are fried sweet pastry bows. When I searched on the internet for them, I found something called *farfallette dolci*. What? There is no way we called them that in my mother's kitchen in Suru-lere, Lagos, Nigeria! I can't even pronounce the words.

I don't remember calling them anything at all because I suspect my mother made them out of some foreign cookbook, but they were the same exact sweet dough, shaped like bows and fried in oil, not dusted with icing sugar because that was too much sweetness for the Nigerian palate. We were always moderating sugariness.

You wanted to wear the bows and eat them and wear them and eat them. We ate them hot-juggled in the mouth before they even landed on the kitchen paper meant to absorb the extra oil, against all dictates of common sense... You kept your mouth open to percolate the burning heat and blew out frantically from the pain of the roof of your mouth peeling off in one piece.

They were good. Almost like puff-puffs or chin-chin but a different texture, in-between somewhere. Sweet and hot and just the right balance of dense and chewy.'

Wild Garlic Dressed in Vinegar

Apart from mushrooms, foraging culture has been largely lost in my part of Ukraine, so it has been satisfying to hear stories of my half-Armenian aunt Nina who grew up in Baku, Azerbaijan and the Karabakh mountains on the Armenian border. Hundreds of wild herbs grow in the Caucasus and people use them. This method of preparing wild garlic is from a 1960 edition of *Armenian Cuisine*.

It says that a similar method can be applied to nettles, goosefoot, purslane, sickleweed and marshmallow plant. If you are not a forager, or want to make something like this in other seasons than spring, use chard or large-leafed spinach. Whatever you do, this is the occasion when you should get that bottle of really excellent vinegar out of the cupboard.

·· 200g wild garlic

·· 3 tbsp very good vinegar

·· nutty oil, such as sesame or unrefined sunflower, to serve (optional)

·· sea salt

• Have a large bowl of iced water at the ready. Put the wild garlic into an empty pot and pour boiling water over, leave for 30 seconds, then drain and immediately immerse into the iced water. The wild garlic will become sweet and lose its harshness. Drain again and spin in a salad spinner if you have one, or pat dry with a tea towel.

• Dissolve ¼ tsp salt in the best vinegar that you have (I often use quince vinegar from Vinegar Shed) and use this to dress the wild garlic. A slick of sesame oil or unrefined sunflower oil on top is very good indeed. It is good as an accompaniment to a sweet, meaty vegetable such as Pumpkin Stuffed with Sour Dried Fruit, Nuts and Rice, or you can use it to top toast and eat that with Dark Greens Soup with Blue Cheese (see pages 86 and 130).

Joza's Octopus with Potatoes, Croatian-Style

I asked a Croatian-Ukrainian friend, Anna Corak, for her family's octopus recipe. This is normally cooked in a special dome-lidded pan in a wood-fired oven (imagine that!). Her response was so good, I'm leaving her words unchanged:

'I called my aunt Ankica to ask for the recipe, her husband Joza used to have a little boat in Zadar, he used to catch octopi and cook them. They even had a special octopus freezer! Anyway, she was quite helpful with the process, but not at all with measurements and timings, you know how aunts are!

'Since I think it's rude to send untested recipes, especially to someone whose recipes I love, I popped by the supermarket yesterday and got myself a nice little frozen octopus. Thankfully, my husband can eat weird things for breakfast, so now I have an adaptation of the recipe that works in the normal oven, which of course is an abomination for purists in Croatia. Fortunately, this turned out to be a very tasty abomination.'

She added that frozen octopus is best, as it's already tenderised. This recipe has been made numerous times in my own home, and is a good initiation if you've never cooked octopus before. It's very easy, trust me and have a go. A word of warning: even an octopus that looks massive when raw will shrink considerably. So don't think, 'Oh this is huge and will actually feed eight,' especially if this is your main dish. It is a good make-ahead recipe, as you can boil the potatoes and poach the octopus the day before and keep them in the fridge, covered. Take them out a couple of hours before putting them in the oven, so they are not fridge-cold.

·· 1–2 octopus (about 2kg), frozen is best

·· olive oil

·· 2 bay leaves

·· 500g floury baby or regular potatoes, scrubbed, skins left on

·· 1 onion, quartered

·· 8 garlic cloves, half left whole, half finely chopped

·· 2 rosemary sprigs

·· 50ml white wine

·· sea salt and black pepper

• Thaw your octopus, rinse under a running tap, then pop into a large pot that you have a lid for. No water is needed here, you will be cooking the octopus *nell'aqua sua* as the Italians say: in its own juices. Pour 1 tbsp olive oil over the octopus and add the bay leaves. Cover the pan with a lid. Once it comes to a boil (you will hear it bubbling), cook it over a low heat (gentle heat is important here) for 35 minutes. By this time, the octopus will have released more water and its colour should have changed from greyish to purplish. If it still looks grey and raw, give it another 10 minutes. How long it needs depends on its size and whether it has been frozen or not, so go by feel (below) rather than timings.

• To test if it's ready, slice off a tentacle and take a bite: it should be soft and not too chewy. If it is very rubbery and chewy still, give it another 10 minutes, covered, over a low heat. If you are using a couple of octopus it may take up to an hour for them to soften sufficiently. Remember the octopus will get cooked further in the oven, so don't let it become too buttery-soft. Let the octopus cool down a bit in the liquid with the lid off. Keep the octopus liquor, do not discard it.

• Preheat the oven to its highest setting. We are trying to emulate a wood-fired oven here, so we need that fierce heat.

• While all this is happening, halve the baby potatoes, or cut larger potatoes into 2cm pieces and put them into a pot of cold water. Season the water with salt, bring to the boil, then simmer for 5–10 minutes or until the potatoes can be easily pierced with a knife, but are not falling apart.

• Drain the potatoes and let them steam off a bit in a colander.

- Take the octopus out of its liquid and nestle it, whole, with the onion and whole garlic cloves in a lightly oiled casserole dish, making sure the tentacles are on top as you want them to get crispy. Drizzle over 2 tbsp olive oil. Make sure you know how salty the octopus is, then season accordingly, if it needs it. Cover with a lid and bake in the oven for 20 minutes. Nestle the potatoes and 1 rosemary sprig around the octopus, add another drizzle of olive oil over it all and cook, uncovered, for another 15–30 minutes, allowing the octopus and potatoes to crisp up. Do check up on it, everyone's ovens are different, mine is quite weak so it takes me the full 30 minutes to get to the crispiness that I desire.

- Meanwhile, put 100ml of the octopus juices into a small pan, add the finely chopped garlic and the other rosemary sprig, bring to a simmer and gently cook it for a couple of minutes. Now add the wine and let it bubble for another couple of minutes, so the alcohol evaporates off. Taste it: the octopus liquor, in my experience, can vary in saltiness, so add salt and pepper if it tastes bland.

- Serve the garlicky wine sauce alongside the roasted octopus and take it to the table with some crusty bread and a big lettuce salad.

Vegetable Gratin Balkan-Style

Whenever my dad spots a cookbook on Eastern European cuisine – in a supermarket, a petrol station, online – he gets it for me, however strange the topic! They are often unassuming looking but contain gems. I spotted a version of this dish (billed as 'vegetarian lasagne') in my dad-curated books, in a volume called *Bulgarian Cuisine* by Olga Kuzmina. This has all my most favourite ingredients: juicy summer vegetables, feta, yogurt, herbs. It is important to make sure the vegetables, especially the potatoes, are finely sliced, so they cook quickly. In the original, the feta is just crumbled in between the layers, but I like whipping it with the yogurt to make sure its flavour gets on every bit of every vegetable.

....

- 1 medium courgette (300g)

- 4 medium tomatoes (total weight 400g)

- 3 medium potatoes, unpeeled but scrubbed (total weight 400g)

- 1–2 fat garlic cloves

- 2 red peppers (total weight 200g)

- 200g feta

- 150ml yogurt

- olive oil

- small bunch of dill, chopped (optional)

- pinch of paprika (I like it hot, but you can use sweet)

- sea salt and black pepper

• Make sure your vegetables and sauce are prepped before you begin and this recipe will be a real doddle! Slice the courgette into thin slices (about the thickness of 1 pound coin). Do the same with the tomatoes, I find a serrated fruit knife is best here. Now slice the potatoes as finely as you possibly can. Slice the garlic finely too.

• Cut the peppers in half and scoop out the seeds, snip off the stalks and compost them. Slice the peppers across finely.

• For the sauce, blitz the feta with the yogurt, or just use a hand-held whisk to mush it all together. Taste it and see if it can do with a small pinch of salt, it will depend how salty your cheese is. You can always add some finely chopped herbs if you like; it's a good way to use up any fridge-tired herbs.

• Preheat the oven to 220°C fan. Pour 2 tbsp oil into a 30 x 20cm baking tray or an equivalent-sized pie dish. Now put the potatoes in so they cover the base of the dish, overlapping the edges, sprinkle over some salt and pepper and pour over some more oil. Then put the courgette on top, overlapping again. Add the peppers. Add the garlic and the dill, if using, drizzle over a little more oil and season with salt and pepper. Now put the sliced tomatoes over, but no more salt as you don't want the tomatoes to release too much liquid.

• Put the tray or dish in the oven for 30 minutes. The tomatoes will look drier, fraying at the edges. Pour the whipped feta sauce evenly over the top and return to the oven for a final 15–20 minutes or until nice and golden on top. Sprinkle over the paprika for the last 5 minutes of cooking, so it doesn't get burned.

My Brother's Salad

Recent events have rejigged so many family dynamics. My older (and only) brother Sasha ended up moving to Kyiv from Lviv and living in the same flat as his older son Nikita and his fiancée Yana. Nikita is a very good meat cook, often roasting big slabs of this or that. My brother, however, who also loves cooking, really missed vegetables and started making this salad, which is both hearty – because of the cooked aubergines and cheese – and fresh, because of the tomatoes. Do make sure to get the meatiest tomatoes you can. It is the simplest thing, with a short ingredients list, but uses a clever aubergine preparation technique, is full of flavour and hits all your vegetable needs. He calls it his 'Armenian salad', but to me it is my brother's.

- 2 (or however many you like) medium garlic cloves
- 2 large aubergines
- 5 tbsp olive oil
- ½ small red onion, finely sliced
- juice of 1 lemon
- 4 large, very ripe tomatoes (such as Bull's Heart)
- 2 tbsp sesame oil
- soft herb leaves, such as coriander, dill, basil, or all of them
- 100g feta, crumbled
- sea salt

- Peel and squash the garlic and chop it roughly.

- You can peel off strips of aubergine skin if you like, as Sasha does; it does help it cook more quickly. Then chop the aubergines into 3–4cm cubes, quite roughly, there's no need to be too precise here. Heat a large non-stick frying pan over a high heat without adding any oil. I don't have non-stick at home, so I use a cast-iron pan, and that works too, but it's a little trickier.

- Now put the aubergines in and fry them dry, moving them around from time to time. You want them to cook through and soften, it will take about 5 minutes. At the very end, add 2 tbsp of the olive oil and the garlic, then stir often. The oil will moisten and colour the aubergines and the garlic will give its flavour; this will take 2 minutes. Switch off the heat.

- Meanwhile, get the sliced onion, put it in a bowl and spritz over the lemon juice and a pinch of salt. Let it sit while you finish the salad.

- Cut the tomatoes into chunks, catching the juices in a bowl.

- Add the aubergines to the tomatoes with the rest of the olive oil, the sesame oil, the onion and its juices, herbs and feta.

Cheese and Grape Muffins

I wasn't sure where to put these in the book, as they satisfy my cake craving as well as my savoury food craving. They make a very good addition to a school lunch box, or any lunch box, or a picnic for that matter. I found the idea for this recipe (the original made in a pre-Soviet bakery in Lviv) in *Lviv Cuisine* by Igor Lylyo. It sounded intriguing and slightly mad, but after playing with the recipe for a while I made it work. These can be transformed into very lovely sweet muffins if you up the sugar to 50g and take out the cheese.

- 18 large seedless grapes (total weight about 150g)
- oil or butter, for the tin
- 2 eggs
- 100g unsalted butter, melted and cooled
- 250ml whole milk
- 40g sugar or honey
- 250g self-raising flour
- 150g feta, crumbled
- sea salt

- Preheat the oven to 180°C fan.

- Halve your grapes. If they do have seeds, take them out. Prepare a 12-hole muffin tin by lightly oiling or buttering it, or line it with paper cases if you prefer.

- Mix the eggs with the cooled melted butter, then whisk in the milk. Whisk in the sugar or honey and a generous pinch of salt. Sift the flour into the mixture and then gently incorporate it with a spatula. Make sure there are no pockets of flour, but do try not to overmix. Fold in the cheese in a couple of movements.

- Gently spoon the mixture into the prepared muffin tins to two-thirds full. Then push in the grapes, 3 halves into each, and bake for 25–30 minutes, until risen, deep golden-brown and firm to the touch. The skewer test might be hard to do here, as if you hit a pocket of melty feta, it won't come out clean. You might need to swap the positions of your tins around towards the end of cooking, if you're using 2 trays or not using a fan oven.

- Let the muffins cool a little in the tin, then, when you're ready to eat, gently run a knife around the edge of each to help release them from their holes.

La Libertà Che Mi Vuole

An Italian Interlude

La Libertà Che Mi Vuole

Despite having formidable cooks in my family, both male and female, I had no interest in cooking as a teenager. But then Dad, who mainly left the exhausting business of teenage parenting to Mum, put his foot down and insisted I cooked with her every weekend. It wasn't a patriarchal thing – he was and still is a natural feminist, championing women at his work and within his family – but he recognised what an invaluable and enriching skill cooking was, because he could also cook very well. We made a deal that I would master basic cooking skills with Mum every Sunday. But Mum could tell my heart wasn't in it. I burned things, and, after a few disastrous attempts, she stopped making me learn.

I did well in my A levels. Even though my dream was to become an artist, my dad – imagining me destitute with an easel under a bridge – insisted I attempted to gain a degree in language and business studies. I applied for business studies everywhere except for at the best university I approached. The University of Warwick accepted me for a degree in Italian and International Relations. To this day, it has been my most cunning move. 'Dad, you cannot deny me one of the best universities in the world. Also, look, I got an "A" and a school award in politics.' I went to Warwick.

Before our second year, all we students were asked to pick an Italian city where we would complete the exciting Erasmus language exchange programme. While everyone fought over Roma and Milano, my equally relaxed friend Natasha and I deliberately picked a place no one else wanted. We ended up in a dreamy medieval castle of a town: Urbino. The experience was well beyond any fantasy I may have harboured.

The halls of residence – designed by legendary architect Giancarlo de Carlo – were a tumbling Brutalist structure cradled inside a hill. Picture the Amalfi coast. Now imagine its famous multi-coloured little houses look like cousins of the Barbican, and replace the sea with a vast forest. Each floor had a broad terrace overlooking a valley filled with grape vines, deer and fireflies. I wish I could be there now to appreciate it even more, and to really take in the food that came out of our tiny shared kitchens.

We immediately made friends with a bunch of older Italian boys and girls. A lot of them seemed to fail their exams and resit them year after year. I wonder if it was deliberate, as student life was filled with so much multi-faceted pleasure. One of those pleasures, central to our student life, was cooking. All our new friends cooked. And how they cooked!

They all received boxes with homemade maroon-coloured *sugo della mamma* (ragù sauce). Pepe, a wide-shouldered, skin-headed, kind-hearted son of a Pugliese butcher, got boxes filled with the best cuts of meat. I couldn't yet speak Italian and the first few months were incredibly hard, but knowing about these parcels made me connect to my new friends on a very special level. It reminded me of my mum sending boxes of whole ducks and Ukrainian-style rillettes to my older brother, who was studying by the Black Sea in Odessa. I would help her pack the box, missing my brother and imagining him on the other end, skipping lectures, playing Duck Hunt on his first-generation Nintendo and munching on ready-cooked home-reared duck.

Back in Urbino, there was also Tommy, who looked like the lead singer of The Mars Volta. He used to tear up sweet cherry tomatoes and throw them into the residual heat of a spaghetti pot alongside clouds of ripped mozzarella. His cooking was effortless. Giacomo, the Sicilian maverick, pretty much single-handedly taught me Italian and made me fall in love with Sicily; I got to try his mother's outstanding cooking in Agrigento by the end of the year. I travelled to my friend Fabiana's Sardinia too, to a tiny town called Gesturi, up in the hills where tiny wild spotted pigs roamed.

Daniele, Natasha's boyfriend, was the best cook of them all. When we tumbled home at midnight, woozy with wine and music, he poured oil into a pan. In went garlic, chilli, parsley. The spaghetti, perfectly cooked, not too soft, not too al dente, was tossed in the red-flecked oil. I don't think I have ever been more ravenously hungry. Near-nude spaghetti, the hit of peperoncino, DJ Shadow organ-buzzing in the background, smoke, more wine, that sensation of freedom and zero responsibility.

I was so inspired by every meal made by my Italian friends, however simple... actually, even more so if it was very simple. By the end of my trip, when I headed back to the UK, I decided to learn how to cook

I returned to Italy the following summer for a stint of work and travel in Sicily. I waitressed at the buzz-filled Vucciria fish market, leaving me memories of heat and noise and bright-eyed fish and seafood, people selling car parts and something to do with the Chinese mafia. Then I was joined by Natasha, Giacomo and Daniele – we were all as close as family by then – and we travelled to the small island of Favignana, where canned tuna is supposed to come from. For a couple of days, we pitched a tent five metres from the sea, fishing in the mornings and cooking the fish over fire for breakfast, and circled the whole island on rented bikes.

There was a tune we played quite a lot, called *Vento in Faccia* ('Wind in my Face') by Bandabardò. The chorus went (in my clumsy translation): 'Wind in my face, arms in the air, ready to receive the sun, soul at peace, when it's quiet like this, because it's the freedom that wants me.' Every time I hear it now, it tightens and tingles inside my chest. We were so young and free, we travelled, we connected, we loved, cooked and ate and compacted five years' worth of events into one. And, for me, the seed of my cooking obsession was firmly planted.

Sea Urchin Pasta

I pinpoint the moment when I first tried this dish as the instant that transformed me forever and made me obsessed with food and cooking. It was 2004, I was in Sicily, working as a waitress in a small restaurant at the famous Vucciria fish market in Palermo. I remember the chef and owner of the restaurant, a husky-voiced character straight out of the 1980s Italian mafia series *La Piovra*. He brought me a dish of naked-looking spaghetti for staff lunch. I tasted it and it was a moment I will never forget: hot spaghetti dressed in the flavour of the sea. I did not know what *ricci* meant, and after some explaining it transpired it was sea urchin. Just pasta, olive oil, a little garlic and sea urchin. If you ever spot some at a fishmonger, treat yourself. Ask the fishmonger to get the flesh out for you if you will be cooking it immediately.

··· 20g sea urchin roe (from about 4 medium sea urchins)

··· 200g linguine or spaghetti

··· 4 tbsp olive oil, plus more to serve

··· 2 garlic cloves, sliced

··· 1 tbsp chopped parsley leaves

··· ½ tsp chilli flakes, or to taste

··· sea salt

• If you will use the sea urchin straight after buying it, ask the fishmonger to get the roe out for you. Otherwise take a towel, fold it in half and hold an urchin in the towel, so it doesn't prick your fingers. With your other hand, go into the mouth of the sea urchin with some scissors. Cut a little bit in and then around; you want to cut a circle out, like a lid. Tip the urchin over a plate and tap it on the plate so the grit and some crushed needles come out. The orange-corally roe will be stuck to the walls inside the urchin. Gently scoop it out into a bowl, making sure no grit comes with it.

• Bring a pot of water to the boil and season it with salt until it tastes like the sea. Drop the pasta in and cook for 2 minutes less than the instructions advise. You want it to be bendy but still al dente, quite firm to the tooth.

• While the pasta is cooking, heat the oil in a deep, large frying pan and add the garlic. Cook it over a very low heat, so it softens and mellows but doesn't colour; a couple of minutes should do it.

• When the pasta is ready, scoop out a cupful of pasta water, then drain the pasta. Immediately add the pasta to the pan with the garlic, add the parsley, chilli and sea urchin, add a small splash of the reserved pasta water and give it all a very good stir. Take it off the heat after 1 minute.

• Add another glug of olive oil, give it all another stir and serve immediately.

White Ragù of Genoa, Naples and Odesa

I spent a summer in Sicily when I was 20. For the first half I worked as a waitress in a restaurant, and for the second I travelled the island with my friends. We were all quite destitute, and we rented a dark, flaky apartment in one of the grand but crumbling buildings in Palermo. One of my Pugliese friends, Daniele Vilardo, a natural cook, started simmering something in a massive pot. I thought the amount of onions he put in was staggering. Then he added minced meat. Then we waited. I remember my raging hunger and the sweet, soft smell of the cooking. After a couple of hours, the dish was ready. It involved just a couple of ingredients but it was incredible. And it also time-machined me back to my childhood, to an

unassuming pasta dish we called *makaroni po flotski* ('navy-style macaroni'). My dad's version also just involved onions, minced pork and beef. His only took 30 minutes and it worked. But this Napolitano *sugo bianco* (white sauce) is something else. I did some research, and confusingly it hails from Naples, but is called *genovese*. The legend goes that merchants from Genoa, who lived in Naples in the 16th century, introduced it to the area. So this dish has a double layer of nostalgia attached to it for me, the first for my childhood and the second for my carefree, exciting year of being a student abroad. I implore you to try it.

- ·· 1kg onions (yes, this much)
- ·· 3 tbsp olive oil
- ·· 1 tbsp unsalted butter
- ·· 400g minced pork
- ·· 400g minced beef
- ·· 1 bay leaf
- ·· splosh of white wine (optional)
- ·· 250g rigatoni (or penne, ziti, bucatini or any other tubular pasta)
- ·· sea salt and black pepper
- ·· healthy grating of Parmesan or ricotta salata, to serve

- Slice the onions, not too finely, but aiming for thinnish. Put the oil and butter into a medium-sized pot, then add the onions and a generous pinch of salt. You are not looking to brown the onions but to make them turn soft and release a lot of their juices; adding salt helps with this.

- Cook them over a medium-low heat with the lid on for about 20 minutes, stirring often, until a lot of the juice gets released. I repeat, please in this instance do not let the onions colour, otherwise the dish will be very different from what I want you to experience. If at any point you notice that the onions start sticking to the pan, your heat was too high, but it's OK, add a splash of water and scrape at the base, then reduce the heat.

- Now add the minced meats, bay leaf, another pinch of salt and plenty of black pepper and stir them through the onions thoroughly. Reduce the heat to its lowest setting and cook it slowly for 2–3 hours, again with the lid on. Check from time to time that it isn't catching at the bottom, add a splash of water if it looks a little dry. But really, you shouldn't need to stir it too often; the onions and meat should release enough juices to do their thing independently from you.

- The sauce is ready when the mixture looks gently brown, creamy and almost homogeneous. You can add a splash of wine here and cook for another 10 minutes, but I rarely add the wine. If there is a lot of liquid in the pot, raise the heat and reduce it down. It should look, as Italians say, *cremosa* ('creamy').

- Look, more often than not I eat it as it is, I like and embrace the softness of it all. But if you are keen to add a little crunch and colour to this cremosity, make my easy, non-greasy pangrattato.

- Of course you can just use good-quality breadcrumbs. But if you have some scrag ends of bread that need using up, do so! Preheat the oven to 170°C fan.

For the pangrattato (optional)

·· 50g good-quality bread

·· finely grated zest of
½ unwaxed lemon

·· small handful of parsley
leaves, finely chopped

·· 1 tsp chilli flakes, or finely
chopped fresh chilli

Chop the bread (crust and all) into small chunks, then put it on a tray and into the oven for 10–15 minutes. I don't add any oil, because there is already so much delicious fattiness in the sauce. When the bread is dry and crispy, I put it into a mortar and pestle and crush it a bit into rough breadcrumbs. Lacking a mortar and pestle, you can always chop through them with a knife. Mix the breadcrumbs with the lemon zest, parsley and chilli.

• Serve the sauce with some penne or other tubular pasta, cooked according to the packet instructions, and make it rain with Parmesan or ricotta salata. Then also sprinkle over some pangrattato – which is supposed to be poor-man's Parmesan – but hey, just have it all, the cheesy and the crisp.

....

• **TIP • If you have leftovers and are bored of eating this ragù white, just put some canned tomatoes into a pan, boil them off a little to reduce, then stir in the ragù to reheat and enjoy one of the best Bolognese sauces there is.**

....

Sardinian Ravioli with Ricotta, Greens and Saffron

We arrived at the Port of Cagliari on a boat at dawn, the morning sun reinforcing the yellow-pink kaleidoscope of the buildings. But Sardinia's capital was not our destination. We were headed for Gesturi, a tiny town nestled in a valley. I remember my heart racing when we passed through the hills and saw lots of wild-looking small pigs roaming around. I remember thinking that my mum calls these kind of pigs 'greyhound pigs' as a joke, because they are so skinny and fast; we saw similar ones in Georgia. I asked if the pigs were wild, but my friend Fabiana said they weren't quite, they belonged to someone, but were just allowed to roam in the hills. Fabiana's mum Patrizia made us a roasted suckling pig later and it was the best I had ever tried. She also made *ravioli campidanesi*. She would have used what she called *cicoria salvatica*, which could have been either nettles or borage, as both are used when in season. You can certainly use spinach here, but nettles do taste very good.

For the filling

·· 100g spinach or nettles, chopped

·· 1 egg yolk

·· pinch of saffron threads

·· 250g ricotta

·· 1 tbsp plain flour

·· finely grated zest of ½ unwaxed lemon

·· sea salt

·· pecorino cheese, finely grated, to serve

For the pasta

·· 350–400g fine semolina or '00' flour, plus more to dust

·· 150ml warm water

- A quick note: if you decide to pick nettles yourself, pick them in spring before they flower, so the leaves will be tender. Be careful and use gloves and scissors and only cut off the top 10–12.5cm of the plant; the top young leaves are what you are after.

- QR CODE • *To make the pasta, put the 350g flour into a large-ish bowl. Add the measured warm water gradually and bring it all together into a rough dough with a fork or spoon. It will look shaggy and quite rough and will be tough to knead, but carry on and squish it together with your hands for a couple of minutes. Don't panic, just leave it to relax: it will be much easier to knead and will smooth out after you cover it (so it doesn't dry out) and leave it be for 10 minutes.*

- *Now your dough will be much more cooperative. Give it a good knead, you will see that it will become smooth quite quickly. Knead energetically for a solid 3 minutes, then cover again to prevent it drying out and leave to rest for 30 minutes while you potter around and attend to your greens.*

- Put the spinach or nettles into a bowl, then pour boiling water over them, making sure to submerge the leaves fully, especially nettles! Leave for a minute (or a little longer for sturdier nettles) in the water, then drain in a colander and run cold water over them. Squeeze them out thoroughly in the colander to get rid of the water; I just cup the greens in my hands over a sink and squeeze, squeeze, squeeze. You will end up with a tight ball; keep it like that, as it will be easier to chop. Slice through it, then chop across. I'd imagine a mezzaluna knife would be quite helpful here, but I just use my regular kitchen knife and chop, chop, chop until the greens are fairly finely shredded.

- To make the filling, mix the egg yolk with the saffron in a small bowl. Then add the bright yellow egg yolk to the ricotta, as well as the 1 tbsp plain flour, chopped greens, lemon zest and 1 tbsp sea salt flakes (or ½ tbsp table salt). Mix it all with a spoon, or your hand, thoroughly. Give it a taste, adding more salt if it feels a little underwhelming and mild. Pasta fillings should really be on the verge of being overseasoned.

For the sauce

·· 2 tbsp olive oil

·· 2 garlic cloves, left whole

·· 400g fresh tomatoes, chopped, or chopped canned tomatoes

·· handful of basil leaves

- QR CODE • *Cut the dough into 3 equal parts (cover those you're not using). Roll out one piece on a well-floured surface as thinly as you can. Dot spoonfuls of filling, in a row, about 2cm apart and 6cm down from the top edge. Now flip the top edge over the filling and press between the mounds, using a wet finger to seal, if needed. Squeeze the edges of the squares really well, letting the air out. Cut off right under the edge you flipped down, then between each filling, to leave neat squares.*

- For the sauce, simply heat the olive oil in a pan, add the garlic and cook it over a very low heat to infuse the oil. As soon as it smells lovely and garlicky and the garlic has got a very gentle golden glow, add the tomatoes and cook for about 10 minutes, then add the basil and cook for another 5 minutes.

- Cook the ravioli in boiling salted water for 2–3 minutes, then drain them and toss in the pan with the tomato sauce. Serve with plenty of pecorino grated over the top.

'I remember eagerly
throwing some coins
into the fountain
afterwards, making a
wish to come back here
and eat octopus again'

Octopus

....

'I tasted octopus the first time I left Ukraine, just a couple of years after the USSR dissolved. It was 1993 and my parents took one of the first (very dodgy) tours to Italy. We were called *russo turisto* and stared at quite a lot. It must have been quite the novelty to see ex-Soviet citizens on the streets of Italy.

The whole tour was a shambles, but it didn't matter to us kids. We went to an aqua park! We saw a street parade – of a non-Soviet kind – in which grotesque papier mâché puppets of Italian politicians were ridiculed rather than lionised! We all squealed in delight (including my parents), it was all so new and exciting.

One of the brightest memories was our trip to Rome. I wore the most beautiful polka-dot dress that my mum made herself. The heat was so intense (close to 50°C) that the dress clung to my body. At the Vatican, I distinctly remember the coolness of the crumpled coral-tinged marble and the golden skeleton embedded in the St Peter's cathedral Gates of Death. I had to skip the tour of the Colosseum, as I started feeling faint in the heat. We eventually ended up by the Trevi Fountain. Its grandeur and beauty filled me with awe in the truest sense.

We sat in a café right opposite the fountain and I ordered seafood salad; I can still remember the fluttering anticipation in my chest. The salad was extremely vinegary, which felt refreshing, and my mouth explored the exciting textures of the reassuringly firm baby octopus. That feeling of awe splashed into me, both with each bite of octopus and with the marbled vista of muscular Oceanus. I remember eagerly throwing some coins into the fountain afterwards, making a wish to come back here and eat octopus again.'

Sugo Della Mamma

Of course, there isn't a recipe for *sugo della mamma*. It was the title my Italian student friends gave to a tomato-based pasta sauce that took a long time to cook. Depending on the region and the mum, it could be a slow-cooked ragù, a minced meat Bolognese, or meatballs in tomato sauce. Jars of the stuff would be sent over, packed into boxes. I feel so lucky to have been able to scoff as many *sughi delle mamme* as I have. Here is an approximation of my friend Daniele's mum's *polpette*, the one I remember eating the most. I am not adding any onion to the meatball here, because I don't enjoy its crunch; it never manages to cook through thoroughly however finely I chop it. But if you absolutely cannot imagine not including onion, add 1 small onion, grated on the coarse side of a grater.

For the meatballs (*polpette*)

·· 60g stale sourdough bread, crusts and all (or dry out 80g fresh bread, cut into chunks, in the oven)

·· 250ml hot whole milk

·· large handful of parsley leaves (about a 20g packet)

·· 400g minced beef

·· 400g minced pork

·· 1 small egg, lightly beaten

·· 2 garlic cloves, finely grated

·· 100g pecorino or Parmesan cheese, finely grated (might feel like a lot, but it isn't!), plus more to serve

·· ¼ nutmeg, finely grated (it won't be too nutmeggy, I promise)

·· sea salt and black pepper

- I like adding sourdough crusts to my meatballs as it's the most flavoursome part of the bread. However, they can be quite tough and take ages to soak. There are 2 things you can do: first soak them in hot milk, and second, once soaked, break the crusts up into small pieces with your fingers when you add it to the meat.

- So, pour the hot milk over the bread in a bowl. The milk might not cover it completely, so wait for 5 minutes and then crush the bread down so it all gets soaked. Cover and leave for at least 15 minutes to soften. Chop the parsley very finely, as finely as you possibly can, really go to town here, you don't want big chunks of parsley in your mouth.

- Mix the minced meats, egg, bread along with its soaking milk, garlic, parsley, cheese and nutmeg together. Don't forget to season well with 1 tbsp sea salt and lots of pepper. Mix some more; I use my hands, it's the easiest way. You can always fry a small piece of the mixture to taste for salt.

- Then wet your hands (this way the mixture won't get stuck to them) and shape the meat mixture into golf ball-sized meatballs. You should get around 30.

- Now, this bit can be annoying if you don't have a non-stick pan. I don't, and I suffer every time. If you do, the following tips may not apply to you, as you should just breeze through the frying easily. Heat 3 tbsp of the oil for the sauce.

- If you are using a cast-iron pan, gently lower in the meatballs (so the hot oil doesn't splash you), depending on the size of your pot – maybe 6 balls at time so they don't overcrowd and stew – and fry over a medium-low heat on a couple of sides, no need to mess around trying to get the whole sphere properly brown. Without non-stick the balls might keep sticking to the pan, I'm afraid. Be patient and don't try to turn them too soon: I use a fish slice and give them a scrape if they get stuck.

- Take the balls out for now and leave them on a plate. Now, if your sticking situation has been tricky and the sticky bit in the pan are too dark, wipe out the pan with plenty of kitchen paper. But hopefully it's all good and you have lots of flavoursome fat. If the stickiness was moderate and it's all looking golden but not burned, do not wipe away the oil and pork fat: it's flavour!

- If there isn't sufficient fat, add another 2 tbsp oil.

For the sauce

·· up to 5 tbsp olive oil

·· 2 garlic cloves, peeled and bruised, but left whole

·· 800g tomato passata or 2 x 400g cans of chopped tomatoes

·· couple of basil sprigs

....

·· 640g tagliatelle, pappardelle or orecchiette, to serve

• Add the bruised garlic to the pan where the meatballs have just cooked and cook for a couple of minutes over a low heat to infuse the oil, then take them out and compost them.

• Now add the passata or tomatoes to the pan. Fill the jar or tin with 200ml water and add that too with a generous pinch of salt. Cook over a medium-low heat for about 15 minutes. Gently nestle the meatballs into the sauce. Cook for 15–20 minutes, letting it bubble gently. Add the basil sprigs for the last 5 minutes of cooking, gently squeezing them to release more flavour into the sauce.

• Cook the pasta according to the packet instructions in plenty of salted water. Drain the pasta, but not too fervently, you want a little of the pasta water to remain. Put the pasta back into its pot, then ladle over some of the sauce and meatballs and stir through. Serve on individual plates with some meatballs plonked on top and more pecorino to grate over it all.

Spaghetti Alla San Giovanni (*San Giuannid* in Dialect)

I remember my friend Tommaso Piccarreda for his light touch with pasta sauces. He would throw a couple of ingredients (fresh tomatoes torn by hand, basil and mozzarella) into a bowl of steaming naked spaghetti and magic would come out. I think these are my most favourite recipes, those where you look at an ingredient list and it's quite basic and even predictable, but then you read the method and there are details, intricacies and idiosyncrasies that make a dish unique. You just feel as if you are being let in on a big, special secret. This recipe is something that Tommy's Pugliese grandma made for him a lot when he came to visit. He also says that, on Christmas Eve, if someone in his family did not like the traditional dish, *spaghetti capitone* (eel pasta!), they were always served San Giuannid.

It is the typical example of a delicious dish that needs only a few humble storecupboard ingredients which are easy to find in every home in the South of Italy. The secrets of this recipe include cooking spaghetti strictly al dente, good creaming (emulsifying the sauce with the pasta cooking water) and top-quality ingredients. Other intel Tommy emailed to me were:

Spaghetti have to be not too thick or too thin, just the regular size. Cherry tomatoes are Datterini, sweeter than classic cherries. A good indicator that your anchovies are good quality is that they will dissolve very easily when cooked. Always avoid capers in vinegar. For olives, the best choice is pitted Taggiasca olives in oil, but if not so easy to find outside of Italy, any olive is OK (except in vinegar). My grandmother always said, 'Never burn the garlic!'

·· 1 tbsp salted capers

·· 6–10 Taggiasca olives in olive oil, or other good firm olives

·· 2 garlic cloves

·· 200g cherry tomatoes (preferably Datterini)

·· 3 tbsp extra virgin olive oil

·· chilli flakes, to taste

·· 5 anchovy fillets in oil

·· 1 tsp sugar

·· 150g spaghetti

·· sea salt

·· finely grated Parmesan cheese, to serve

• Soak the capers if they come salted; about 15 minutes should do it. If your capers are in brine, just rinse them well under a tap.

• For this recipe, if you haven't found Taggiasca olives, just use any 3–5 good-quality olives per person, depending on the size of the olives. If your olives are firm, and have stones, be nice and destone them. The best way to do this is to crush each olive, either with the flat side of a knife (as you would when bruising garlic) or with something heavy… a heavy pestle comes to mind, or a meat mallet. Just bash each olive until it's crushed and pick out the stones!

• Fill a large saucepan with water, put the lid on and bring to the boil over a high heat. Don't forget to season the water with salt; it should be sea-salty, but more at the level of the low-salinity Sea of Azov than the Dead Sea! Remember you have quite a few savoury-salty ingredients in the sauce.

• Meanwhile, peel the garlic and squash it lightly with the flat side of a knife. It should be gently bruised or cracked, but if you are heavy-handed like me and you squashed it too clumsily, it will still be OK.

• Cut the tomatoes in half across the 'equator' (in the middle but not through the stem end), just so they look pretty.

• Before we begin frying in good olive oil: that legend you've heard about that being a bad thing? Forget it. Get it out of your head. You absolutely can fry in good extra virgin olive oil, especially in a dish which is as pared down as this.

Continued →

Continued...

- OK, so put a large saucepan over a medium-low heat and add the oil. Add the cracked/squashed garlic cloves and chilli flakes and give them a swirl around the pan so the garlic cloves get covered in oil. Cook for 3–5 minutes over a lowish heat, stirring from time to time. You want the garlic to release its flavour but not burn or colour too much at all.

- When the garlic begins to become ever so slightly golden, add the anchovies and 1 tsp of their oil (I don't always measure it to be honest, just splash it in, so it can be more than 1 tsp). Keep frying gently, prodding the anchovies in a leisurely manner from time to time until they dissolve in oil.

- Now, using Tommy's technical term, which I love, gently 'scrunch' in the tomatoes to help them release a bit of their juice, then increase the heat, add the sugar and stir.

- Put the lid on (if you don't have a lid, use a baking tray), reduce the heat right down to its lowest and put the spaghetti into the boiling salted water. The sauce will be ready by the time your pasta is perfectly al dente for the next step (check the packet instructions, but this is usually 3–4 minutes less than the advised cooking time). I don't normally like my pasta mega al dente but I do it here, because it gets cooked a bit more in the sauce itself. So taste your pasta; it should be bendy but still have a bit of a bite.

- When the pasta is nearly ready, add the capers and olives to the sauce and remove the garlic; always keep the lid on.

- Scoop out a cupful of the pasta water. Drain the almost-done spaghetti, then transfer the pasta to the pan of sauce and stir well. Add a splash of pasta cooking water, increase the heat and agitate the pasta in the sauce a bit more. Let the sauce boil and the pasta finish cooking in the sauce, absorbing all its savoury-sweet flavours, for 2–3 minutes. Taste the pasta: it should still be firm of course, but not as toothy as before.

- Serve with plenty of Parmigiano grated over the top.

....

- TIP • You may never ever have leftovers of this sauce, but just in case you start making it and then discover you do not have any pasta in the house (happened to me once!), this whole tomato-anchovy-caper situation is beautiful squished into some thick slabs of porous, hot sourdough toast.

....

Chicken Cotoletta Sandwiches with Marie Rose and Lettuce

This was my staple lunch when I was a student in Urbino. Along the really steep cobbled hill to the town centre, surrounded by an ancient fortress, there were many little places to grab a bitter espresso and a rectangle of pizza or a focaccia or ciabatta sandwich. You don't have to sandwich the chicken, you can just have it with potatoes or rice. But there is something about this bread-on-bread action that is just so incredibly comforting. I *love* Marie Rose sauce, so that is what I am giving here. My son Sasha likes to add chilli flakes, sriracha or chaat masala to the sauce, but you can use garlic mayo, mayo with pesto, or just pesto. People complain about Iceberg lettuce, but I really love the crunch and freshness it adds to the whole affair... though annoyingly I can't always find it, so Gem lettuce it is. If you have skin to remove from your chicken and you like Crispy Chicken Skin, see page 288.

·· 50g plain flour

·· 1 tsp garlic granules

·· 1 large egg, lightly beaten

·· 100g breadcrumbs or panko

·· 2 skinless chicken breasts

·· 3–6 tbsp vegetable oil

·· knob of unsalted butter (optional)

·· 4 tbsp shop-bought mayo

·· 2 tbsp tomato ketchup

·· sea salt

To serve

·· 4 ciabatta rolls (for homemade, see page 274)

·· 4 lettuce leaves, ideally Iceberg

·· Crispy Chicken Skin (optional, see page 288)

·· sliced tomatoes

Shown overleaf →

- You'll need 3 shallowish soup bowls for the crumbing action.

- Mix the flour with the garlic granules and 1 tsp salt and put it into the first bowl. Put the egg into the second bowl and the crumbs in the third.

- Separate the mini fillet from the chicken breasts: they are the flappy bits that separate easily. You can overlap them with the main chicken breast part and bash them using a meat mallet, moulding the pieces together, or bash them separately into a little schnitzel for a small child. Cut each chicken breast horizontally so you get 2 flat pieces. You will have 4 pieces of chicken plus the extra mini fillets.

- I beat them with a meat mallet (but you can use anything heavy) in their thicker places. Basically you want the chicken breast slices to be as even as possible and rather thin, so they cook before the breadcrumbs burn.

- Dip each piece of flattened chicken first into the seasoned flour, then into the egg, then coat in breadcrumbs, shaking off excess after each dipping.

- Have a large plate lined with kitchen paper at the ready. Heat 3 tbsp oil in a large frying pan over medium-high heat. If you want extra luxuriousness, add a knob of butter too. When it sizzles, add half the chicken gently, so the hot fat doesn't splash you. Fry for 90 seconds, then turn and cook for another minute. If you managed to get your chicken very thin, it will be ready. You can take it out of the pan and slice it at the thickest part to check, cooking for another minute on each side if needed. Be conscious of the heat, reducing it a little if you feel the crumbs are becoming too brown. When ready, lift the chicken pieces out with tongs and drain on kitchen paper. Repeat to cook the remaining chicken.

- You can slice the larger cotoletta pieces across into 2 pieces to make it easier to fit into the sandwich.

- To make the sauce, simply mix the mayo and ketchup together.

- Open the ciabatta rolls and spoon sauce on the bottom half. Put the lettuce on top, then the chicken, maybe a bit more sauce and crispy chicken skin, if using, followed by the tomatoes and the other slice of ciabatta. Enjoy enormously.

Bobbie's Chicken and Pork Adobo

One of my best friends from university, Natasha Carella, has the most welcoming and also exciting family. Her dad is half-Eritrean half-Sicilian and her mum Bobbie is half-Spanish and half-Filipina. Because of Natasha's father's roots I tasted and fell in love with injera, and because of her mum Bobbie I have been able to taste the most spectacular adobo. Her mum came to visit us at university and made this dish. It tasted both new and familiar, like all the best food does. When she listed the ingredients, I thought, 'Wow, something so simple can taste so good and interesting.' I have been meaning to ask for the recipe for years, and I finally did. Bobbie comes from the Bulacan province of the Philippines and this recipe was taught to her by her cousin Nene. You don't have to use pork belly – it is very good with just chicken – but if you can, do try it with the pork belly. Bobbie likes the belly to have a bit of texture rather than being completely fall-apart, but if you would like a super-soft pork belly, just cook it for longer before you add the chicken. This is a great storecupboard ingredient dish and you can also make it vegetarian using aubergines or green beans in place of the meat.

- 200g pork belly, cut into 2cm cubes
- 8 bone-in chicken legs and/or thighs
- 100ml soy sauce
- 5 garlic cloves, finely chopped
- 2 tbsp coconut oil
- 450ml water
- 5 bay leaves
- 2 tsp whole black peppercorns
- 100ml cider vinegar, or, if you can find it, coconut vinegar

- First marinate the meat. Put the pork belly at the bottom of a bowl and the chicken on top. Mix the soy sauce with the garlic and pour it over the meat, rubbing it into the meat. Marinate it for at least 30 minutes at room temperature, or for a minimum of 2 hours or up to overnight in the fridge.

- When ready to cook (make sure to bring the meat out of the fridge in advance, if needed, to return to room temperature), drain the marinade from the chicken into a bowl. If there are visible pieces of garlic on the meat, try to get them off so they don't burn when you brown it. Reserve the marinade and garlic for later.

- Heat the oil and brown the pork belly pieces. They will release some of their fat which will be good to brown the chicken pieces in after. When the pork belly is nice and brown, remove it with a slotted spoon and keep in a bowl while you brown the chicken. Resist the urge to move the pieces around too soon, just let them sit on one side for a while to allow them to brown properly. Again it should be golden. Because the chicken has been marinating and is a bit wet, it won't necessarily become crispy, this is not what you are trying to do here. But you are trying to get colour, which equals sweetness and depth of flavour.

- Take the chicken out, return the pork belly and pour in the measured water, reserved marinade and garlic, bay leaves and peppercorns. The liquid should almost cover the meat. Scrape at the base of the pan as there are bound to be slightly sticky soy bits. Cook for 30 minutes with the lid on. Now return the chicken and cook for another 30 minutes, again covered. Finally add the vinegar, stir once, bring to a simmer and cook for a final 10 minutes, uncovered. The dish should look stewy, not soupy. If you feel like there is too much liquid, you can take the chicken out and boil some of the liquid off to reduce and intensify the sauce. Serve with plain rice and pickled or steamed green vegetables.

Potatoes and Cabbages

The Food That Shaped Me

Potatoes and Cabbages

When you are told something many times, you start believing it.

I left Ukraine aged nearly thirteen. I lived in Cyprus, the UK, then for a year in Italy, and finally settled back in the UK. For years, whenever I mentioned Ukrainian or Eastern European food, I was asked if there was anything beyond potatoes and cabbages. I don't blame the people who were asking those questions: stereotypes can stick as readily as flies to a fly trap. The strange thing is that although I knew how fantastic the food was at home, how delicious, how fresh, how skilled one must be to make it, I half-suspected that it was only delicious to me. Maybe its tomato-stained sour cream juices at the bottom of a bowl, its dumplings and noodles, were directly entangled with neurons in my brain.

With time, I developed what I can see now was an actual complex. 'So is it all potatoes and dumplings, Olia?' 'Yes, I guess, and also cabbage!' Blush.

I didn't realise food from my home country was worthy of attention until well into my late twenties. Even then, when I was pitching my idea for a feature about Ukrainian cuisine, I remember meeting the editor of a national newspaper magazine. He spoke of his experiences of Czech canteen food in the 1970s. Of course, he talked about bland potatoes, dumplings and overcooked cabbage. My recipe pitch was rejected, my complex deepened.

When I was little, Ukraine was always beautiful to me. Its post-Soviet darkness was lit up by the candles of my family's love and by the glimpses of nature bursting through cracks in the concrete, which enlivened the otherwise drab, rectangular high-rises we called 'anthills'. The regular power cuts felt like an adventure. Doing homework by candlelight every other night was kind of fun. As to the rest – the corruption, racketeering and other post-Soviet peculiarities that made it difficult and even dangerous for businesses such as my dad's (he produced sunflower oil) to develop – I was happily almost oblivious.

I knew things weren't quite ordinary. We once sheltered a family on the run – from whom, I do not know – I am still too nervous to ask my dad. I remember their kids had a PC and real Barbies; *beyond* luxury in the Ukraine of the early 1990s. I remember my dad saying they were heading towards the Turkish border. Ukraine in the 1990s was a strange place: a corrupt, inefficient system collapsing into another system that, yes, was more free, but was just as corrupt and inefficient.

Besides that, I had suffered crippling asthma since I was two, though I have only recently made the connection with the time it happened – summer 1986 – and the Chernobyl disaster. When we went on holiday to Cyprus in 1997, my asthma felt better. There, we were shocked to see cars with keys sticking out of them and owners nowhere to be seen (WHAT!?). We had never lived in a society where there was so much trust and so little crime. My parents did everything they could and ended up relocating to Limassol, where we lived in a small flat and I worked really hard at adapting to the new English school (I spoke very little English at the time).

My dad would spend one month in Ukraine, one month with us, which created an interesting family dynamic. My mum and I embraced Cyprus, its culture and its food wholeheartedly. We especially loved its simple fresh seafood, something I still consider the biggest treat, a true luxury. Tiny *barabulka* (red mullet), so small that I imagine it is probably illegal now to catch and eat them, were crisply deep-fried and tasted like crustaceans. Red mullet remains my favourite fish to this day.

My mum cooked at home a lot, but as a treat we would go to an ancient trattoria in the old town, order a massive Greek salad with a snowy layer of finely grated feta and all the seafood. Sometimes we would travel to the mountains, eating at a famous homely restaurant run by a Czech woman. We spent most of our time by the sea. It was bliss.

After the first awkward years of assimilation, I thrived in my studies and my friendships. Not all was rosy; it rarely is for teenagers. But I still have the warmest memories of my five years there, and I wanted to include some recipes from that period in this book, both those that Mum brought from Ukraine and cooked at home, and those that we came to love in Cyprus.

Easy Crunchy Vegetable Salad-Pickle

This is a very good salad-pickle that works with a whole bunch of different crunchy vegetables and fruits. Use a combination of any of the produce suggested below. It is good in so many things: inside a pitta bread with grilled chicken or cheese, or as a side dish with a rich dumpling stew. And yes, raw parsnip, swede and pumpkin are a thing. This is also a good way to use up those tough outer layers of fennel that we usually discard; just slice or shave them as finely as you can and then cut into fine matchsticks. Anything fibrous such as this benefits from being cut as finely as possible, so it becomes easily digestible. For the spices, you can just choose any one of them or go for the lot. I recommend using them all, as it makes this taste extra delicious.

Total 500g of any of:

·· apple, beetroot, carrot, celeriac, fennel, green mango, kohlrabi, parsnip, pear, pumpkin, swede, turnip

For the pickling liquid

·· 1 tbsp coriander seeds (optional)

·· 1 tbsp caraway seeds (optional)

·· 1 tbsp fennel seeds, crushed (optional)

·· 70ml sherry vinegar, or other flavoursome vinegar

·· 1 tbsp honey

·· 2 garlic cloves, crushed or finely grated

·· pinch of cayenne pepper (optional)

·· sea salt

• Place all the seeds for the pickling liquid in a dry frying pan over a medium heat and cook, stirring constantly, until they turn a shade darker and smell toasted. Immediately tip into a mortar and crush them with the pestle.

• All you need to do now is to cut your vegetables or fruits into fine matchsticks; the technique is called julienne and it's a very good thing to do if you want to practise your knife skills. If you don't, but you still want to eat this, you can use a special julienne peeler that gives the long strands. Or maybe if you have a dusty spiraliser tucked in a cupboard, its time has come!

• Mix the vinegar with the honey and ½ tbsp salt in a large non-reactive bowl or other container and stir; the vinegar will dissolve them both easily. Then add the garlic, seeds and cayenne, if using. Stir in the fruit or vegetable matchsticks.

• You can use this straight away or you can stick it in the fridge and let it pickle for a few days or even weeks.

• I sometimes drizzle it with a little unrefined sunflower or sesame oil and scatter on some toasted sesame seeds and coriander leaves. But it is good without any embellishments, too.

• TIP • Having a jar of this in the fridge can save many potentially lacklustre lunches. Stuff it into a pitta with leftover roast chicken or veg, or grilled halloumi or feta. Top a Dhal (see page 54) or bean stew with a small handful. You can also add it to broths: caramelise some chopped onions in a pan, then add a handful of this pickle and cook down until soft. Put the mixure into a meat or vegetable stock to add a welcome sour note.

Dark Greens Soup with Blue Cheese

I have found a lot of interesting out-of-print cookbooks at Ukrainian and Georgian flea markets. One of the best sources for vegetarian recipes are church-affiliated books. I have a lot that contain a fasting angle. I also have a Russian book called *Monastic Kitchen* by the sinister-sounding All-Russian Bureau of Fiction Propaganda, printed in December 1990, which marks it as one of the last books printed in the Soviet Union. This pamphlet-like book is subtitled: *Prayers, advice, recipes of simple and tasty healthy food (from the experience of Orthodox monasteries)*, and it is full of fascinating vegetarian dishes. A lot of them use foraged herbs, berries and vegetables. The soup in this pamphlet is called *polevitsa* which refers to various grasses. During the 'hunger gap' in April, apart from nettles and wild sorrel, the Orthodox monks advise using young shoots of goosefoot, chickweed, hogweed, oxalis (called 'hare's cabbage' in Russian), buckhorn plantain, mallow, fireweed and clover. Nettles and sorrel are the only two that I am comfortable identifying, so I use those. Of course, the blue cheese here is not in the original recipe, but my mum uses it on top of sorrel soup a lot, so I do too.

- 200g nettles or spinach
- 2 tbsp vegetable oil
- 1 tbsp unsalted butter
- 1 onion (200g), roughly chopped
- 2 medium carrots (total weight 150g), scrubbed
- 2 medium potatoes (total weight 400g), unpeeled but scrubbed
- 650ml vegetable stock (optional)
- 150g sorrel
- 50g blue cheese, crumbled
- sea salt and black pepper

- To prepare the nettles, if using, put them into a large stockpot, cover with boiling water and cook over a medium heat for 5 minutes. Drain over a large bowl, or take them out with a spider strainer or tongs (you will need that hot water again), then refresh in iced water. Now that you are safe from their bite, cut off any thicker, fibrous stalks and compost those.

- Heat the oil and butter in a medium saucepan or cast-iron pot. Add the onion and a pinch of salt and cook for about 15 minutes over a medium-low heat until it softens and starts colouring a little bit. Chop the carrots quite small. Add them to the onion and cook over a medium heat until they too soften and catch a little bit of colour here and there.

- If your potatoes have a thin skin and you have a powerful food processor, keep their skins on and cut them into 1cm cubes (otherwise peel them first). Add them to the pan, stir through the other vegetables and cook without disturbing for a little bit, again to catch a little colour here and there.

- Now add the blanched nettles or spinach and the stock or 650ml of reserved nettle cooking water. Season and bring to a simmer. Cook for about 15 minutes or until the potatoes and carrots are soft and blendable.

- Finally add the raw, chopped sorrel – the residual heat will be enough to wilt it – and blitz everything in a food processor. Taste the soup and season depending on how salty the cheese you are serving with it is. Serve with the crumbled blue cheese and some bread or croutons.

Serves 2–4 (I can eat more than half of this in one go, but I am a total pig)

Potatoes of My Childhood

Mum said, 'Is this even a recipe?' Yes, it is and what a recipe! In fact, this is one of the most classic, probably most-often-cooked 'quick family suppers' and student staples there is in the whole of ex-USSR. The beauty of this dish is that the potatoes get cut a little higgledy piggledy… you know when you try to cut them really finely and you get some really fine and some a bit thicker? In this recipe, that is exactly what you want! Do not use your mandolin, they are evil things in general (my poor knuckles, so many times). With this imperfect cutting, some of the potatoes become brittle and crisp, some meltingly soft, while the onion catches a little colour. With some kraut or a gherkin and sometimes a chunk of cured sausage on the side, I cannot think of a more comforting thing to eat. To me, this dish is a main event, it takes centre stage. Everything else – whether a token bit of meat or a very welcome pickle – plays a secondary role. Do get good butter and sunflower oil for this, if you can.

·· 1kg potatoes, peeled

·· 1 large onion, peeled

·· 50g unsalted butter

·· 50ml sunflower oil

·· sea salt

• Slice the potatoes in half and make sure they are stable on their cut sides. Then slice them into fine half-moons, as fine as you can, and of course rejoice, this time, at the different thicknesses. Some will become super-crispy like crisps, some will turn soft: that's the beauty of it, the irregularity, the mixture of textures.

• Slice the onion in half and then into fine slices, as fine as you can.

• Heat the butter and oil in the largest, deepest frying pan you have (mine is a 26cm deep stainless-steel frying pan) until sizzling. The heat should be medium-high-ish, but you may need to play around with it throughout the cooking process; if you see anything catching too much, reduce it, or if it feels like the potatoes are stewing and not colouring at all, crank up the heat.

• Put all the potatoes in and add a generous pinch of salt. Stir once to distribute the salt evenly, then leave them be for a few minutes, then stir them in one big sweep and leave them alone again. Be patient: give the potatoes that are at the bottom time to catch and crisp a little bit. The whole process will take you about 15 minutes. The potatoes should be looking crispy and brown in parts.

• Now add the onion and another pinch of salt and stir it through. Repeat with the stirring and then leaving it be for another 5 minutes, until the onion is translucent and soft. The onion does not need to get caramelised, but if a few slices do get some colour, it's all good. Now reduce the heat to its lowest setting and cover with a lid. Cook for another 5 minutes, adding a splash of water and scraping the bottom of the pan with your spoon if things get sticky, until all the potatoes are soft. Just prick the fattest-looking one with the tip of a knife: if it gives, you are ready to rock and roll.

• I love serving these with Easy Crunchy Vegetable Salad-Pickle and Chicken Cotoletta *sans* bread (see pages 129 and 119), or some chunks of dry-cured sausage or roasted English sausage on the side. Try it and figure out what side dish will make it your own.

Broth with Those Bits
from the Depths of Your Freezer

Do you buy whole chickens and ducks and sometimes forget they have those little bags inside the cavity with the giblets in? And then you start roasting them and remember halfway through. No? Oh, no, that has never happened to me either (grimaces). What do you do with those bits? It's brilliant if you use them cleverly to make gravy. I don't, as gravy-making is not something I do naturally. What I do is panic and throw them in the freezer. After a while, when I realise I have nothing in the fridge but I need to feed the kids, I fish the little bags out and make broth. It's absolutely acceptable to mix both duck and chicken bits, if that's what you have. Also, of course, if you happen to have a chicken carcass, add that too. Use everything in the bags, apart from the livers as they will make your broth bitter. Normally I fry those in butter and eat them on toast (cook's treat). The rest of the giblets are all perfect to make a little stock and then this broth, to which I have added easy spoon dumplings.

·· 2 onions

·· a few poultry necks, gizzards and hearts (but not livers)

·· 1 chicken carcass (if you have it)

·· 1 bay leaf

·· 1 tbsp unsalted butter

·· 1 carrot

·· 1 tbsp tomato paste (optional)

·· 1 large potato, scrubbed but unpeeled, then chopped

·· 1 egg

·· 50g buckwheat flour, or plain flour

·· sea salt

·· soft herb leaves, to serve

• Peel one of the onions, but leave it whole. Put the chicken bits, whole onion and bay leaf into a medium saucepan. Pour in 1.5 litres of water if you're just using giblets, or 2.5 litres of water if including a carcass. Bring to the boil, reduce the heat and simmer for 40–60 minutes. Remove the carcass, if you used one.

• Peel and finely chop the other onion and fry it in a frying pan with the butter. Grate the carrot coarsely, add to the onion and cook for about 5 minutes, stirring from time to time. You want them both to soften and even colour ever so slightly. At this stage, you can add this mixture to the broth, cook for about 10 minutes, then use it as a base for any other soup in this book. It also freezes very well.

• If you want a little bit of tomato acidity in the broth, you can add the tomato paste to the onion at this point. Cook it with the onion and carrot for a couple of minutes, then scrape into the stock. Add the potato and cook until it can easily be pierced with a knife (about 10 minutes). We never considered what type of potato we used in broths, sometimes they would be floury and sometimes waxy! Whatever you use will be fine. At this point you can add more vegetables, such as chopped celery or celeriac or Savoy cabbage, but I like this spartan version.

• To make little spoonable dumplings, mix the egg and flour with a generous pinch of salt into a thick but 'droppable' batter. You can use almost any flour; my mum would use plain, but I like the flavour of buckwheat (as you'll see).

• Using a soup spoon, drop spoonfuls of batter into the boiling broth. Depending on size, they should take about 5 minutes. You can always fish a bigger one out and cut into it: if it doesn't have any dry flecks of flour inside, you are good to go!

• Serve with plenty of dill or other soft herbs that you love.

• **TIP** • **This beautiful poultry stock can be used in so many dishes in this book and beyond: just omit the dumplings, potatoes and tomato paste.**

Sunshine Broth with *Frikadelki*

This is an old childhood comfort blanket of a dish. Whenever we were a bit ill, or when it started getting colder in the autumn, we would crave simple things, and request either chicken broth or this from my mum. It is a great thing to make when you have leftover rice, but, if you don't, the meatballs can be shaped without the rice. My mum always grates the carrot for this soup on the fine side of the grater; she says it brings a certain injection of gaity to the soup, giving it a golden shimmer. I hasten to add that my mum also dislikes the texture of cooked carrots, so making them melt into the broth is one of her typical moves. Sometimes I use floury potatoes, sometimes new potatoes, it really is up to you.

·· 3 small potatoes (total weight about 300g), peeled and chopped into 2.5cm cubes

·· 1.5 litres meat or vegetable stock, or water

·· 2 onions, peeled

·· 400–500g minced chicken or pork

·· 100g cooked brown or white rice (optional)

·· 1 tbsp chopped parsley leaves

·· 2 medium carrots, scrubbed

·· 2 tbsp unsalted butter

·· 1 bay leaf

·· sea salt and black pepper

·· handful of soft herb leaves, to serve (dill or parsley work best)

• Put the potatoes into the cold stock or water in a saucepan, bring to a simmer and cook for about 5 minutes.

• To make the *frikadelki*, grate one of the onions on the coarse side of a grater and mix it in a bowl with the minced meat, rice, if using, and parsley. Make sure to season well with salt and pepper. For this amount, 1½ heaped tsp salt should do it, but you can always fry a little bit to check the seasoning. Mix everything thoroughly with your hands and shape into small walnut-sized balls. Wetting your hands will help the shaping. You should get 15–18 balls in total.

• Meanwhile, grate the carrots on the fine side of the box grater. The good fine side, not the one that traps everything in its holes! That side should be forbidden. Chop the other onion very finely. Heat the butter in a frying pan, add the onion and carrots and cook over a medium-low heat until soft; it will take 5–8 minutes while the joyful orange of the carrot infuses into the butter. Add this to the potato pan with the bay leaf and enjoy the sight of the water blushing with a happiness-inducing orange glow (thanks, finely grated carrots and Mum).

• Season the broth well and taste it to make sure it tastes good; if it's at all underwhelming, add more salt. Now add the *frikadelki* to the broth and simmer for 10 minutes.

• Serve with some soft herbs, especially dill (game changer) and crusty bread.

• **TIP** • **Let's assume you've scoffed the *frikadelki*, but you have some broth left over. Don't chuck it! It is so beautifully flavoured, so use it as a base for a stew. Simply add a (drained) can of something starchy such as butter beans or chickpeas and a generous amount of shredded greens, like kale, cavolo nero, spring greens, Brussels tops or good old chard… and you have another pot of something tasty and nutritious.**

'The butter was smooth and
rich, the crystals crunchy
and gritty, together the two
made the most delicious
thing I'd ever tasted'

Elisabeth Luard, Food Writer and Illustrator

Butter and Sugar

....

'The leathery chewiness of dried banana is my earliest food memory. It tasted like soapy flannel but they made me eat it anyway. As a war baby born in London in the middle of the Blitz, it wasn't until I was five or thereabouts that I first tasted sugar. It happened after I'd been sent to my room without any supper as punishment for quarrelling with my brother on his birthday. My brother had been mean to me and was bigger and older, so this was unfair.

I waited until everyone was busy with the birthday, then crept downstairs and stole a scraped-out bowl of butter icing from the kitchen table under the nose of our mother's cook, a battle-axe who shouted at everyone but had a soft spot for a five-year-old who loved to roll out pastry and pod peas, even if half of them rolled on the floor. Butter and sugar were strictly rationed at the time and kept for special occasions. Even the scrapings were precious. I took the bowl to a nest I'd made with an old blanket under the stairs and scooped the remains of the buttery, sugary sludge from its sides with my fingers, licking them clean. The butter was smooth and rich, the crystals crunchy and gritty, together the two made the most delicious thing I'd ever tasted. Still is – at least in memory.

I finished it all up and hid the evidence: a small triumph in a world where you could be made to eat dried banana and sent to your room without supper. It was a secret that no one else shared. These days, I still feel a twinge of happiness when I spread butter on my morning toast and take just a little sugar in my tea.'

Nina's Cabbage Pie

My aunt Nina, who is half-Ukrainian and half-Armenian, lives in Kyiv, the capital of Ukraine. Every time I travel home to see my parents, who live in the South of the country, we have to travel through the capital. We take an old rickety Soviet sleeper train, which is both as romantic and as uncomfortable as it sounds. Despite our protestations, my cousin Alyona, a successful and busy opera singer, always insists on meeting us at the airport and taking us to the train station. Invariably she brings a massive carrier bag with our 'train snacks' prepared earlier by her mum, Nina. In a regular snack bag we may find a whole(!) roasted chicken, pickles, potatoes, boiled eggs, sweet treats and invariably this cabbage pie. It tastes so fresh and moreish, and makes for a very good lunch or a picnic dish. Shop-bought puff pastry is great here.

- 1 tbsp unsalted butter, softened, or sunflower oil
- 250g white cabbage
- 200g (1 large) red pepper
- 2–4 garlic cloves
- bunch of dill, leaves and stalks, chopped
- 100g (1 medium) onion
- 1 large egg, separated
- 325g pack of puff pastry
- plain flour, to dust
- 4 heaped tbsp tomato paste
- a little milk, if needed
- sea salt

- Preheat the oven to 180°C fan.

- Rub the softened butter or oil all over the base and sides of a 25 x 15cm baking dish. If you don't have one with those dimensions, don't be discouraged, it will work with slightly different-sized tins (as long as it's not too large).

- Slice the cabbage as finely as you can and put it in a bowl. Feed the core to your children or yourself (it's so sweet!). Cut the pepper in half, scoop out the seeds and slice it as finely as you can, then add it to the cabbage. Slice the garlic finely and put it in with the cabbage and peppers. Add the dill.

- Slice the onion in half and then very finely into half moons. Do really try to slice this as fine as possible – the thinner the better – but there's no need for a mandolin (they are evil and should be banned). Keep the onion separate from the cabbage, as it can release water and make your pie soggy.

- Now add the egg white to the cabbage mixture (so as not to waste it) and mix gently but thoroughly. You can use a spoon, but I use my hand as it's more efficient and satisfying.

- Mix sea salt through the cabbage mixture just before you're ready to fill and bake the pie, otherwise too much water will leach out; 1 scant tbsp of it is good. I know it sounds like a lot, but it needs to be seasoned properly, or the whole thing will be insipid.

- You now need to roll the pastry out slightly on a well-floured surface, to make it a bit bigger, the whole sheet should measure 30 x 25cm. Cut it in half to get two 25 x 15cm rectangular sheets. Put one sheet of the pastry in the buttered pie dish, with some of it going up the sides, so you can seal the edges with the other half of the pastry later.

- Brush the tomato paste on the bottom pastry sheet and scatter over the raw onion. I strongly advise you follow this step: I did once mix the tomato paste, onion and cabbage together and it didn't work: it tasted different to Nina's and also made everything soggy. Put the seasoned cabbage mixture on top and cover with the other half of the pastry, pinching the edges to enclose and seal.

- Glaze the top of the pie with the egg yolk. If my eggs are small, I add a little milk to the yolk to make it stretch further and be easier to brush; 1 tbsp will do. Prick all over the top of the pastry with a fork.

- Cook on the middle shelf of the oven for 50 minutes. As always, do check on it halfway through, especially if your oven has hot spots, and rotate the dish to get it golden evenly. If at any point you feel like the top is becoming too dark, you can always cover it loosely with foil. The top should be dark golden when ready. The filling will be cooked but still fresh. I like eating this once it cools down. Once it cools and sets, it makes for a good lunch or travel snack.

Cabbage Fritters

A memory of this recipe was shared with me by Latvian-American chef and teacher Anna Gershenson. It is such a simple dish, but so delicious and moreish. It's actually popular all over Eastern Europe, as cabbage is so widely available in all seasons. I like to use spelt or buckwheat flour here, just to take a break from white wheat flour from time to time. But you can use pretty much any flour you like; there is so little of it, it won't make much difference. Anna likes to add a handful of soft herbs to the mix, but I leave them out. I sometimes jazz up the yogurt I serve it with instead by whisking in a spoonful of harissa, or blitzing tired soft herbs into it.

·· 250g white cabbage

·· 3 eggs, lightly beaten

·· 2 tbsp spelt, buckwheat or plain flour

·· 4 tbsp vegetable oil

·· yogurt or crème fraîche, to serve

·· 1 garlic clove, grated

·· sea salt and black pepper

- Slice the cabbage really finely into thin strands, then cut across it all. You should have tiny pieces of cabbage. Add 1 tsp salt and plenty of black pepper and gently mix it through, then mix in the eggs and flour. The mixture should be ever so slightly sloppy.

- Heat half the oil in a large frying pan and make sure it is sizzling hot. Spoon in dessertspoonfuls of the cabbage mixture; the oil should be hot enough for you to hear it sizzle as soon as you spoon the first one in. Depending on the size of the pan, you should be able to cook 4 x 8–10cm fritters. Cook for about 3 minutes over a medium heat, turning them one by one as soon as the edges turn golden brown. Cook on the other side until light brown and crispy. You may need to turn them a few times and you may also need to add more oil between batches, if your pan looks dry.

- Serve with some yogurt or crème fraîche, spiked with the grated garlic. I also sometimes like to mix in some soft herbs, or, to go in another direction, Tabasco, sriracha or Quick Fermented Chilli Sauce (see page 285).

Savoury Eggy Bread

I tried sweet French toast for the first time in my early twenties in the UK. We only eat it as a savoury dish back in the motherland. I asked my husband Joe, 'Remember those French toasts that my mum made for me as a child, that you made from my description when I was really ill?'

'The ones with garlic, cheese and mayo?' 'Yes (blushes). Do you think I can include them in my new book? Or too weird, people wouldn't get them?' 'Oh no, they are nice, they are just horrifically filthy, aren't they?' Thanks, Joe.

· 2 eggs

· 60ml whole milk

· 1 small garlic clove, halved

· 4 slices of stale-ish bread (Mum used shop-bought fluffy white, I use Bread for Eating, see page 215)

· unsalted butter, to fry

· 2–4 tbsp mayonnaise (shop-bought is fine, Japanese Kewpie the best)

· 100g Gouda cheese or similar, coarsely grated

· sea salt

• Whisk the eggs with the milk in a broad, shallow bowl and season with salt. Take the garlic clove and rub it on the crusts of the bread, then dip the bread in the egg mixture and let it soak for a few minutes on each side.

• Heat a good knob of butter in a pan until it froths up and add the bread, frying for 2 minutes on each side or until set and golden brown. It will start smelling biscuity, like brown butter, soon enough.

• Now for the mayo. I am a purist, and, when it comes to childhood recipes, swapping out less rubbish bread is as far as I go. I like shop-bought here. The Soviet stuff we had was quite acidic, almost spiky; Japanese mayo tastes similar. You can go crazy and add other things to the mayo as an experiment, but mine remains untouched. Spread a little bit (1 tsp) on the warm toast and then make it snow with the cheese. Now, when Joe made it for me he used a fine grater. He doesn't know this, but that ruined it for me a bit. The cheese must be grated on the coarse side of the grater. Enjoy.

Rice Salad to Get Creative With

One of the recipes Mum has been making from the *International Family Favourites* cookbook for 25 years (see overleaf) appears in the South American section and is called 'Brazilian Lover's Salad'. It was served in little lettuce boats and had lime in the dressing; all very exciting for us at the time. With the years, I have changed it a bit, and this version is also influenced by author and Italian food importing supremo Rolando Beramendi's grandly named Italian Contessa salad. The trick is to use whatever crunchy seasonal things you have in the fridge, and to chop them very very small, as small as the grains of rice if you can. Get creative with the dressing as well, using the proportions given below. Just use any acid – a mild vinegar or lemon juice work well – a sweetener such as maple or agave syrup or sugar and a good amount of salt. Use very good olive oil. I serve this as is for my vegetarian husband, and, for my sons and me, add a little canned fish on the side. Beramendi likes a version with chopped raw courgettes and shrimps. I still serve it in lettuce boats and it may feel a little retro, but there is much comfort in that. It can be a meal in itself, or part of a bigger spread, a barbecue or picnic.

- 200g brown rice, soaked overnight, if you remember

- 1 celery stick

- 1 carrot, scrubbed

- ½ cucumber

- ½ red onion

- 1 green, yellow or red pepper

- large handful of soft herb leaves, such as dill, chives, coriander… (optional)

- olive oil, to drizzle (optional)

- sea salt and black or white pepper

For the dressing

- 1 ripe tomato

- juice of 2 limes, or to taste

- 1 tbsp honey, or to taste

- 1 small garlic clove, crushed or finely grated

- Put the rice (drained, if you soaked it) into a pan and pour over 500ml cold water. Season with salt and bring to a simmer. Cook for 30 minutes if unsoaked, or 20 minutes if soaked, until nice and soft. Remember brown rice may never become very soft; by nature it has a firmer texture. Drain and let it cool down.

- Cut the tomato for the dressing in half and squeeze the juice into a bowl. I just salt the squeezed-out halves and eat them there and then. Whisk the lime juice, honey and garlic with the tomato juice, taste and adjust the seasoning. It should be very well-seasoned, almost on the verge of being overseasoned.

- Slice all the vegetables into fine strips and then across, so you get tiny squares of them, almost as small as the rice grains if you can. (If raw onion upsets your constitution you can soak it in some iced water or lemon juice for 10 minutes or so, then drain and use.) Mix all the vegetables through the cooled rice and add the dressing. Taste it now: it should be really well dressed and flavoursome. If you feel it is lacking something – acidity, sweetness, salt – it is not too late to add any of those elements.

- This can stay in its bowl in the fridge for a couple of hours, so if you won't use it straight away, wait before adding the herbs, if using.

- Stir through the herbs, if using, just before serving. My husband likes to drizzle olive oil over his salad, but I like it without.

'I cannot explain just
how exciting it was to
have a cookbook with
comprehensive recipes
and a photograph
for every dish'

First Cookbooks from Behind the Curtain

'When the first cookbooks arrived on the post-Soviet market, our family friend Uncle Vadik bought a thick tome for both his wife and for my mum. I am pretty sure it was for International Women's Day, March 8, which was also Mum's 37th birthday. (She was my age then! How is that possible?) It was the Russian edition of *International Family Favourites: a World of Great Recipes* by Ron Kalenuik, a Canadian chef from Alberta. The book was divided into different continents, and then into countries. My mum marked around 50 pages of the book and she has been cooking those recipes regularly for the past 25 years.

I cannot explain just how exciting it was to have a cookbook with comprehensive recipes and a photograph for every dish. And to see recipes for so many exotic dishes, even if we didn't have the ingredients for them yet. My rice salad (see previous page) is inspired by the recipe in that book.

I also have a number of old Soviet cookbooks that were printed in Bulgaria. Quite a few of them of them are vegetarian (very unusual for 1980s USSR), or at least vegetable-heavy, which is more expected because Bulgarians *love* their salad and vegetables so much. There is one book called *A Man in the Kitchen*, written by a musician, Petr Saraliyev, whose hobby was to cook and the recipes include (allegedly) super-quick-to-make dishes.

In the introduction he, progressively, states that cooking should not be a woman's job. He also writes that, "Every man with a medium intelligence should be able to cook something that would satisfy him and his guests," and even states that setting the table should bring pleasure, talking of "aesthetic feelings", taste and skill. The book does have some meaty recipes, including a couple involving brains and three(!) involving garden snails. But there is also a recipe called Turkish *plov* (see overleaf for my version) and it is a delight.'

Tomato Rice

This makes a great lunch with some fried chorizo on the side, or a side dish with roast chicken or lamb. Most of the time I make it, eat a portion and then use the deliberate leftovers to make the rice cake(s) on the next page, which are the real bomb. I use brown rice at home as it is more nutritious and flavoursome, but in this recipe method I include a method for using white rice, too. If you decide to use brown rice, I recommend soaking it in advance: it takes two minutes to pour some water over the rice, but then it cooks much more quickly.

·· 360g brown or white rice

·· 2 tbsp sunflower or olive oil

·· 2 tbsp unsalted butter

·· 1 onion, finely chopped

·· 400g can of chopped tomatoes

·· 1 tsp paprika (optional)

·· sea salt

• If you are using brown rice and feel organised/are planning this meal in advance, pour 500ml water over it and keep it in the fridge for 4 hours or – even better – overnight. This cuts the cooking time dramatically. If this is a spur-of-the-moment thing, don't worry, you can still use white rice or unsoaked brown rice.

• Heat the oil and butter in a pan that you have a lid for (I use a 20cm cast-iron pan). Add the onion and cook over a medium-low heat, stirring from time to time, until it softens and starts becoming golden. About 10 minutes of cooking should get you to where you want to be, no need to caramelise too avidly here.

• Empty the canned tomatoes into a bowl and weigh them. If you are using white rice, add enough water to the bowl to make its total weight 700g. If you are using brown rice (soaked or unsoaked), add a little more, enough to make it up to 850g. Whisk in the paprika, if using, and a scant 2 tsp salt. Taste the liquid and add a bit more salt if needed.

• Now, if you used brown rice and soaked it, drain it. Add whatever rice you are using to the buttery onion, toss to coat and then add the tomato mixture. Cover with a lid and bring to a simmer. From the moment the liquid starts simmering (the lid is always on), either soaked brown or unsoaked white rice will be ready in 20–25 minutes, while unsoaked brown rice will take closer to 40–45 minutes. When it's ready, the liquid will be absorbed and the rice will be soft to the tooth.

• Another thing that you may discover, especially if you keep your heat a little higher, is that the rice might develop an amazing crispy layer at the bottom, not unlike an Iranian *tahdig* or Spanish *socarrat*. Even if you haven't, but you have leftover tomato rice, turn the page to find out how to get it.

Fried Tomato Rice Cake

Everyone loves and wants the crispy *tahdig* of Iranian rice or the *socarrat* at the bottom of paella and now you can have it! Here it is: your own personal *tahdig* cake. Sometimes I add other bits: ends of chorizo, feta, or cooked or raw chopped chard or beetroot tops, or tired-looking herbs, or some spices, or 3 tbsp harissa. The possibilities are endless and I invite you to create your own versions. Because, really, this is all about the crispy bits. I like to make a bigger cake (that you see in the picture), but my friend Caroline prefers making smaller individual cakes to make the flipping easier. (If you want to make individual cakes, I recommend doubling the recipe.) See what you think. If you go for a big cake, don't stress if it breaks up a bit while flipping, you can press it back together. It's not about keeping it whole, but getting lots of rice bits crispy. This is a meal in itself, especially if you add a fried egg on top and some kimchi on the side.

· · 250–300g leftover Tomato Rice (see page 150), at room temperature

· · 1 large egg, lightly beaten

· · 50g Parmesan or other cheese, finely grated
or
· · 2 tbsp harissa and 50g feta

· · 2–4 tbsp sunflower or olive oil

- Mix the tomato rice and egg. Add either the Parmesan, or the harissa and feta.

- I wouldn't normally advise using a non-stick frying pan, but sadly they are best for this job. After watching the movie *Dark Waters*, I threw all mine away, so now I suffer, but I am proof that these cakes can work without non-stick too.

- Heat 2 tbsp oil in a 20cm pan for a big cake (separate cakes may need a bigger pan) over a medium heat until it's properly hot (this step is important).

- When it's hot, carefully, so as not to splash yourself, spoon the rice in, pushing it in with a spoon or spatula to fill the bottom of the pan. It should be sizzling as you put it in. Cook it for 3–6 minutes, checking if it's crispy underneath by gently lifting the edge.

- Now to turn it. Cover the pan with a large flat plate or a flat roasting tin, hold the pan and plate or tin firmly together (wearing oven gloves!), then carefully flip it out on to the plate or tin. Then slide it back into the pan to fry the other side. Don't get stressed if it breaks, just push it back into a pancake shape using a spatula. Cook for another 3 minutes or so. I cut it while it's inside the pan and serve it with some kraut or kimchi and a little mayo, or just a salad, or a poached or a fried egg if it's one of those days when you really need extra comfort.

- If you are frying separate little cakes, don't expect them to look like perfectly round patties; they will resemble rough little latkes. Again, it's important you put them into properly hot oil. I shape them into a ball in my hands, then lower the balls into the hot oil, leaving space around each one, then squash them down with a spatula and resist the temptation to turn them too soon. Let them sizzle and set, then turn one by one and let them sizzle and set again.

Cypriot Keftedes

These do hold a special place in my heart. One of the first ever cookbooks that I owned, way before I actually started cooking, was *Kopiaste* by Ivy Liacopoulou. When I did start cooking – in the UK in my twenties – I was married to a half-Cypriot man, and these were in my home-cooking rotation. I'd make them as often as once a week. When we divorced, I also divorced myself from keftedes, which I now feel quite mournful about. I do love these meatballs, the flavours of cinnamon and dried mint, their crispiness, the inclusion of raw potato which I always found so interesting. It is worth making a kilo, as they are good the next day cold, and are my son Sasha's favourite packed lunch, stuffed into a pitta with a small tub of tzatziki to spoon into it all in the school cafeteria.

·· 1 medium potato (about 250g), scrubbed

·· 2 small onions

·· 1kg minced pork, the fattier the better

·· 4 tbsp dried mint

·· 1–2 tsp ground cinnamon

·· 25g parsley leaves, finely chopped

·· 2 eggs, lightly beaten

·· olive oil, to fry

·· sea salt and black pepper

For the tzatziki

·· 2 small cucumbers or ½ regular cucumber

·· 300ml Greek yogurt

·· 1 garlic clove

• I don't bother to peel the potato. Grate it on the coarse side of a box grater, then squeeze it in a sieve placed over a bowl (reserve this potato liquid).

• Grate the onions, too, on the coarse side of the box grater. Place them in a separate bowl and add the potato. Mix in the minced meat, mint and cinnamon, parsley and eggs. Add 1½–2 tbsp sea salt. I know it seems like a lot, but you need it to flavour this much meat, potato and onion. Grind in pepper, to taste.

• I use my hand to mix everything really well. The more you manipulate the mixture, the more protein strands develop, binding everything properly. You can also scrape at the bottom of the potato water, lift out the starch and add that too; it will help things bind.

• You can now leave the mix covered in the fridge overnight, or for an hour or so, or use it straight away. If you do keep it in the fridge, make sure to bring the mixture to room temperature before frying.

• To shape the keftedes, do wet your hands as it will make it easier. I go for a slightly oblongish shape, each 55–60g. Traditionally these are deep-fried, but deep-frying makes me feel uneasy (not for any health reasons, I just find dealing with huge amounts of oil daunting).

• Preheat the oven to 180°C fan (if it's not your first time making these, you might not need it).

• Have a plate lined with kitchen paper at the ready.

• Use a deep-ish and wide frying pan for this job. Fill it with oil so it comes 1–2cm up the sides. Heat the oil until it is hot enough that, when you pinch a tiny bit off the keftedes and throw it in, it sizzles immediately.

• Fry the keftedes in batches (6 at a time) over a medium heat on 3 sides until golden brown. This should take 7–8 minutes. Reduce the heat if you feel they are colouring too much. Once they are brown, you can always cut one open to see if the meat and potato are cooked through. The meat will be opaque if done, and do have a nibble to see if the potato feels raw. You can always put them on a lined tray into the oven while you fry the rest. I feel like the first batch needs this oven treatment, but the consequent batches don't as the oil in the pan becomes a good enough temperature. Set on the lined plate to blot off excess oil.

- To make the tzatziki, cut the cucumbers in half lengthways and scoop out the watery seeds with a small spoon. I just sprinkle some salt over the cores and eat them right there and then (I never chuck them). Grate the cucumber on the coarse side of the grater and add it to the yogurt. It will seem like a lot of cucumber, but I think that's how it should be.

- Grate the garlic on the fine side of the grater and mix that through. Add some salt and you are good to go. These little meatballs are good with so many things, as part of a bigger meal, with Cypriot (and Also Bulgarian) Salad (see page 158), or – my and Sasha's favourite – stuffed into a pitta with shredded lettuce, ripe tomatoes, sliced red onion and green pepper, grated feta and tzatziki.

Cypriot (and Also Bulgarian) Salad

There is something extremely comforting about this version of what we know as 'Greek salad'. In Bulgaria they call it *shopski*. In Cyprus, where I lived, it was very often undressed (oil and vinegar or lemon juice were provided for DIY dressing), served with a massive slab of feta on top for you to separate with a fork. But in one particular place, an ancient taverna in the old town of Limassol, the feta was finely grated over the salad, which I found especially pleasing, as it eventually melts and forms part of the dressing. I serve this with Cypriot Keftedes (see page 154) or very simply grilled prawns, and transport myself back to my teenage years. I can still feel the coolness of the stone walls of the taverna, shielding us from the sun. Serve it undressed if you have people coming over and provide dressing ingredients on the table. For my family, I dress it just before serving it.

···

- ·· ½ small red onion
- ·· 4 tbsp red wine vinegar, or juice of 1 lemon
- ·· 2 very ripe tomatoes
- ·· 1 regular cucumber or 2 small cucumbers
- ·· 1 green pepper
- ·· 1 carrot
- ·· handful of (ideally) Kalamata olives, the best you can get
- ·· 1 tsp dried oregano
- ·· olive oil
- ·· 200g feta
- ·· sea salt

- Slice the red onion as finely as you can into half moons. Put it in a salad bowl (a shallow bowl works best) and pour over half the vinegar, or squeeze over half the lemon, to temper its harshness.

- Slice the tomatoes into slim wedges. If any of the juices seep out, swipe them with your hand into the lemony onions. Put the tomatoes into the salad bowl.

- Slice the cucumber into quite chunky rounds and put them with the other veg.

- Cut the pepper in half, deseed, and, if it is a big one, cut it in half lengthways again and then slice it across. Add it to the bowl.

- Grate the carrot on the coarse side of a grater and add it, too, to the bowl.

- Throw in the whole olives. If you have kids eating, you can pit the olives beforehand; I just smash them with the flat side of the knife and remove the stones.

- Finally, make the dressing by whisking together the remaining vinegar or lemon juice and the oregano with oil and salt to taste. Stir it through the salad. Finely grate half the feta on top. I leave the remaining feta and the grater on the table, so everyone can top themselves up when needed.

Celebrating Together

The Magic of Festive Food

Celebrating Together

I am not a religious person, I have never been; nevertheless, I have always resented the Soviet-imposed secularism of my childhood. I feel it robbed us of a lot of beautiful tradition and a sense of being united by a deeper history.

As a child, I didn't understand secularism and the Soviet efforts to standardise everything: people of a huge multinational country forced to speak the same language, eat the same food, read the same books, think the same thoughts. When I was little, New Year's Eve was the biggest holiday of the year and January 6 – the Orthodox Christmas Eve – was celebrated half-heartedly and on the down-low. I remember the traditional sweet wheat berry porridge with dried fruit, called *kutya*, was made and passed around the table with a shot of vodka and a plate with food was left at an empty space at the table for the spirits of the ancestors. But overall, it was all rather unremarkable, a bit of a let down.

My non-eventful Christmases happened in a small town called Kakhovka, in the South of Ukraine, not too far from the Crimean border. Unless covered by thick snow, Soviet tower blocks stuck out like scraggy ribs along the Dnieper's shores. Only in warmer months did nature overwhelm the grey cityscape of my home town, when tall poplars, willows and flowers covered the ugly bones of Stalinist neo-renaissance architecture like newly grown skin and hair; winters completely exposed it for what it was. Like the architecture, cultural expression where I grew up was also suppressed and dumbed down.

All the colour and spirit of the Ukrainian folk tradition was trapped inside our hard-cover set of Nikolai Gogol's books. The illustrations were so beautiful. It was as if such things existed in a different dimension somewhere, in the past and far away.

My perception of the Ukrainian Christmas changed drastically in 1994. Once the USSR crumbled, we suddenly felt it was safe and desirable to reconnect with long-lost customs. My family decided to take a pilgrimage to Western Ukraine, a thousand kilometres away. Being further away from the centres of power, communities in these remote parts of the Carpathian Mountains were in more of a position to resist the iron fist of Soviet standardisation.

We took a sixteen-hour train journey to get to a small station between Ivano-Frankivsk and Ternopil, arriving to visit a friend of friends a day before Christmas Eve. Sadly, we can no longer recall where the village was. Just outside the train station, we appeared in a landscape of dreams. There were rolling cobalt-blue hills interrupted by darker rows of frozen fir trees. When we walked near the trees, I recall the branches were stuck together by heavy crystals of snow. I have never seen anything sparkle more brightly.

This friend of friends met us at the station and explained that the walk to his house was not long. He assured us that the locals hardly used transport, and that walking was the done thing. Enlivened by mountain air after the stifling, sweaty train atmosphere, we enthusiastically agreed. We were three families, all with kids about my age (ten).

We started walking, taking in the otherworldly alpine views, but little did we know that the people of the Carpathian mountains were used to walking or skiing everywhere… for hours. The 'short walk' took an hour and a half in heavy snow. Red-faced and exhausted, we trudged through a thick pine forest, out of breath but still able to marvel at the yellow-chested blue tits, and finally arrived at our destination. What awaited us made one of the biggest impressions on me and has helped me form the perceptions of the world and nature that I retain today.

A large wooden house stood alone in the forest, a noisy brook gushing by just five metres from the front door. We were to wash our faces in its sweet, freezing waters the next morning, and that night we heard wolves howl nearby. Christmas celebrations the next day – which really lasted at least a week – were straight out of those tangerine-splattered pages of Gogol's stories I had pored over at home.

From December 19, for about a month, people went from house to house singing special Christmas carols called *kolyadky*. It wasn't the half-hearted attempt we made as kids, carrying a pillow case for a sack and concluding with a quick plea for some sweets or rubles. It was a real, folk opera performance. People, both adults and children, would arrive by our host's door, wrapped in heavy, brightly embroidered sheepskin coats and feathered hats, one of them wearing an impressive goat mask. And they sang and played dulcimer and violins like true virtuosi.

There were two bedrooms with fireplaces in the big wooden house. The third, larger room with stags' heads on the walls was not heated. This is where the enormous Christmas table stood. It was always laid with cold dishes, for a couple of days at least. There was a beetroot and mushroom dish called *shukhy*, the ceremonial *kutya* porridge, cheeses and pickles, bean dishes, as well as sweet yeasted buns and a plaited *kolach* bread covered in poppy seeds. The performers would sing and play, and were then invited into the cold room with its rustic wooden table, hot dishes suddenly appearing alongside the spread of cold appetisers. The performers would eat and drink for a while. When they left, dirty plates would be swapped for fresh crockery and it would all be repeated again with the next set of performers.

I have always known the warmth of my big extended family, but I had never before experienced such a spirit of openness and camaraderie between people who were not related to each other. It was my first experience of a community. A community with a spirit that is only possible when not everyone is wearing the same grey coat. We saw that unity in a group of people was attainable when individuality was allowed to flourish.

Pumpkin and Orange Kolach

I adapted this recipe from my Ukrainian friend and baker Katrya Kaluzhna's recipe. Kolach is a very traditional festive bread, like a circular challah. Pumpkin and orange is not a traditional flavouring, but it is definitely an amazing feature of this recipe. Katrya uses a sourdough starter, but I thought a yeasted version would be a bit less demanding. If you are an experienced sourdough baker, use 100g of a revived starter. It's nice to break this recipe up: prep the poolish and the pumpkin purée the evening before and then it is a doddle the next day to bake and eat it. On its second day, toast it and eat with butter… it is just such an extraordinarily tasty thing.

For the poolish

·· 7g fast action dried yeast

·· 100ml water

·· 100g plain flour

For the bread

·· 200g peeled, deseeded pumpkin

·· finely grated zest of 1 orange

·· 2 eggs, lightly beaten

·· 150g caster sugar

·· 450g strong white bread flour, plus more to dust

·· 60g unsalted butter, softened

·· salt

For the glaze

·· 1 egg

·· 2 tbsp milk

·· 3 tbsp mixed seeds

- Make a poolish by whisking the yeast and measured water in a bowl. If you are not sure how fresh your yeast is (I keep it in the fridge), let it sit in the water somewhere warm for 10–15 minutes or until you see froth and bubbles. When you are positive the yeast is active, add the 100g of flour. You should have a thick mixture. Smooth it out, cover tightly and leave the bowl in the fridge overnight.

- Chop the pumpkin into even 5cm chunks. I then steam it. The easiest way to do this, if you don't have a steamer, is to pop it into a metal or enamel colander and put it over a pot of boiling water, then cover with a lid that will fit as tightly as possible on top. Steam for 20 minutes or until very soft. Blitz into a smooth purée. If doing this the night before, let it cool down and keep it, covered, in the fridge, or on your work surface if your kitchen is cool.

- QR CODE • *In the morning, take the poolish out of the fridge. It should look bubbly and slightly raised. If it doesn't, I am sad to confirm that your yeast was dead. Whisk in the pumpkin purée, zest and eggs, then about 1½ tsp of salt and the sugar. Now the flour: I just dump it all in and stir with a fork or spoon. Knead it well and leave for 1–2 hours to rise somewhere warm.*

- *Now, if you have one, fit your food mixer with a dough hook. If you don't, you can do this by hand in a large bowl; it will be a slippery business, but embrace it and remember you are also moisturising your hands. Add the butter, bit by bit, kneading it with a wet hand using the stretch and fold technique (see page 274), or with the machine, until fully incorporated. The dough will be shiny, soft and sticky.*

- *Leave the dough, covered, for 30 minutes somewhere warm. Then give it a knead on a well-floured surface, it might feel sticky at first, but that will stop.*

- *Divide the dough into 4 equal parts and knead each into a ball. Make sure your surface is still well floured, then roll each ball into a long sausage. I do this by lifting each piece of dough and rolling it between my palms, letting gravity stretch it, then put it on the barely floured (so it can stretch by sticking to the table) surface and roll from the centre to the edges, stretching it out to 45cm or so.*

- *Put the dough sausages parallel to each other, perpendicular to you. Squish and stretch the top ends with your fingers, so they become a little thinner, then pinch them together. Now we work from right to left. Take the sausage on the right, feed it over its neighbour to the left, then under the next sausage, then over the final sausage. Again take the sausage on the right and feed it over, under and then over. Keep going until you have plaited the full lengths of the dough.*

- *Now pinch the bottom ends together. The middle will look a bit bulkier, so stretch the whole thing delicately to even it up. Gently but confidently transfer the plait to a tray lined with floured baking parchment. Connect the ends together, to form a plaited circle, making sure the centre is well open. Cover and leave for 1 hour.*

- Brush the kolach with the egg and milk beaten together and sprinkle over the seeds, then, if using chunky seeds that tend to fall off (such as pumpkin), dab a little bit more of the egg wash on top to make sure they really stick. Leave somewhere to prove again for 30–60 minutes. Preheat the oven to 200°C fan.

- Bake for 30 minutes or until golden. Leave to cool down on a wire rack.

....

- TIP • I very much doubt you'll have leftovers. If you do, I highly recommend just toasting slices and slathering over butter and marmalade. But this can also be turned into a kick-ass bread and butter pudding (see page 237).

....

Christmas Cheese and Quince Shortbread

In 2015, a national newspaper held a Christmas fair and invited me, a budding young writer, to come and sell some baked goods. As a freelancer and single mum, my finances were extremely limited. So I asked my best friend Caroline to help me make something out of nothing. I had a lot of quince jelly at home from the previous year and a large piece of a Swedish equivalent of Parmesan – Västerbotten – from the *Observer Food Monthly* award's legendary goody bag. I had an idea to combine them in a biscuit. I roughly based the biscuit recipe on Nigella Lawson's Parmesan shortbread recipe, and that was that. We baked all night and completely sold out the next day. It is such a good, moreish biscuit that will satisfy all your cheese and sweet cravings at once! As always, feel free to use plain flour if you like, but as you may have noticed I have a slight buckwheat flour obsession; it works so well here and makes these biscuits gluten-free, for those who care.

- 150g buckwheat flour, or plain flour
- 75g Västerbotten cheese, or Parmesan cheese, finely grated
- 100g unsalted butter, softened
- 1 egg yolk
- 100g quince jelly

- Mix all the ingredients except the quince jelly together, either by hand or in a food mixer. If you are doing it by hand and the dough refuses to come together, sprinkle over ½ tbsp water.

- Knead the dough, cut it in half and roll each half first into a ball and then into a 16cm log. Wrap it tightly in clingfilm and keep in the fridge for 30 minutes minimum, or for a couple of days, until ready to cook. (You can also stick it in the freezer instead, for 20 minutes or so, if short on time.)

- Preheat the oven to 170°C fan. Cut each log into 1cm-thick coins and then make an imprint with your finger in each of the pieces. Put the biscuits on a lined baking sheet, they can be quite close to each other as there will be minimal spread.

- Bake for 15 minutes or until they look firm and are starting to become golden.

- Take them out of the oven and gently spoon a little quince jelly into each indentation, then return them to the oven for another 3–5 minutes. Let them cool down on a wire rack and then eat them with a glass of lovely fizz.

Fiadone

I met Gabriella Buttarazzi at the University of Warwick. We became friends fast and she and her family often took me under their wing and had me over at their home near Loughborough, especially during the holidays. Gabri's mum Enza Santina Pinto is originally from the little-known region of Italy called Molise in Campobasso. This fiadone is a kind of a delicious crispy Easter pie, and Enza asked me to emphasise that it is very different from versions in other regions of Italy. It is the most wonderful thing and I must admit I make it at least once a month, as it freezes well, my son loves it and it makes for a great packed lunch. If you do make it during Easter, serve it with an aperitivo glass of wine as a snack or a starter. You can experiment with different cheeses and hams, I've tried it with all sorts. Gabriella makes an amazing vegetarian version using potato, spinach, caramelised onion, pine nuts and Gruyère cheese.

For the pastry

·· 250g pasta flour ('00' flour), plus more to dust

·· ½ tsp baking powder

·· 2 medium eggs, plus 1 egg yolk, to glaze

·· ¼ glass (80ml) white wine (this makes the dough elastic)

·· 50ml olive oil

For the filling

·· 200g provolone or cacciocavallo cheese

·· 200g Parmesan cheese

·· 200g stracciatella cheese

·· 150g mature Cheddar cheese

·· 4 eggs, lightly beaten

·· 100g cured Italian sausage with fennel, finely chopped

·· leaves from ½ small bunch of parsley, finely chopped

- QR CODE • *If making the pastry by hand, mix the flour and baking powder in a large bowl, make a well in the middle, then crack in the 2 whole eggs and pour in the wine and olive oil. Using a fork, mix the flour into the wet ingredients; it will be a bit rough and shaggy. Flour a work surface lightly and then knead the dough briefly by hand. It will refuse to smooth out, but if you cover it and leave it be for 10 minutes, it will relax enough for you to get a smoother result when you knead again. Shape the dough into a long fat sausage and cut across into 4 pieces.*

- If making the pastry with a food mixer fitted with a dough hook (which I do often), put the wet ingredients into the mixer bowl first, add the flour and baking powder and mix at a low speed to combine, then increase the speed and knead well into a smoothish dough.

- Now, Enza and Gabriella warn that a pasta machine gets you the best results because you need even, thin pieces of pastry. The other reason why it is good to do with a pasta machine is because you fold the layers when you work it in the machine, which means you get a beautiful flaky result. But of course, you can also roll it out by hand. Either way, let the dough rest, covered, for about 1 hour.

- For the filling, grate all the cheeses on the coarse side of a grater and mix in a bowl with the eggs, chopped sausage and parsley.

- QR CODE • *To roll the pastry by hand, take one-quarter of the dough and roll it on a floured surface into a rectangle or oval shape. Fold into thirds as if you were folding a business letter, first folding one end (from the short side) into the middle, then covering it with the other end. Turn it seam side down and roll it out again, perpendicular to the way you rolled it before, then fold it again in the same way. Repeat to roll and fold a total of 4–5 times. If it becomes too stiff to roll, set aside to relax for a few minutes while you roll another piece of dough.*

- *Now roll each piece of dough on a lightly floured surface into a thin rectangle the width of the baking tray you intend to use (35 x 25cm is good). Put one-quarter of the filling in a lengthways strip, lightly brush the edges with water to help it all stick, then fold the dough over lengthways. Seal the seams with the tines of a fork and snip holes on top with scissors. Repeat to roll and stuff the other 3 pasta pieces.*

- Preheat the oven to 180°C fan. Your baking tray needs to be long enough for the length of a pasta roll, but I have also bent a fiadone before to fit it on and it was all good. (Or you might need 2 trays.) Line the tray(s) with baking parchment, put your fiadoni on the tray(s), brush with egg yolk and bake for 35 minutes.

- Leave to cool, then slice it. Enjoy slightly cooled with a gorgeous glass of white wine, or cut into pieces and stash into a packed lunch.

Lamb Shoulder with Herbs and Preserved Lemons

I had to go back to work when my son Sasha was six months old. I was lucky that a friend of mine, Rachel Sweetapple, ran a catering business from her house only two streets away from our rented flat. I would go and help her prep, and my mum, who would sometimes be looking after the baby, could pop in whenever Sash needed a feed. We often made a version of this lamb for Rachel's clients and I have been making it for friends and family ever since. In fact this is my go-to for dinner parties and Easter. The marinade ingredients might sound fusion-y and improbable, but they work so well. When you pull the lamb and mix it through the marinade juices, it's just incredible. This recipe is fantastic for using up tired, soft fridge-forgotten herbs: feel free to use any, such as parsley, chives and basil. Serve it with any grain, too – I like couscous or freekeh – but any slightly plain carb that can soak up the sauce is good: rice, boiled and crushed potatoes, flatbreads… you name it. Lamb shanks or pork or beef ribs will also work here if you want something smaller or cheaper than a lamb shoulder!

·· 3 garlic cloves, peeled

·· 1 tbsp soy sauce

·· ½ tbsp honey

·· 15g finely grated ginger (I don't bother peeling it, but that's up to you)

·· 1½ tsp ground coriander seeds

·· 1½ tsp ground cumin seeds

·· leaves from ½ small bunch of mint

·· leaves from ½ small bunch of tarragon

·· ½ small bunch of dill, leaves and stalks

·· ½ small bunch of coriander, leaves and stalks

·· 1 tbsp olive oil

·· 1 preserved lemon, chopped

·· 1 shoulder of lamb (2kg), or 4 lamb shanks

·· sea salt

• Preheat the oven to 200°C fan. Put all the ingredients (bar a handful of soft herbs and the lamb) into a food processor, add ½ tsp salt and blitz them up into a paste. Cover the lamb with it. If you can leave it in the marinade overnight, all the better, but if you don't have time, it is ready to be baked straight away.

• Put the lamb and marinade into a cast-iron pan and cover it with a lid. Otherwise, especially if you are using a shoulder, you can also use a roasting tin and cover it tightly with a foil tent (just use 2 large pieces of foil and tent them over the meat without touching it). Cook for 30 minutes, then reduce the oven temperature to 160°C fan and cook for another 2 hours. Then lift the lid or foil off and have a look. The meat should be soft and coming away from the bone. If it is not quite there, cover it again and put it back in for another 30 minutes. Be careful not to dry out the lamb and keep checking, as a shoulder can take up to 3½ hours.

• Take the lamb out of the oven, cover and rest in its juices for at least 20 minutes.

• Pull the meat off the bone, discard the bones and large bits of fat, roughly shred larger pieces, then return to the tin. Taste, it may need a light sprinkling of salt.

• If the lamb has been resting a while, you can pop it and the juices in the roasting tin under a hot grill to warm through and crisp up the meat on top.

• Of course you can shred the lamb and mix it with the juices up to a day before and keep in the fridge, then just reheat in a lidded pan with a splash of water mixed in, or in a foil baking tray, before serving. Serve with any plain grain you fancy, or even crushed boiled potatoes, sprinkling over the reserved herbs.

• **TIP** • **With leftovers, I love doing what my friend Laura Jackson from Towpath Café does. Melt some ghee or oil in a pan and add the shredded leftover lamb. Fry until crispy, then spoon the meat over a bed of hummus, top with toasted pine nuts and scoop up with crispy pitta or flatbread.**

Christmas Duck with a Cabbage, Kraut and Chestnut Stuffing

This is partly influenced by my mum's preparation of duck and also by a Lithuanian stuffed goose recipe Anya von Bremzen has in her seminal *Please to the Table* book. Everything about it screams huge flavour, and it's very little effort as it all goes into the same roasting tin. I make a vegetarian version for my husband: I just stuff a small pumpkin with the stuffing, cover it in foil and bake at 180°C fan for two hours. This is a great Christmas dish as it takes care of so many elements. Do feel free to add some spices to the stuffing, perhaps some coriander seeds, allspice or a little bit of nutmeg.

·· 6 potatoes, peeled

·· 3 apples, skin on, cored

·· 1 duck (about 2.35kg)

·· 1 large onion, thickly sliced

·· ½ tbsp coriander seeds, lightly toasted and ground

·· ½ small Savoy or white cabbage (about 300g)

·· 200g sauerkraut

·· 150g chestnuts, roughly chopped

·· sea salt and white or black pepper

• Halve or quarter the potatoes and boil them in salted water for 10 minutes, or until the edges become a little rough when you drain them in a colander.

• Leave small apples whole, but quarter any larger ones.

• Take the duck out of the fridge to come to room temperature and pat it as dry as you can. The drier it is, the crispier the skin will get. Prick the skin all over with a fork to help release the fat when it cooks. There are some fatty bits at the back and the neck ends of the duck. Really get as much as you can out, as you will need the fat to cook the large amount of cabbage. (You can also use a little cooking oil or jarred goose or duck fat, if your duck is unusually svelte and you don't get enough fat.) So pull the fatty pieces out and put them into a large, dry frying or sauté pan. Set it over a low heat and start rendering the fat. When there is enough fat to cover the base of the pan, add the onion, coriander seeds and a generous pinch of salt. Increase the heat slightly and cook until the onion softens and starts to colour ever so slightly, about 5 minutes.

• Meanwhile, trim off the dry-tough stalk of the cabbage, then slice it fully, including the core (just slice the core very finely).

• Add the cabbage to the onion and cook for 5 minutes, so it softens. Add the kraut and chestnuts and cook over a medium heat, covered with a lid to speed things along, for 5–10 minutes. If it looks a tad dry, add a splash of water. You can pick out the bits of fat now if you like; I often have very little, so leave it in.

• Give the stuffing a taste. Depending on how salty the kraut was, you may need a pinch of salt and definitely give it a few grinds of pepper. Let the filling cool down, I just take the pan outside and leave it to cool for 10 minutes.

• Preheat the oven to 220°C fan.

• Then, following Simon Hopkinson's advice, put the duck into a deep bowl so the bottom cavity is upwards; this frees both your hands to pack the stuffing in. Scoop all the cabbage inside the duck and put it, breast up, on a rack over your largest roasting tin or tray. If you can't fit all the stuffing in, just add it to the tray later with the potatoes and apples. Rub the breast and legs with salt. Cover the tray with foil, like a tent, so it doesn't touch the duck.

- Cook in the oven for 40 minutes. Then, taking care with handling the hot duck, pour most of the fat from the tray into a bowl (you can use it to cook potatoes another time). Now put the duck back on the rack over the tray, turning it by 180° so it cooks evenly, and cook for a further 40 minutes.

- Reduce the oven temperature to 190°C fan, remove the rack so the duck is in the roasting tray and surround it with the potatoes and apples. Cook for another 30 minutes, turning the potatoes halfway through. The potatoes should be golden and crispy, the apples softened and caramelised, the stuffing slightly sour from the kraut and sweet and textured from chestnuts, everything moistened and enriched by luscious duck fat. I cannot think of a better dish to have over the Christmas holidays. Well, unless it's the hash that you can make from the leftovers (see overleaf)!

Duck (or Any Other Roast Meat) Hash

This is the perfect Boxing Day recipe. I often roast a duck for Christmas and there aren't many leftovers, but I always pick at the carcass thoroughly, especially its back, as it often gets forgotten but contains quite a lot of meat. I use potato and cabbage stuffing here, but you can use any meat and leftover roast veg. Pull the meat if it's slow-cooked, or slice it very thinly if it's, say, beef cooked rare. This may be one of those slightly filthy and ugly-delicious dishes, but dress it up with a fried egg on top and serve with a gorgeous Easy Honey and Caraway Kraut (see page 282) to cut through all the fat and it will not only look beautiful, but will fix the sternest of hangovers.

- 100g leftover roast potatoes, in larger chunks

- 150g leftover roast duck, or other leftover roast meat

- 100g leftover cabbage stuffing (see page 172), or any other leftover vegetables

- 2 tbsp goose fat or oil, plus vegetable oil to fry the eggs

- 2–4 eggs

- pinch of chilli flakes (optional)

- sea salt

- gherkins, kraut, or kimchi, to serve

- If your potato chunks are large, crush them with a fork. Pull the duck meat into smaller strands (or thinly slice firmer meat), add the cabbage stuffing or other vegetables and moosh it all together with a fork or your hand.

- Heat the 2 tbsp fat in a large frying pan. Make sure it sizzles properly. Now put the mixture into the fat. Hear it sizzle. Cook it all over a medium-high heat, without disturbing too soon. You want crispy bits to develop. Now turn it over and fry on the other side. You want everything to get a little crispy; don't worry about it not being a cohesive thing. It will all be a little bit of a delicious mess. Reconcile yourself to that.

- Fry the eggs in a little oil in another frying pan and serve the hash with the fried eggs on top, sprinkled with chilli flakes, if you like, and with a tasty pickle, such as a gherkin, kraut or kimchi, on the side.

'In the night, the rice
kernels absorb the water,
expand and come apart.
The bones cook down to
their cores, infusing with
the aromatics and rice'

Adrian Chang, Cook and Food Writer

Christmas Morning *Jook*

'My family has roots in the tropical and lush wilds of Guangdong Province in Southern China. Being a descendant of countless generations of rice farmers, you could say the stuff is in my blood. I often say: "Rice is life." The glorious golden grain which nourishes our bellies, sustains our communities' welfare, and whose life cycle marks the seasons. Rice is everything to my people. Rice is community. Rice is family.

And even now, when all the living generations of my family are California-born, our love for rice has never waned. On Christmas Eve, before bedtime, my grandmother and my mother would fill a giant pot with jasmine rice, crushed knobs of ginger, spring onions tied into bows, add the leftover turkey carcass from that night's roast and cover it all with water. After bringing it to the boil, they would turn the heat down to a simmer, cover the pot and leave it until morning. In the night, the rice kernels absorb the water, expand and come apart. The bones cook down to their cores, infusing with the aromatics and rice.

In the morning, the rest of us would awaken to the scents wafting through the house. Three generations would sit around a breakfast table already laid with small serving bowls of peanuts, chopped spring onions, pork floss, soy sauce and chillies. Everything and everyone gathered around the large pot of steaming rice porridge – or as we call it in Cantonese, *jook* – slurping back bowl after bowl, laughing, teasing, sighing and even burping. Rice is family.'

Christmas Chocolate Log with Chestnut and Sour Cherry Cream

This is a bit of a mash-up of my mum's chocolate log and a Croatian dessert. The Croatian pud has ground walnuts in the sponge cake and buttercream instead of cream. If you want that version, google *biskvitna rolada s kremom* *od kestena* and do some nifty Google translate action, but this version is brilliant: light and rich at the same time. If you can't get hold of chestnut purée, just omit it and up the cream!

- ·· 5 eggs
- ·· 200g caster sugar
- ·· 30g cocoa powder, plus more to dust
- ·· 200g plain flour
- ·· sea salt

For the cream

- ·· 250g double cream
- ·· 200g chestnut purée
- ·· 50g frozen sour cherries, pitted

For the ganache

- ·· 80g dark cooking chocolate, finely chopped
- ·· 100ml whipping or single cream
- ·· 50g icing sugar, to dust (optional)

- Preheat the oven to 180°C fan.

- Whisk the eggs in a food processor on their own first, then gradually add the caster sugar, whisking all the time and beating until really light and foamy. It is really important to beat in as much air as possible here, as we are not using any other raising agent, it should rise just from all the air in the eggs. It should take about 7 minutes; you are looking for a slight ribbon stage (this is when the mixture from the beaters drips into the batter, but leaves a risen trail and doesn't sink into it for a few moments).

- Sift the cocoa and flour together, stir in a good pinch of salt and gently but surely fold through the egg and sugar foam. I do this in 2 batches.

- Spread the sponge over a large shallow baking tray lined with baking parchment; mine measures 32 x 23cm. Bake for 10 minutes. You can always pierce it with a skewer to check, but it should be ready in this time.

- Meanwhile, line another tray with baking parchment and lightly dust it with cocoa powder. When the sponge is ready, turn it out on to the cocoa-dusted tray and roll it up from a short end. Leave it to cool a bit.

- Now whisk the cream a little with a hand-held whisk, stopping before it holds any peaks. Fold in the chestnut purée. Unroll the sponge and spread the cream over, then scatter over the cherries and roll it up again.

- Trim the end and attach it to the side of the log to make it look more log-like (as in the photo, right).

- For the ganache, put the dark chocolate into a bowl. Heat the cream in a pan and then pour it over the dark chocolate. Allow to sit for 2 minutes before gently stirring together. If you find your ganache splits, whisk in 2 tbsp boiling water at a time until it becomes glossy again. Leave to cool.

- Spread the cooled chocolate ganache over the log and use a fork to make it look like bark. Dust over a little icing sugar, if you like, or decorate with a couple of sour cherries and non-poisonous leaves (warn children not to eat the leaves!).

Ginger and Honey Keks

This tastes to me like I think the Austro-Hungarian empire would have tasted in cake form! The ginger, the spices and the use of sour cream has a Galician (West Ukrainain) feel to it. My mother bakes this cake in winter a lot. She calls it *keks*, and it is one of our favourite things to cook at Christmas. We love the warm smells of ginger, honey and allspice lingering in the kitchen until they get replaced by the yeasty smells of the kolach bread that we start baking closer to Orthodox Christmas in January. Mum uses a very rich *smetana* to make this when she is in Ukraine, but full-fat crème fraîche works well. I don't usually peel ginger, but I do here, because, well, it's Mum's recipe and that's what she does…

- 100g unsalted butter, softened, plus more for the tin
- 100g honey (chestnut or buckwheat are great, but any works)
- 50g dark muscovado sugar, or any sugar
- 50g light brown sugar
- 150g full-fat crème fraîche or 150ml yogurt
- 4 large eggs, lightly beaten
- 30g piece of ginger, peeled and finely grated
- 300g plain flour
- ½ tsp freshly ground allspice
- ½ tsp freshly ground black pepper
- 1½ tsp baking powder
- pinch of sea salt

For the lemon drizzle

- 200g golden icing sugar
- finely grated zest and juice of 2 unwaxed lemons

- Preheat the oven to 170°C fan. Butter a 22cm bundt cake mould.

- Melt the butter in a small saucepan with the honey and both the brown sugars. It just needs to melt together and be homogeneous, but shouldn't boil. If it does, no big deal, just cool it down slightly before the next step. Take it off the heat and briskly whisk in the crème fraîche.

- Beat the eggs gradually into the warm mixture, then add the ginger. I don't use a machine for any of this, just a fork or a whisk.

- I very rarely bother with flour sifting, but in this case I do as I feel the spices and baking powder get distributed more evenly. So sift the flour, spices, baking powder and salt together, then fold them into the wet ingredients.

- Pour the cake batter into the prepared mould and bake for 1 hour. Use a skewer to check whether it's cooked through inside. If it comes out clean, you are good. If it has lots of sticky batter on it, return the cake to the oven for another 10 minutes.

- Meanwhile, in a separate bowl, whisk the icing sugar into the lemon zest and juice. It's good to have it ready, as you will pour it over the warm cake. It will be thin; more of a drizzle than a true icing.

- Pour the lemon drizzle over the warm cake. Serve with a cup of tea or a coffee in the morning.

Walnut Esterhazy Torte

I often find cake-making daunting, especially when chocolate is involved (I find chocolate capricious and annoying). So I love to split the jobs up a bit here and do things in advance. I make the sponge and the cream two days ahead, layer them together, wrap and keep in the fridge. I then do the dreaded chocolate ganache bit on the day before the event, cover the top of the cake with apricot jam and pour the ganache over. This way, on the actual birthday or other festive occasion, the cake is ready! All you need to do is stick the candles in.

For the sponge

·· 200g walnuts

·· 3 tbsp plain flour

·· pinch of ground cinnamon

·· 200g icing sugar, plus more to dust

·· 8 egg whites

·· sea salt

For the cream

·· 300ml whole milk

·· 8 egg yolks

·· 150g caster sugar

·· 3 tbsp cornflour

·· 200g unsalted butter, softened

·· 100g cooked condensed milk (bought ready-caramelised, or homemade in the can)

·· 2 tbsp kirsch (optional)

·· 1 tsp almond or vanilla extract (optional)

·· 2 tbsp apricot jam

- First we need to make the 'meringue sponge' layers (otherwise known as dacquoise). These can be made up to 2 days ahead and kept covered in the fridge.

- Preheat the oven to 180°C fan. Put the walnuts in 1 tray and the flaked almonds for the decoration into another and put them in the oven. Check the almonds after 6 minutes. You want the walnuts to be pretty well toasted and you want the almonds to go properly golden brown (like in the photo). They both should take 8–10 minutes. Give them a shake halfway through, especially if your oven has hot spots. For the walnuts, as you can't always tell from the colour, just taste one after 8 minutes: you will know when a nut is properly toasted if it is irresistibly tasty. When both are brown and taste very very good, take them off the tray (otherwise they will keep cooking and might burn) and let them cool down slightly.

- Reduce the oven temperature to 170°C fan.

- Line 2 large baking trays with non-stick baking parchment and use a 20cm cake tin or plate to draw 2 circles on each.

- In a food processor, blitz the walnuts with the flour, cinnamon and half the icing sugar. The flour absorbs the nut oil and helps the mixture to remain dry.

- Whisk the egg whites and a generous pinch of sea salt to stiff peaks, then gradually add the rest of the icing sugar until they reach stiff peaks again. Fold the nut mixture into the egg whites, incorporating them as best you can without beating too much air out of the egg whites. But also remember this is more of a 'sponge' layer rather than a true meringue, so don't be too stressed about this process.

- QR CODE • *I tried not to use a piping bag here, but it really does work better with one. It does not need a nozzle, and is very easy to do. Spoon the mixture into a large piping bag and snip a 1cm hole at the bottom. Pipe the mixture in concentric circles inside the templates you drew. Be quite generous with the thickness piped out: it should be 1–2cm thick.*

- Bake for 15 minutes, checking after 10, until lightly golden, still a little bouncy and cooked through.

- As soon as the meringue layers are out of the oven, take the baking parchment with them on off the baking tray. I just gently slide it out of the tray on to a large wire rack to cool completely (a tabletop will also be OK). They will look puffed when you take them out, but will deflate as they cool and will also feel a little sticky to the touch. That's all fine! You can stack them one on top of the other with baking parchment in between (just make sure to dust a little icing sugar on

For the decoration

·· 80g flaked almonds

·· 80g dark chocolate, finely chopped

·· 150ml whipping cream, or single cream

·· 50g white chocolate, finely chopped

the sponge before putting baking parchment on top), if you are making the cake in advance.

- When they are cool you will need to peel them off the baking parchment. I flip them over on to an icing sugar-dusted table and gently peel off the paper.

- Have a large mixing bowl to pour the custard in at the ready.

- To make the cream, heat the milk in a medium saucepan. Whisk the egg yolks with the sugar and cornflour until slightly pale. Add a splash of hot milk to the yolks, stirring the yolks as you do this.

Continued →

Continued...

- Pour the yolk mixture back into the pan with the milk, put a timer on for 5 minutes, and cook over a medium-low heat, whisking all the time. At first it will all be loose and liquid, but after about 2 minutes, the custard will suddenly thicken and will look lumpy. Don't worry. Just keep whisking, reduce the heat to its lowest and cook until your timer goes off. Switch off the heat but keep whisking the custard for another minute or so, as you want to cook the raw flour out. Taste it: if it doesn't taste floury, it's ready. Scrape it into the bowl. It will look like a big jiggly blob. Let the custard cool down to room temperature, then, using a spatula, smooth out the top evenly and cover it directly with baking parchment if you are not using it that day.

- Using electric beaters (or lacking those, the sheer force of your muscles), beat the softened butter with the cooked condensed milk until very fluffy. Now beat in the custard in 3 batches until homogeneous. At the very end, whisk in the kirsch or any other alcohol you like, if using. If you are making this for a child, add the almond or vanilla extract. Put into the fridge for at least 30 minutes, but longer is better. (If you find the mixture splits, put it in a blender or use a stick blender to bring it back, then chill as normal.)

- When you are ready to assemble, put one-fifth of the cream into a small separate bowl. Now put a sponge layer on a work surface. Cover it with some cream from the main, big bowl, and continue with all the sponge layers, building it up. Do not put any cream on the top layer. Heat the apricot jam in a pan gently until more spreadable, then brush it over the top layer.

- Put the dark chocolate into a bowl. Heat 120ml of the whipping or single cream in a pan and then pour it over the dark chocolate, allow to sit for 2 minutes, then gently stir together. If you find the ganache splits, whisk in 2 tbsp boiling water at a time until it becomes glossy again.

- Put a pan of simmering water on the hob and turn the heat to medium. Put the white chocolate and remaining cream in a heatproof bowl and set over the pan of water, making sure the water doesn't touch the bowl. Heat until melted.

- Pour the dark chocolate ganache over the cake. I start in the middle, then coax it to the sides with a spatula, making it run down the sides. Once that's done, add blobs of white chocolate all around the top. Then, using a knife or a chopstick, drag the white chocolate blobs around, creating a marbled pattern. Use a spatula to scrape any chocolate dripping down the sides around the cake, then allow to set in the fridge for 10 minutes.

- Spread the reserved cream around the sides of the cake and stick on the flaked toasted almonds.

- Keep the cake in the fridge overnight to let the meringue layers get saturated with the cream. Take it out of the fridge 10–15 minutes before you are ready to serve. Cut into pieces and enjoy with unsweetened lemony tea or a black coffee.

Esterhazy Torte

'The history of Esterhazy torte is rooted in the Austro-Hungarian empire. It was named after Prince Paul III Anton Esterházy de Galántha (1786–1866) and was created by 19th-century Budapest confectioners. The original was made using almonds, which were gradually replaced by walnuts, and my recipe (see page 182) is a riff on my mum's. I won't lie to you, it is probably the most involved recipe in the book, but it is worth it if you are trying to make something truly impressive.

It is my go-to for my son Sasha's birthday. I believe a child's birthday should also be a celebration of the mother, so I always want a cake to please us both. After all, we both did a lot of hard work on his original birthday… Esterhazy fits the bill perfectly as it has plenty of chocolate (his favourite) but also nuts and cooked condensed milk (my favourites).

The original has a very specific feathered pattern on top, so please do look it up if you want to be super-authentic. But, personally, I have nozzle anxiety. "Where is the piping bag? Where is the right nozzle? I found them! Bah, the attachment just popped through the bag hole with all the chocolate. I hate you, piping bag!" So I made a conscious decision a while ago never to use a piping bag and nozzle again. Therefore, mine is a marbled effect Esterhazy, which some might say means it is no longer an Esterhazy… but hey, if it reduces anxiety, I don't mind the semantics. It still tastes like the most delicious Esterhazy and will please a variety of palates. This is quite an intense cake; portion it out carefully and with restraint, as a little goes a long way.'

Easter Loaf

Easter is the biggest holiday in Ukraine, when we make yeasted enriched breads called *paskha*, which are not unlike panettone or brioche. Everyone makes an inordinate amount of them, as you also give them to friends and family. Mum would make an enormous dough – enough for at least 15! – and recycle large used food cans to bake them in. For the past few years we haven't had a chance to celebrate Easter with my extended family, but I still wanted to make the bread, so I came up with this simple loaf version for a regular-sized family. In fact this is almost a mixture of Ukrainian *paskha* bread and an English hot cross bun. Soaking the raisins in tea comes from Richard Snape's brilliant hot cross bun recipe in his *Bread and Butter* book. I remember Mum using multi-coloured sprinkles and an egg white and icing sugar glaze, but I prefer poppy seeds and an English-style lemon drizzle.

- 100g raisins
- 200ml hot, strong Earl Grey tea
- 200ml whole milk
- 70g caster sugar
- 7g fast action dried yeast
- 2 egg yolks
- 400g plain flour, plus more to dust
- 80g unsalted butter, softened, plus more for the tin
- sea salt

For the drizzle

- 100g icing sugar
- finely grated zest and juice of 1 unwaxed lemon
- 1 tbsp poppy seeds

To serve (optional)

- 50g unsalted butter
- grating of nutmeg
- 1 tsp ground cinnamon

- Put the raisins in a medium bowl, pour over the hot tea, cover tightly and leave to soak for at least 30 minutes. Then drain (I drink the raisiny tea, but you don't have to).

- Heat the milk a little, so it's warm but not hot, add 1 tsp of the sugar and whisk in the yeast. If you are not confident about how old your yeast is, leave for a little while, 5–10 minutes, to make sure the yeast activates and froths up. Then add the egg yolks, remaining sugar and 1 tsp salt and sift in the flour. Mix really well in the bowl, first using a spoon and then your hand to make it easier. The dough will be sticky and wet, but don't worry as it will change structure and will be easier to work with once it rises. I wet my hand, smooth the top over a bit and leave it to rise, covered, for 1 hour, or until it doubles in size.

- When it has doubled in size, it is time to mix in your butter. You can put everything into a food mixer fitted with a dough hook and mix in the softened butter and drained raisins gradually until incorporated. If working by hand, dust a work surface with flour and knead the dough gently, sprinkling in the drained raisins and little bits of butter as you go, kneading them in. Keep sprinkling on flour if you feel it's too sticky. Shape the bread by flattening it slightly, then fold the edges underneath to create a tight ball.

- Now butter a 900g loaf tin and pop the bread in, cover and leave to rise again. You want it to double in size. This may take up to 1 hour depending on how warm your kitchen is.

- Preheat the oven to 180°C fan. Bake the bread for 40 minutes.

- For the lemon icing, mix (or, if you can be bothered, sift) the icing sugar into the lemon juice. In a separate small bowl, mix the zest and the poppy seeds to sprinkle on later.

- Take the bread out of the oven and cool on a wire rack over a baking sheet lined with some baking parchment. When the loaf is cooler, drizzle on the icing and sprinkle over the lemon zest and poppy seeds. Joe, who is used to the spiciness of hot cross buns, toasts slices of this loaf the next day, mixes soft butter with nutmeg and cinnamon and spreads it over. Each to their own!

Food
and Love

Cooking as Self-Care

Food and Love

At the moment of writing this I am a self-employed working mother of two boys – a nine-year-old and a toddler – and, like everyone else, on a daily basis I am painfully short of time. But I love cooking. I love all the stages: picking ingredients, choosing what to make, taking my time to cook it. And when I get an opportunity, I cook something special, which more often than not involves some kind of dough, or hand-made pasta, or dumplings. I put a binge-able podcast on and I get to work.

Although I can't even call it work. As long as the kids are taken care of by Joe, and I don't have any deadlines looming, I find more involved cooking projects so incredibly relaxing. After all, the repetitive actions – folding dumplings, or slicing vegetables – take the focus away from the thoughts in our heads and really force us to be 'in the moment', which is every meditative practice's trope. Apart from being good for you, from being essentially 'self-care', it is also good for your loved ones. Nothing gives me more pleasure than knowing how excited my older son will be if dumplings are on the menu. I also believe in the concept of cooking with intention, putting positive energy and love (read: attention) into my dishes. Those you cook for will never forget it.

Another positive result that comes from time-consuming tasks such as making dumplings is that it really is an investment in time-saving in the future, when you may not be in the mood to spend any time cooking at all. I make a big batch of dumplings and freeze them, then I have a delicious instant lunch whenever I am a bit stuck or short of time. They take only a few more minutes to cook from frozen than if they were fresh and they taste just as good. Take the second recipe in this chapter – the Rose Dumplings – the easiest dumplings to shape. Freeze them as soon as you shape them, then steam from frozen and serve as a starter (or as part of a dumpling feast) to your guests… all you need to do is melt or brown some butter and make a garlic yogurt. Remember that you have QR codes which take you to videos of me guiding you through the trickiest bits, too. Also bear in mind that a lot of these recipes are designed so you can choose which part of the dish to make by hand and where you can cut corners. For example, with the Lazanky and Dark Greens and Noodles with Yogurt (see pages 204 and 212), feel free to use cut-up shop-bought lasagne sheets and just make the sauces.

So dive into this chapter: learn a skill, make delicious food for the freezer, meditate as you do so, and direct love and good intentions to everyone you are cooking these dishes for, including yourself.

Dumplings Over a Potato and Mushroom Stew

My grandmother Lusia used to make this amazing dish called *noodli*, a simple pork rib or duck, onion and potato stew with kefir dumplings leavened with bicarbonate of soda cooked on top. It was one of those celebratory meals we used to make when the extended family got together. My mum was so keen for my vegetarian husband to experience this important family dish that she created this version. I have played around with the original dough and created these feather-light dumplings, almost like airy steamed buns. They are not better than the original, but different, very puffy and light. You can use these dumplings over any stew you love as long as there is sufficient liquid in it. Serve with some kraut, kimchi or pickles on the side… heaven.

....

For the dough

·· 200ml kefir (or 150ml yogurt let down with 50ml water)

·· 15g fresh yeast, or 7g fast action dried yeast

·· 1 tbsp brown sugar

·· 1 egg, lightly beaten

·· 450g plain flour (or 350g plain flour plus 100g wholemeal or spelt flour), plus more to dust

·· a little vegetable oil

·· 50g Clarified Butter (see page 289) or regular unsalted butter, melted

·· sea salt

....

Continued →

• Mix the kefir with the yeast and sugar in a large bowl and whisk it well. Wait a little bit until yeasty froth appears, to make sure the yeast is alive. Then add the egg and 1 tsp salt and give it all a good whisk. Add 400g of the flour and mix it first with a spoon. Then put your hand in. The dough might be very wet, so stretch out and then slap the dough against the sides of the bowl for as long as your patience and muscle power allow you. If you feel like the dough is waaaay too wet, add the extra 50g of flour (but keep in mind: the wetter the dough, the lighter the dumplings).

• Wet your hands, fold the dough into a rough ball and put into a large oiled bowl to rise (I just use the bowl I mixed everything in to save on washing-up). Cover tightly with clingfilm or a tea towel and leave somewhere warm to rise. It should double in size, and, depending on the temperature in your kitchen, can take up to 1–2 hours. Or you can leave it in the fridge overnight.

• QR CODE • *Have 1–2 large and lightly oiled trays at the ready, to place your dumplings on for proving after you have cut them. When the dough is proudly puffed up, flour a work surface well and gently help it out of the bowl. It will be very soft and will deflate as it hits the surface. Gently give it a knead. Enjoy this brief process and be tender. Then, making sure the surface really is well floured, so the dough doesn't stick, roll it into a 30cm sheet. Now drizzle the clarified or regular butter all over it, and, using the palm of your hand, spread it all over the dough. Roll it all up into a sausage shape, evening it up along its length if needed, and cut across into 16–18 pieces. They will look similar to cinnamon rolls. Put them snail side up and a few centimetres apart from each other on the oiled trays and loosely cover with tea towels. (Be careful with the choice of towels, as they can get stuck to the tops if the dough is quite moist.) Leave to prove for 30 minutes.*

• Meanwhile, for the stew, pour the hot stock or water over the dried mushrooms in a bowl and soak them for at least 30 minutes.

Continued →

Continued...

For the stew

·· 500ml hot vegetable stock,
   or hot water

·· 50g dried mushrooms

·· 4 tbsp vegetable oil

·· knob of unsalted butter

·· 2 onions, thickly sliced

·· 400g chestnut mushrooms

·· 500g potatoes, scrubbed but
   unpeeled, cut in wedges

·· 2 large garlic cloves,
   roughly chopped

·· black or white pepper

- Fish the mushrooms out of their soaking liquid and put them into another bowl. Then strain the liquid over the bowl with the mushrooms through muslin, to make sure no grit passes through.

- Heat 1 tbsp of the oil and the knob of butter in a large pan for which you have a tight-fitting lid. Add the onions and a generous pinch of salt and cook over a medium-low heat for about 15 minutes. If the onions start catching a little, just add a splash of the mushroom liquid to deglaze the base of the pan. Cook the onions for as long as you have the patience or time for: another 15 minutes on a low-ish flame is great, but if the onions look softened and have taken a little bit of colour, it will be good enough.

- Take the onions out and put them into a bowl. Quarter or halve the chestnut mushrooms, depending on size. Add another 1 tbsp of oil to the pan along with the mushrooms and a pinch of salt. Fry over a medium-high heat until they are brown all over, then add them to the onions.

- Heat another 1 tbsp of oil in the pan and put in the potatoes. Cook them on each side until lightly browned. Now return the mushrooms and onions to the pan, add the garlic and cook for a minute or so. Pour in the mushroom stock, the rehydrated mushrooms, another pinch of salt and a healthy grinding of black or white pepper and give it a gentle stir. Cook for about 10 minutes over a medium heat.

- Now, be ready! Have your stew bubbling away over a medium-high heat. If your dumplings feel quite soft and a little sticky, use an oiled spatula or dough scraper to scoop them off the tray. Otherwise, pick them up with your hand. Add the dumplings pretty/curled side up on top; they will puff up, so leave at least 1cm between each. Cover with a lid immediately after putting the last dumpling in. Cook over a medium-high heat for 20 minutes. The dumplings will puff up and be soaked with delicious stew juices at the bottom and fluffy on top.

- I cannot describe the satisfaction this dish brings. Serve it with a bright winter slaw or some pickles on the side. It is also good with a glass of kefir. It is best eaten on the same day, but we do love to scoff it cold the next day if some is miraculously left over. It is also light enough to be eaten on a rainy summer's day.

- **TIP** • **The dough for these dumplings is so versatile. You can shape it into regular round buns, steam them in a steamer and then fill with pulled pork or anything else you like in a bao bun. Or you can bake them and use as burger buns, or just as white rolls. The stew, equally, can be made without the dumplings, just serve it with crusty bread to dip into the savoury juices.**

Rose Dumplings with Sweet Potato, Onion and Barberries

This is inspired by Central Asian dumplings called *gul khanum*. Traditionally, finely sliced raw pumpkin and onion would be used, seasoned and spiced. I find that sweet potatoes are good all year round and are similar to pumpkin, they also cook in no time at all. Frying the onion adds a deeper sweetness, while barberries give a welcome sour tang. If you don't want to use dried fruit, finely crumbled feta will add acidity; just mix it into the cooled filling. You can serve just one of these as a starter, or two or three as a main dish. They freeze beautifully from raw, so it is worth making more than you need. I just pop them on a tray lightly dusted with flour and put them into the freezer. If your freezer is full (mine always is) take some non-meat stuff out and put it in the sink; it won't defrost in the 20 minutes you need for the dumplings to firm up. When the dumplings feel firm and as though they won't crumple in a bag, pluck them off the tray, pop them in a bag and put them and the stuff in the sink back into the freezer. You can steam them from frozen, they will only take an extra 5 minutes.

- 200g sweet potato
- 1 tbsp flavourless oil, plus more for the steamer
- 150g onions or banana shallots, finely chopped
- 2 tbsp dried barberries or dried sour cherries, chopped into smaller pieces
- 1 tsp ground cumin, or to taste
- 1 tsp ground coriander, or to taste
- 1 quantity Dumpling Dough (see page 270)
- plain flour, to dust
- 50g unsalted butter, cut into very small pieces
- sea salt and black pepper

Continued →

- Preheat the oven to 200°C fan.

- You can keep the sweet potato skins on if you care about the nutrients, it will not be unpleasant! Otherwise, peel the sweet potato and cut it into small pieces. I do this by slicing a little 'cheek' off one of the sides so I can rest it on that side and it will be stable and won't roll around on the work surface. Then I slice the potato lengthways into 5mm slices. Cut each slice into 5mm strips, then across into 5mm dice.

- Heat the 1 tbsp oil in a small-ish frying pan, then add the onions and season well with salt. When they become translucent, add the barberries and the spices. I put some wet baking parchment on top of the onions to help them steam and catch a bit of colour at the same time; just remember to stir them every so often. If you see any of them becoming too dark and catching at the bottom, add a small splash of water and scrape at the bottom of the pan with a spatula, the water will also help the barberries to plump up.

- The onions should become golden and soft and the barberries will swell up nicely. We are not necessarily caramelising them here, just frying them, so if your onions were chopped quite small, after about 5 minutes of cooking over a medium-low heat they will be nicely golden.

- If you chopped the sweet potato very small, you don't need to pre-cook it. But if you feel as though your chunks are not tiny-tiny, you can roast or fry them in oil just to help them along.

- Mix the onions with the raw or par-cooked sweet potato – depending on how good your chopping skills were today – and let cool completely. Taste and add more salt, if needed, and plenty of black pepper.

Continued →

Continued...

To serve

·· 50g melted butter, or brown butter (see page 230), or chilli oil

·· 100ml yogurt, mixed with either 1 grated garlic clove and sea salt, or 1 tbsp harissa, or to taste

·· sumac

·· Crispy Pickled Shallots (see page 287), or toasted sesame seeds

• QR CODE • *Halve the dough, roll each piece into a sausage shape, then cut it into 30–35g pieces, keeping those you are not working with covered, so they don't dry out.*

• *Flour a work surface lightly. Shape each piece of dough into a rough, flat 7 x 5cm puck. Flour your surface and roll this puck into a 30 x 10cm strip. The thinner the strip, the more delicate the dumpling. Especially the edges benefit from being very thin, so you can always go over them with a rolling pin. Put 2 tbsp of the filling evenly along the length of each strip and dot 6 small pieces (2g each) of butter all along. Then flip one of the longer edges over the filling and gently tap along the length of the dough, over the filling, to flatten it out a little. Roll from the short end closest to you upwards into a rose shape. Pinch the end to the base of the 'flower' to seal. You can open up the 'petals' a little if they look tight.*

• Make sure you oil the steamer, or use special perforated paper, so the dumplings don't stick to the steamer. Steam the dumplings, petal sides up, for 45 minutes. If you feel like your dough wasn't rolled out very thinly, steam them for up to 1 hour, or even longer. I would rather you steam them a bit longer rather than understeam. You can always take a dumpling out and cut it in half: if it doesn't have any white-looking dry floury bits in the centre, they are ready. Immediately drizzle with plenty of melted or brown butter or chilli oil.

• Mix the yogurt with the garlic and salt, or harissa (start with 1 tsp and taste until it is hot enough for you), spoon it on to a platter, smooth it out and sprinkle with sumac. Put the dumplings on top, drizzle with more butter or oil and sprinkle over the crispy shallots or toasted sesame seeds.

....

• **TIP** • **If you, miraculously, have cooked rose dumplings leftover, stick them in the fridge in a container. Then, when ready, put them on a tray, brush or drizzle with oil and bake in an oven preheated to 200°C fan for 10 minutes or until crispy all over. You can also fry these in a pan, but it's hard to fry the sides, so I often roast them in this way.**

....

'I am sitting at the big
wooden table with my
mother, grandmother
and great-grandmother.
A winter evening is
setting in'

Alissa Timoshkina, Writer and Chef

Pirozhki Sessions

....

'The most grounding memory involving food for me is interwoven with the women in my family. As I close my eyes, I can see myself so clearly as a little girl in Omsk, Russia. I am sitting at the big wooden table with my mother, grandmother and great-grandmother. A winter evening is setting in as we snuggle up to large cups of sweet black tea and a big platter of freshly fried *pirozhki* buns is placed in the middle of the table.

The air is still heavy with all the scents and smoke from frying the flavoursome meat encased in the pillowy dough, as I try to bite into one of the hot buns without burning my fingers and my tongue. My favourite part of the *pirozhok* is the contrast between the crispy, nearly burned surface of the dough and its steamed soggy, fatty and salty meat filling within. Washing it down with overly sweet tea was the cherry on the top of the cake for me. And speaking of "cakes", the sweet version of the meal would follow in the form of fried dough cakes – *pyshki* – that we would generously smother in condensed milk.

I always think so fondly of those *pirozhki* sessions and a warm sense of cosiness washes over me.'

Zhenia's *Zrazy*

This is my mum's sister's recipe. It is worth making twice as much mashed potato whenever you feel like eating it and keeping the leftovers to make this the next day; this way, it honestly isn't that much of a faff. Having said that, I often make mashed potato specifically to use for this dish, as my son Sash and I love it so much (if you're doing that, you'll need 600g raw potatoes, 20g butter and 40ml whole milk). We like this simple, nursery-food version, but you could always mix some favourite spices into the meat mixture. I don't always bother with the mushroom sauce, I mainly make that to jazz up the veggie version for Joe. For him, I just fry the potato patties without filling them, and serve alongside the mushroom sauce.

For the patties

·· 100g minced beef

·· 100g minced pork

·· 4 eggs, lightly beaten

·· 50g onion (1 small onion), finely chopped or grated

·· 500g cold mashed potato

·· 100g fine semolina

·· 1 tbsp flavourless oil

·· 2 tbsp unsalted butter

·· sea salt

For the sauce (optional)

·· 25g dried wild mushrooms (I used trompettes de mort, but any are fine)

·· 1 tbsp flavourless oil, or as needed

·· 20g unsalted butter

·· 1 onion, finely sliced

·· 200g button mushrooms, finely sliced

·· 1 garlic clove, sliced

·· 100g crème fraîche

- If you're planning on making the sauce, cover the dried mushrooms in 100ml boiling water and leave to soak for 15–30 minutes.

- For the filling, mix the minced meats, half the eggs, the onion and 1 tsp salt together really well with your hand. The filling must be seasoned with salt properly, you can always fry a little bit off to make sure it's super-nice.

- Take roughly 80g of mashed potato, put a 40g spoon of the meat over it, then mould the potato around the meat to encase it. It will look like a ball, but you will squash it into more of a patty in the pan in a bit.

- Put the remaining eggs into a bowl and the semolina on a flat plate. First dip the patties into the eggs, then into the semolina to cover. This step will help keep the potato together.

- Heat the oil and butter in a large frying pan until sizzling. The patties might be quite soft, so use a spatula to lower them into the hot oil and butter, taking care not to splash yourself. Do not overcrowd the pan, otherwise they will steam instead of fry. If your cakes are stuffed with meat, fry them for 2 minutes on each side. You may need to be gentle when turning them; if a bit of the potato ruffles, just pat it back with a spatula. Cover the pan with a lid and cook over a low heat for another 5 minutes on each side to make sure the meat inside is cooked. If they are not filled, simply fry for 2 minutes on each side or until light golden and warmed all the way through.

- Now for the sauce, and again, I hasten to say that I only make it when Joe is around, otherwise the stuffed cakes are good as they are. Strain the wild mushrooms over a bowl, saving their soaking liquid.

- Heat the oil and butter in a pan, add the onion and cook over a medium heat for about 10 minutes, stirring from time to time, adding little splashes of the mushroom soaking liquid to deglaze if things are looking a bit dry and sticky. Then add the mushrooms and wild mushrooms (and a little more oil if the pan is dry) and cook, again stirring occasionally until they brown here and there and soften, about 7 minutes. Add the garlic, reduce the heat and cook for 1 minute, then swirl in the crème fraîche. Serve with the potato cakes, especially any that are unfilled.

Lazanky with Tomato Sauce

Lazanky is kind of what it sounds like: lasagne! The dish was brought into Poland by the Italian royals, though to me this pasta shape is closer to *maltagliati* ('badly cut'). In Ukraine and Poland they are often served with cooked kraut and mushrooms, but at home we love the simplicity of a tomato sauce. Adding full-fat crème fraîche to a tomato sauce is a very Eastern European thing and it makes for a simultaneously decadent and simple sauce.

As my friend Anna said, it is 'different and original' (music to my ears). You can use some grated Parmesan or pecorino here, but more often than not I sprinkle some breadcrumbs over. It is worth making pasta by hand if you want something a little special, but regular pasta works too, as the sauce is just so delicious. (Cook regular pasta for a couple of minutes shy of what it says on the packet, so it will finish cooking in the sauce.)

For the pasta dough

·· 2 medium eggs

·· 200g pasta flour ('00' flour), plus more to dust

·· Parmesan or pecorino cheese, finely grated, to serve

For the sauce

·· 30g unsalted butter

·· 1 tbsp olive oil

·· 3 fat garlic cloves, 2 finely sliced, 1 finely grated

·· 400g can of chopped tomatoes, or tomato passata

·· pinch of sugar (optional)

·· 1 heaped tbsp full-fat crème fraîche

·· sea salt and black pepper

- Put the eggs and 1 tbsp water into a large bowl and beat them into a homogeneous mass. Now just tip the flour in, first mixing it into the eggs with a spoon, then going in with your hand, squashing and kneading it, trying to collect all the little dry bits into a rough ball of dough. Knead it over an unfloured surface – to bring it together more than anything – for a minute or so. It will look wrinkly and uneven, but should hold together. Cover it tightly and leave for 10 minutes, after which it will be so much easier to knead. Once it relaxes, knead again – it will be smoother – and leave for another 15–30 minutes while you make the sauce. The longer you leave it, the easier it is to work with.

- Heat the butter and oil in a medium frying pan, add the sliced garlic and cook it over a very low heat for a minute or so. The garlic should soften and mellow but not colour (watch it like a hawk). Now add the grated garlic, pick up the pan and swirl it quickly off the heat, then put it down and immediately add the tomatoes and a pinch of salt. My mum would also add a pinch of sugar, but I don't. (Do if your tomatoes are quite acidic.) Cook for 15 minutes over a low heat. Scrape at the base of the pan with a spatula, so the garlic does not stick. At the end, whisk in the crème fraîche and cook for another few minutes. Taste and season.

- QR CODE • *Take half the rested dough and mould it into a flattish disc with your hands. Roll it out over a well-floured surface into a rough circle, 45cm in diameter if you can, but no need to go overboard and make it see-through or anything. Roll it up around your floured rolling pin. Slash lengthways with a knife, once, along the pin, without dragging the knife. The dough will drop to the surface in layers of dough strips. Cut them in half lengthways, and then on the diagonal at 6cm intervals. You will have lots of diamond-shaped pieces of pasta. Put them on a floured tray so they don't stick together. Repeat with the other half of the dough.*

- Put a pot of salted water on to boil. Drop the pasta in and give it a good swirl with a spatula to make sure the pieces do not stick together. Cook the pasta for 2–3 minutes if using fresh, or cook according to the packet instructions if using ready-made pasta, though stop a couple of minutes before it is as ready as you like it, because it's nice to finish cooking it in the sauce. Drain the pasta, or fish it out with a spider, and toss it through the sauce, cooking for a further minute over a low heat. Serve with loads of grated cheese.

Double Garlic Poached-Roast Chicken

A lot of authors will tell you the same, but this is one of the best chickens you will ever try. (If you want a slightly less involved roast chicken, see page 28.) But if you want a different roast chicken experience, stay with me here. This chicken recipe is based on one made by the Galghai people of Ingushetia (the mountain dwellers of Northern Caucasus, now part of Russia). I love this recipe (which I adapted from one I found in the *Gastronom* cookbook), because you get so much out of one chicken. It is lip-smackingly garlicky, but not as much as you'd expect. Keep in mind that you don't need the seasonal addition of wild garlic. Do add it if you can find it easily, otherwise either leave it out entirely or up the amount of dark greens. Apart from chard, spring greens or even kale work well. Please, do read the whole recipe first. Trust me, it may sound wordy, but I just wanted you to be guided through this process properly. You will do it once and next time you won't even need to look at the recipe. The method may go against everything you know about roasting a chicken – especially when it comes to poaching directly in hot water before roasting – but trust me, you will have the most succulent, seasoned throughout and delicious bird. In terms of skin, it may not be the crispiest you will ever encounter, but it will be brown and delicious all the same. All you need to serve with this are simple boiled new potatoes.

· 1 medium free-range chicken (mine for these timings was 1.8kg)

· 1 small onion, peeled

· 1 wet garlic bulb, or regular garlic bulb

· cayenne pepper, or other chilli powder you like

· 20g unsalted butter, or ghee

· 400g new potatoes (optional)

· 200g chard (or 400g, for beautiful leftovers)

· 100g wild garlic, or sorrel, or both (optional)

· sea salt

• For the first step, if you remember, do take the chicken out of the fridge in advance, to come to room temperature. Put a big enough pot to hold a chicken (I use a 26cm cast-iron pot) on the stove. Now boil lots of water in a kettle to speed things along and measure out 2.5 litres into this pot. Add 2 tbsp salt. If your chicken is trussed, leave it trussed, just make sure to take out the plastic pouch of giblets (see page 134 for what to do with those).

• Put the chicken, breast side down, into the hot water gently, so you don't get splashed. Add the whole onion. If the back of your chicken is bobbing up and exposed, add a little more boiling water. This situation happens to me quite often, as my pot is probably just not quite big enough. To try to rectify it, I cover the pot with a lid and set it over the lowest heat possible. Bring it to a simmer and put a timer on for 40 minutes. Shift the lid ever so slightly to let some of the steam escape and poach the chicken until the timer goes off. The water should be just barely bubbling.

• While this is happening, chop the garlic cloves roughly and put them with a generous pinch of sea salt and cayenne into a mortar and pestle. Bash it about into a paste, then add the butter or ghee and bash some more. It should look paste-ish; some garlic may still be squashed rather than properly pulverised, but don't worry. It's OK like this.

• Preheat the oven to 200°C fan.

• If you are bothering with small potatoes, put them into a pot of cold, well-seasoned water, bring to the boil and cook for 20 minutes or until they can be easily pierced with a knife. Drain and keep in their pan, covered with a lid, until later.

• When the chicken has had its 40-minute hot bath, have a deep-ish roasting tray with a rack in it at the ready.

Continued →

Continued...

- What I do, when lifting the chicken out, is use tongs. If it's trussed, I grab on to the feet, if it isn't I hook the tongs inside the cavity (from the neck end), then tilt the chicken away from me, so as many juices as possible run out and back into the stock. Those might look bloody, but don't worry, just cook the stock for 15 minutes and make sure to skim off the scum once it rises. Compost the onion.

- So even if the juices were a little pink, it's cool. Just put the chicken on the wire rack in the roasting tray, breast side up. Rub it with the garlic butter all over the breast and legs and stuff the rest inside the cavity. Put 2 large ladlefuls of the stock into the tray underneath. (Don't tip the remaining stock away! It's nectar.)

- Put it into the oven and roast for 20–25 minutes. But again, please remember ovens and chicken sizes vary. This is how to check if your chicken is done. Take the tray with the chicken out, hook the chicken with the tongs again and tilt to release the juices from its cavity: those should run clear. Also when you pull at one of the legs where the thigh bone meets the breast, the meat should look… well… cooked! Not pink. And the leg can be easily pulled off. If it's not quite there yet, give it another 5–7 minutes in the oven. Then test again.

- A note: leave that tray with chicken juices be! Do not put it in the wash or anything, those juices are pure gold, you need them.

- Leave the chicken to rest somewhere. A platter with a bit of a lip is good, as the juices can't run off like they do from a chopping board.

- Now quickly chop the chard and wild garlic and/or sorrel (if using); the stalks quite finely, the leaves roughly. Put the greens into the roasting tray and drag through all the garlicky chickeny juices. Put the tray back in the oven and cook for 5–10 minutes or until the greens wilt nicely. Don't be too worried about overcooking, they will be fine even for 15 minutes. If you did boil some new potatoes, they can be stirred through the chickeny warm wild garlic and chard tray as well. Now scrape the greens and all the juices, and potatoes if using, into a platter. Pop the chicken on top. This is a meal in itself. The leftovers, if there are any, are good chopped up and put into a small pie dish. Cover with a little shop-bought puff pastry, glaze with egg and bake for 30 minutes.

- TIP • This recipe is Leftover Central, so if you live alone or with one more person and make this, it's an investment for weekday lunches. You can use leftover shredded chicken and greens in Fried Tomato Rice Cake (see page 153). Or reheat leftover greens and chicken in the stock and add a grain (or some noodles) and grated ginger for an instant broth. You can also freeze the stock the chicken was cooked in to make any soup or broth in this book.

Anna Ansari, Food Writer (and Lawyer)

Dr Frugh's *Koobideh*

'The 1980s were a hard time to be Iranian in America. I remember my father dancing around in his underwear the day Ayatollah Khomeini died, and I remember not being invited to sleepovers because other kids' parents in our Detroit suburb didn't like where my father came from. I didn't understand prejudice and fear then as I do now, but I did understand that my family was different.

Our Thanksgiving dinners had turkey, sure, but also saffron-laced basmati rice and crispy potato *gazmakh* (in addition to – not instead of – mashed potatoes). Our Fourth of July barbecues included hamburgers, hotdogs and potato chips, as well as juicy, lamby Iranian kebabs and salad *olivieh*. My father's best friend from medical school in Tehran, Dr Frugh, was always in charge of the *koobideh*, a seemingly simple kebab of ground lamb, onions and spices.

Thirty-plus years have passed, and I can still taste Dr Frugh's *koobideh*. I can still see it, oozing with fat and yellowish turmeric juices, as he cavalierly sprinkled sumac on top, and I can still taste it: the best *koobideh* I have ever had and will ever have. Every time I eat *koobideh*, I want it to be as good as Dr Frugh's and it never is. It never will be. It never can be. All *koobideh* has lamb, onion, turmeric, but Dr Frugh's *koobideh* was more than that.

And every time I have the dish now, I think of a lazy summer's day in metro Detroit. I think of childhood, of running around barefoot, catching lightning bugs in Mason jars, hands sticky with watermelon juice, hair stiff from our undoubtedly over-chlorinated swimming pool. I chase that feeling, that flavour, that memory with every bite of *koobideh*, each of which is nowhere near as good as Dr Frugh's, but also tastes just enough like it to keep me coming back for more.'

Almost Dr Frugh's *Koobideh* Kebab

As soon as I read Anna's memories of Dr Frugh and his kebab (see previous page), so many signals went 'ping' in my head. The kebabs I tried travelling in Azerbaijan, the kebabs we ate in The Syrian Club restaurant in Limassol, Cyprus. Every experience magical, because the kebab was so *so* juicy. I emailed Anna and asked if she was up for developing an approximation of Dr Frugh's magical recipe, she enthusiastically agreed and here we are!

We worked on the method together, then we asked Joe, who is a skilled fire cook, to stand in for the late Dr Frugh. We hope you have an uncle or aunt, family friend, father or mother who loves to cook over fire, who will make this and create super-special memories for you or your kids. I cannot emphasise enough that you need a lot of fat to make a super-juicy kebab, so make sure to get the fattiest minced lamb you can find.

·· 150g onions, peeled

·· 500g fatty minced lamb

·· 2 tsp ground turmeric

·· ½ tsp bicarbonate of soda

·· sea salt and black pepper

....

To serve

·· Iranian (or other) flatbreads (for homemade flatbreads, see page 271)

·· sumac

- Grate the onions on the coarse side of a grater, making sure to catch the juices. Now mix the minced lamb, onions, turmeric, bicarbonate of soda (it helps the meat to bind together), 1½ tsp salt and 1 tsp pepper in a large bowl… and I mean *really* mix it. Get your hand in there and massage and push it with your fist, you want proteins to develop and hold it all together better. After 4 minutes of such manipulations, if you have time, put it, covered, in the fridge for at least 30 minutes or overnight. This again helps it all hold really well together.

- You know how I always bang on that you need to bring meat to room temperature before cooking it? Here it is not necessary because, by the time you handle it and squash it around the skewer, it will have warmed up anyway.

- Get 5 long metal skewers and have a bowl of warm water nearby to wet your hands during shaping; this helps the meat to not stick to your hands. Now, what I do is divide the meat into 5 (100g each max), and with wet hands shape each into an oblong burger with a smooth surface (no cracks: that's important). Then I mash the meat around the top bit of a skewer and move it down, so you have an even, long layer of meat along the skewer. You can keep wetting your hand and also rotate the skewer as you squash-distribute the meat. There should be no air pockets inside. Make sure both ends of the kebab are tightly attached to the skewer, so there are no gaps. If your mixture fails to cooperate and will not stick to the skewer, sack it off and fry the mix as oblong sausages without the skewers.

- Fire up your barbecue or oven grill, but obviously fire is where the magic is. Wait until the embers have calmed down; they should be still glowing red but there shouldn't be any actual fire. Put the skewers on the grill, about 20cm away from the embers, and now the trick is to keep turning the skewers. If you have one of those fancy grills, you are sorted, otherwise keep turning and making sure the kebabs get cooked evenly. They should be lightly golden all over and cooked through and juicy inside. You can always cut into one to check.

- Grab a flatbread, then grab a skewer (wearing heat-resistant gloves!) and point its sharp end into the chopping board, then use the flatbread to slide the kebab off. Put the kebabs on a pile of flatbreads so all the juices go into the bread and sprinkle liberally with sumac. Enjoy with A Small Herb and Sour Cherry Salad or Sweet Water Salad (see pages 74 and 71), or with whole grilled tomatoes.

Serves 2 as a main dish

Dark Greens and Noodles with Yogurt

Here, you can use any greens that will wilt! Chard, kale, spinach… but a combination of spinach, wild garlic and nettles (as you see in the photo) is exceptionally good. This recipe is inspired by an Azerbaijan minced meat *khingial* recipe, but as always, I try to create a vegetarian version so my husband can enjoy it with the rest of the family. You absolutely can buy ready-made fresh lasagne sheets and cut them into 6cm diamonds, or break up dried lasagne sheets, but if you are making this for a special occasion, do make the homemade pasta so it's extra-special. If you decide to make fresh pasta, please, don't be scared. It's easy, you do not need a pasta machine, in fact hand-rolled is preferable. If it's your very first time, give yourself a break and don't stress if it comes out just a little thicker than you are used to.

·· 100ml water

·· 1 large egg

·· 250g pasta flour ('00' flour), or plain flour, plus more to dust

·· 600g onions (you won't use them all, but they are so good)

·· 60g Clarified Butter (see page 289), or regular butter

·· splash of vegetable oil

·· 300g any dark green leaves or

·· 100g each nettles, wild garlic and spinach

·· sea salt and black pepper

To serve

·· 150ml yogurt

·· 1 garlic clove, crushed

·· sumac

·· fine crispy breadcrumbs (see page 109)

• Pour the measured water into a large bowl and add the egg. Whisk it in well. Then add the flour, mixing it with your hand thoroughly into a soft dough. Sprinkle a work surface with more flour and knead the dough until it stops sticking to your hands and is smooth. Leave it to rest, covered, for at least 30 minutes, or up to 24 hours in the fridge overnight.

• You won't need all the onions in this recipe, only half. But there is no point doing this in smaller quantities, also the onions are so good you can use them in a myriad of other dishes (such as Rose Dumplings, see page 195).

• So, cut the onions in half and slice finely along the grain. Melt 30g clarified butter, or use a knob of regular butter and a splash of oil. Add the onions and a generous pinch of salt. Cover with a lid if you have one, or with a cartouche (a round piece of baking parchment), and let them sweat over a medium-low heat for 20 minutes. They will become soft and translucent. Now uncover, increase the heat to medium and cook for another 10 minutes, stirring from time to time. If they become dry and start catching, add splashes of water and deglaze. See what they are like after the 10 minutes, chances are you will need another 5–10 minutes of cooking. You want them to be deeply amber and caramelised.

• QR CODE • *Take half the rested dough and mould it into a flattish disc with your hands. Roll it out over a well-floured surface into a rough circle, 45cm in diameter if you can, but no need to go overboard and make it see-through or anything. Roll it up around your floured rolling pin. Slash lengthways with a knife, once, along the pin, without dragging the knife. The dough will drop to the surface in layers of dough strips. Cut them in half lengthways, and then on the diagonal at 6cm intervals. You will have lots of diamond-shaped pieces of pasta. Put them on a floured tray so they don't stick together. Repeat with the other half of the dough.*

• If they are not to be used immediately, you can freeze them to be used another time. If you freeze them, again make sure they are well-floured so they don't merge and form a giant pasta monster.

• If you are using nettles, have a bowl with cold water and ice at the ready. Pop them into a saucepan and cover with boiling water, boil for 3 minutes, then take out with tongs or a spider and plunge into the iced water. Now that the nettles are disarmed, cut off any of the thick stalks and chop across the leaves.

- Now add the nettles and sliced wild garlic and spinach to a pan and cook over a medium-low heat in the remaining clarified butter for 5–10 minutes.

- If using other greens, there's no need to blanch them, just put them into a pan sliced and raw with the remaining clarified butter. Season well with salt and pepper and cook until they look soft and wilted (kale will take longer than spinach). Mix together the yogurt and garlic in a bowl.

- Cook the pasta in well-salted water for 2–3 minutes. Then drain, but not too vigorously, you want a little bit of the pasta water. Put them into the pan with the cooked greens, add half of the caramelised onions (save the rest for later) and mix them through thoroughly as well. Put everything on a platter, dot garlicky yogurt around and sprinkle over sumac and crispy breadcrumbs.

Bread for Eating

This is a recipe for *shokupan* or 'milk bread' as it's called in the West. The Japanese name 食パン literally means 'bread for eating'. It was given to me by my California-based friend Adrian Chang (see page 177). Adrian says: 'I am not sure where the "milk bread" bit comes in as there's so much more in it than milk.' Adrian uses a poolish starter called tangzhong, from which the bread gets its fluffy, mochi-like texture. He explained: 'Heating the starter gelatinises the starches in the flour, allowing it to absorb more moisture, thereby making the bread more mochi-like. That's the idea anyway. This recipe is adapted from a recipe by our friend's mother, Ikegami-san, in Chiba, Japan, whose favourite way to eat this bread is with strawberries and whipped cream.' And that makes total sense to me.

For the tangzhong

·· 2 tbsp strong white bread flour

·· 3 tbsp water

·· 3 tbsp milk

For the bread

·· 1 tbsp fast action dried yeast

·· 35g sugar, plus 1 tsp

·· 50ml warm water

·· 125ml whole milk, plus more to brush

·· 450g strong white bread flour, plus more to dust

·· 3 tbsp powdered milk (optional)

·· 1 medium egg, lightly beaten, plus 1 egg yolk, to brush

·· 50g unsalted butter, softened

·· a little flavourless oil

·· sea salt

- QR CODE • *For the tangzhong, mix everything together and then heat over a medium-low heat in a small pan, whisking constantly, until it thickens into a paste and starts to leave a slight film at the bottom of the pan as you are whisking. Scoop out into a mixing bowl and allow to cool to room temperature.*

- *Mix the yeast and the 1 tsp sugar with the measured warm water and set aside for 10 minutes; you should see tiny bubbles forming to show your yeast is activated.*

- *Now mix the activated yeast water with the tangzhong and milk, 1 tsp salt and the 35g sugar. I whisk it very well to dissolve the tangzhong.*

- *In another bowl, mix the flour and powdered milk, if using, and make a well in the centre. Pour the liquid mixture in and knead until smooth and elastic, then let it rest for 10 minutes. Wet your hands if you are making the loaf by hand (though I often put it all into a food mixer fitted with the dough hook attachment). Now gradually mix in the whole egg and softened butter, bit by bit, and let it rest for a further 10 minutes. Give it a stretch and fold (see page 274), then a quick knead on a floured surface until it stops sticking to your hands. Roll into a rough log.*

- *Cut the dough into 3, quickly knead each piece, then roll each out into a rectangle. Fold into thirds by overlapping the short ends into the centre. Roll out into a rectangle again, perpendicular to the direction you last folded the dough, then into a little Swiss roll shape. Pinch the seams closed. Repeat to roll all 3 pieces of dough.*

- *Lightly oil a 23 x 13cm loaf tin, line with baking parchment and tuck the 3 rolls in, seam sides down. Cover with a tea towel and allow to rise somewhere warm for about 1 hour.*

- Preheat the oven to 180°C fan.

- Brush the surface of the loaf with milk and egg yolk lightly beaten together. Bake in the oven for about 30 minutes until it is golden brown and has a hard crust. The internal temperature should be about 90°C.

- Allow the loaf to cool on a wire rack before slicing and eating.

Bisque-Style Red Mullet Pasta

Versions of bouillabaisse were among the most impressive dishes that I tried during my year training at Leiths School of Food and Wine. I couldn't remember who exactly made it, and in the end, after some digging, I discovered it may have been a product of memory aberration (when your brain rewrites and deconstructs memories). I know that I loved two demos by my biggest food heroes: Henry Harris – who cooked at Racine restaurant in London at the time – and Theo Randall, possibly the nicest man on Earth. One of them cooked a bouillabaisse, the other a pasta dish, both using red mullet, and it all jumbled in my head and this is the result. I loved that a fish carcass was the most prized part of the recipe. Ask your fishmonger to fillet the red mullet for you, but ask them to give you the bones too. They are almost more important than the fish here. You can even sack off buying the fish and, if friendly with the fishmonger, ask them to keep some red mullet (or other fish) bones for you. If you manage this kind of hustle, you will have the most luxurious-tasting but also most economical sauce.

- 3 medium red mullet, gurnard, or other fish, on the bone (or see recipe introduction)
- pinch of saffron threads
- 1 onion
- ¼ garlic bulb
- 1 large fennel bulb
- 1 leek
- 4 tbsp olive oil, plus more for the fish fillets, if using
- 3 bushy thyme sprigs
- 1 bay leaf
- 50ml Pernod, or white wine, or 1 tbsp white wine vinegar and 2 tbsp water
- 2 x 400g cans of plum tomatoes
- 600g linguine, or other pasta
- sea salt

- If you are filleting and cleaning the fish yourself, make sure that the carcasses are clean, the gills are taken out and all the bitter blood is washed off, especially from the head. Or ask your fishmonger to do all that for you.

- Pour 50ml hot water over the saffron to infuse. Leave it while you do the rest.

- Coarsely chop the onion, garlic, fennel and leek. Take a large pan and heat up the olive oil. Add the vegetables, season well with salt and fry, turning occasionally, for 5–7 minutes or until lightly coloured here and there, then reduce the heat. Check if anything got stuck to the base of the pan and, if so, add a small splash of water and scrape at the pan to deglaze.

- Cover and cook gently for 10–15 minutes or until the vegetables are soft. Check occasionally and stir to make sure the veg aren't catching. Add the thyme sprigs and bay and cook for a further 5 minutes over a medium heat, stirring often. Add the Pernod, or wine, or vinegar and water, give the bottom of the pan another scrape and cook for another minute. Finally add the heads, tails and fish bones and the tomatoes and cook it all over a medium heat for about 20 minutes. You want to occasionally stir it so it doesn't catch on the bottom, but you need to move everything round very gently so you don't break up the fish skeletons and tails. You're looking for it all to be reduced down to, in Harris's vivid words 'a gunk-like compote'!

- Now, fish out the big bones, heads and tails, thyme sprigs and bay leaves and compost them. Make sure there are no bones in the mixture and put the gunk into a food processor (do not wipe out the pan).

- Blitz the sauce in a food processor until homogeneous. If you have a fancy processor you may get a super-smooth sauce, in which case ignore the next step. If the sauce is quite lumpy still, using a spatula, pass it through a fine sieve over the pan where you cooked everything. You need to extract as much smooth sauce as possible and the remaining pulp can be composted. I won't lie, this is the laborious part, and you may be cursing me as you do it (every time I do it

I consider buying a cheffy blitzer) but it will be so very delicious, smooth and elegant, you will forgive me at the first mouthful. Even if it looks like a lot of the pulp remains in the sieve, you should have plenty of sauce in the pan.

- Now add the saffron water and put back over a gentle heat to keep warm and reduce a little more while you cook the pasta. Taste the sauce for seasoning and adjust.

- Cook the pasta according to the packet instructions. Then drain it briskly, or lift it out of the pan and into the sauce with tongs, so a little pasta water clings to the pasta, and stir it through the hot bouillabaisse sauce, agitating it quite a bit.

- If using fish fillets as well, oil them lightly and season them well. Heat your largest frying pan. Put the oiled fish in carefully, away from yourself, skin side down. Fry over a medium heat first for 2 minutes, then turn and fry for another minute or until cooked through. Serve the fish on top of the sauced pasta. If your fish broke down while frying, please, as always, do not stress, just style it out like you meant to do it and stir the broken fish through the sauce. It may arguably be even better this way.

Lime Tree Honey in the Air

Sweetness

Lime Tree Honey in the Air

It was high summer. Lime trees, or linden as they're sometimes called, were strewn densely across the grid of Forest Gate. The streets were thick with their honeyed fragrance. It was my second year in this corner of East London, but during the previous July I had been completely oblivious to it. How did I manage to miss this ambrosial mist? It was becoming clear: 2020 was the year when you noticed things more.

We make tea with dried lime tree blossom in Ukraine. Mum used to pick up a wispy cellophane bag at the market or local pharmacy, inside which cockatiel bracts and flowers fluttered. All the while, a bounty of boughs whorled right above our heads for free, but we never foraged them. A missed opportunity.

Apparently Victorians loved lime trees, planting them as decorative avenues to grand country houses, which is probably why there are so many in the streets of London. And tea was not the only thing on the menu. British social historian Dorothy Hartley, in her 1954 book *Food in England*, gives a pretty irresistible recipe for lime leaf sandwiches:

'While the shell-pink scale leaves still cling to the opened leaf buds, the new soft leaves of the lime tree make a most delicate sandwich filling. Gather scissors, cutting off the stalks; rinse under running water. The leaves are too soft and lack the essential crispness for salad, but the flavour is delicious as sandwich spread. (1) White bread and butter, spread with lime leaves sprinkled with lemon juice. (2) Brown bread and butter, cream cheese, and lime leaves. (3) White bread and butter, lime leaves shredded up and sprinkled with pepper and salt, and a moistening of cream.' Who knew!?

Drawn equally by this description and the saccharine scent of lime trees, I went curb-side picking. Earlier that day, I had happened to inspect the leaf curls of my baby peach tree, tacky with aphids. So when I touched the lime tree leaves and blossom and felt they, too, were sticky, I balked. And then (imagine it in slow-mo and me poker-faced) I licked my hand. There was a possibility that I was about to taste aphid juice, but the impulse was beyond me. And then – Eureka! – my hand was sweet. It wasn't aphid juice at all, it was lime blossom nectar. I looked around and touched a nearby car bonnet and – guess what? – it too was awash with honey.

The Ukrainian word for lime tree, *lypa*, finally made sense. *Lypa* comes from *lypnuty*: 'to stick'. I love when this mixture of serendipity and synchronicity happens, both that Victorian Britons and Ukrainians together shared a love for lime trees – both an aesthetic and a culinary attachment, at that – and the satisfaction of discovering that a familiar word has shapeshifted semantically.

I took a basket full of lime bracts and blossom and rustled their frothy heads across our garden table to dry for making tisane. Before they crisped up and stiffened in the sun, I swept some into the hem of my apron and brought them into the kitchen. I drowned them in the glow of a sugar syrup. Strawberries that were on the turn were swirled in, too. There, they bled and softened, their life extended from hours to days.

It makes me happy to know that in a few months (it's almost summer now, as I write), there will be sweet air to get drunk on. Our daily walks will have more purpose and there will be gold-filled sandwiches, as well as tea taken with strawberries that taste of flowers and honey.

Baked Apples
with Ricotta and Raisins

I have a very specific memory connected to this recipe, when I must have been five years old (1989!). It is still the Soviet Union, but something exciting is happening on TV at 6pm. It was the first foreign-language series shown in the USSR, the Brazilian drama called *Escrava Esaura* (aka 'Isaura: Slave Girl'. Read the Wiki page on it, it's *fascinating*). The series, made in Brazil in the 1970s, earned cult status in the USSR. A Portuguese word, *fazenda* ('ranch') entered the Russian lexicon to describe our tiny Soviet allotments (our sense of humour ever-present). I can still hum the theme tune in my head.

We watched it with my granny Vera, religiously, waiting for each episode with excitement. We had a particular ritual: an hour before each episode began, Vera would mix some curd cheese with sugar, vanilla and raisins. She would hollow out some apples, stuff them with this mixture and bake them until the skins burst, the flesh was fluffy and the cheese caramelised on top. (I won't lie to you, I do miss the flavour of the artificial vanilla sugar Vera used.) I miss that ritual, I miss the excitement of early television, I miss her baked apples. I miss her.

·· 20–50g raisins

·· 250g ricotta cheese, or *tvorog*, or cottage cheese

·· 1 egg yolk

·· 30g Demerara sugar, plus more for the tops

·· 1 tsp vanilla extract, or vanilla seeds, or 1 sachet of vanilla sugar

·· 6 cooking apples (total weight about 1.2kg)

• Soak the raisins in a small bowl of hot water for a minimum of 15 minutes. Drain them really well, so they are not too watery. Mix the ricotta with the egg yolk, sugar, drained raisins and vanilla.

• Preheat the oven to 180°C fan.

• Take the cores out of the apples. Cut the tops off, like a lid. Then, using a regular soup spoon, stick it in about 5mm away from the hole made when you took out the core and move it around, scooping out some of the flesh. Then go in and dig a little deeper.

• Now you will need 50–60g of filling per apple. Fill the apples, put them in a baking dish and sprinkle some extra Demerara sugar on top.

• Bake the apples for 20 minutes first. Depending on the type of apple that you use it may take longer. They should be soft and can be slightly split, but not falling apart. Although to be honest, if Vera forgot about them, especially the new season's summer apples, and they did rise out of their skins like puffed soufflés, we were happy, because the fluffy flesh and curd cheese is what we were after, the skin eaten just at the end or given to grandma to finish (she never wasted anything ever). These are good warm, and very good indeed cold. Enjoy while watching your favourite series, and hug your grandmother if she is by your side.

• TIP • The curd cheese filling can be used in many ways. My grandma used to make simple thin pancakes, then roll the filling inside them, fry in butter until crispy and serve with plain sour cream on the side. You can also use it to fill yeasted dough (try the doughs for Big Baked Snail with Tangerines or Pumpkin and Orange Kolach, see pages 236 and 164), then bake, so you get the most delicious baked *pyrizhky* buns with a curd cheese filling.

Rye Bread and Apple *Sharlotka* with Spiced Custard

This is a very easy, quite old-fashioned-tasting recipe. I have dark rye bread at home often and it takes minimal effort to make it into this wonderful pudding, which is a brilliant way to use up lots of kinds of stale bread.

It is very good served with spiced custard, which makes it a brilliant Christmas dessert. It is also a nice recipe to assemble with a child, or even a toddler.

····

- 300g dark rye bread, or stale sourdough bread, blitzed into rough crumbs
- 50g unsalted butter, melted, plus more for the tin or dish
- 800g apples, cut into cubes
- 5 tbsp honey
- 3 tbsp Demerara sugar

For the custard

- 400ml whole milk
- 1 cinnamon stick
- a little nutmeg
- 2 egg yolks
- 50g caster sugar
- 20g cornflour

- Preheat the oven to 180°C fan. Toss the breadcrumbs in the melted butter, spread them over a baking tray and cook for 10 minutes, or until the crumbs are dry.

- Mix the apples and honey in a pan and stew over a medium-low heat without stirring, with the lid off, until the liquid evaporates and the apples soften.

- Take a round cake tin or a pie dish, brush it with butter and sprinkle with the Demerara sugar. Cover the base with a layer of breadcrumbs, then a layer of honeyed apples. Keep layering until it is all used up.

- Cover with baking parchment and press down with your hands to compact it. Cook for 15 minutes.

- Meanwhile – or earlier in the day, if you were more organised – for the custard, heat the milk with the cinnamon in a pan and grate in a little nutmeg. Let the milk cool down and infuse for as long as you have time. Fish out the cinnamon stick. Reheat the milk to almost boiling.

- Have a bowl and a fine sieve at the ready. Mix the egg yolks with the caster sugar and cornflour in a small bowl, whisk in a splash of the hot milk, then pour this into the pan of the spiced milk. Cook, stirring with a wooden spoon, until the custard is thick and clings to the spoon. As soon as it does that, pour it through the sieve into the bowl. Let it cool down a little, then spoon the pudding into little bowls and serve it with the custard.

227 • Lime Tree Honey in the Air

Strawberries Macerated in Lime Tree Syrup

Lime tree blossom is now my favourite thing to forage. You can use it to make tea (very good for those who suffer from insomnia). All you do is dry the blossom and leaves, then cover with hot water. Or you can make this syrup and use it either as a cordial or to macerate strawberries, as I do here. It is a very good way to preserve strawberries, which I feel deteriorate so quickly. This method keeps them fresh-tasting rather than jammy. Of course, lime tree blossom is not necessary, but it does add a beautiful floral note.

- ·· 300g caster sugar
- ·· 300ml water
- ·· large handful of freshly picked linden (lime) blossom
- ·· 400g strawberries (especially if on the turn), halved

- Put the sugar and measured water into a small saucepan and bring to a simmer, stirring often to help dissolve the sugar. Add the blossom and turn off the heat.

- When it is cooled down to just warm, or, even better, room temperature, pick or drain the blossom out (I didn't do this for the photo, but that was really just to show you how beautiful they are) and add the strawberries to the syrup. Leave the berries, submerged by the syrup, in the fridge until needed. They should last, if fully covered with syrup, for 3 days.

Hedvig's Brown Butter, Miso and Walnut Cake

At the beginning of 2020, I gave myself permission to have as much cake as I wanted to eat, and I have never regretted that decision. I will admit that my cake hedonism was easily sustained because of Hedvig Winsvold, who made the best cakes in her cosy Scandi-furnished café called Tromsø (just in case you are curious it's pronounced 'Troom-suh'). This is for all the salty-sweet lovers. Just be mindful of the potency of your miso: some are saltier than others, so try the recipe with less if you feel yours may be extra-flavourful and salty. I often use a reduced-salt version for this cake.

For the cake

·· 250g unsalted butter

·· 30g reduced-salt miso paste

·· 225g caster sugar

·· 3 eggs

·· 225g self-raising flour

·· 50ml full-fat yogurt

·· 40g broken walnuts

For the syrup

·· 50g white sugar

·· 50ml water

·· 20g reduced-salt miso paste

·· 40g walnuts, chopped

- QR CODE • *A couple of hours before you bake, put the butter in a small pan and heat until it bubbles gently. Use a whisk to scrape the base and sides of the pan, so the milk solids don't burn. From the moment all the butter melts it should take 3–4 minutes over a medium heat. Have a bowl ready, to tip the brown butter into when it is ready. It will start smelling like butterscotch, its colour changing from light gold to amber, and its bubbling sound will quieten. Pour it into the bowl.*

- Whisk the miso into the warm butter; you should have 225g of butter mix. Put it into a container and leave it to cool and firm up (stir it a couple of times while it sets, to re-emulsify). You want it to be soft, like room-temperature butter.

- Preheat the oven to 170°C fan. Line a 20cm square or round cake tin, or a 900g loaf tin, with baking parchment.

- Put the cooled brown butter-miso mix in a mixing bowl, or the bowl of a food mixer, together with the sugar. Beat for 5 minutes with electric beaters or the food mixer at a high speed. (If you're doing it by hand, beat it for a little longer.)

- Beat the eggs one at a time into the mixture, scraping down the bowl in between each. Add the self-raising flour and fold it in carefully by hand with a spatula. I know this bit will feel weird – to add yogurt at the end, after the flour – but don't worry. It works. So mix in the yogurt, again by hand. Spread the batter into the prepared tin, scatter the walnuts over, then push them into the batter slightly.

- Bake for 40–50 minutes, or until a skewer comes out clean. Leave to cool.

- While it is cooling, in a pan dissolve the sugar in the measured water. Take it off the heat, add the miso and whisk it all together. Add the chopped walnuts and put the pan back over the medium heat for a couple of minutes, stirring the whole time. Spread the syrup over the cake, let it cool slightly, then enjoy!

- TIP • **You can use the miso brown butter to spread on toast, or to toss your Christmas Brussels sprouts in, or to glaze roast carrots. Any slightly sweet roast vegetable will love being coated in it.**

Life-Giving Rhubarb Crumble Cake

I will never forget the first time I tried this cake. It was the day after giving birth to my son Sasha. I was alone with him in our flat, and my friend Caroline came over along with her seven-month-old son Reggie and this cake. The crumble on top was so unusual and delicious, I remember having two huge pieces and then just nibbling at big pieces of crumble for the rest of the day. I remember feeling that particular mixture of elation and extreme exhaustion. The cake – and my friend's love – definitely helped tip me over to the shores of euphoria, tiredness momentarily hushed. Caroline has been making this cake for the past 10 years, especially in times when our moods really really needed a boost. It turns out it was originally written by brilliant Debbie Major for the March 2011 issue of *delicious.* magazine… the year feels almost vintage now! I cannot recommend this cake enough. I guarantee, you too will never forget the first time you try it. It works particular magic when a friend needs a pick-me-up.

....

For the crumbs

· 50g unsalted butter

· 25g light muscovado sugar

· 40g caster sugar

· ¼ tsp vanilla bean paste

· 100g plain flour, sifted

· sea salt

....

For the rhubarb

· 275g rhubarb (untrimmed weight), washed

· 50g caster sugar

· 2 tsp plain flour

· icing sugar, to dust

....

Continued →

• For the moreish crumbs, cut the butter into chunks and melt it in a small pan over a low heat. Remove from the heat, add both types of sugar and stir constantly until dissolved into a smooth, toffee-like sauce. If the mixture looks split, don't worry, it will be OK once the flour goes in. Stir in the vanilla bean paste, pour into a small mixing bowl, then stir in the flour and a pinch of salt to make a stiff, biscuit-like dough. Press the mixture together and set aside to cool.

• Cut the dry bits off the ends of the rhubarb, then cut the rest into 2.5cm pieces. Put it into a mixing bowl over some scales. You should be left with about 225g rhubarb (if it is 50g more or less, it's OK). Add the sugar and flour to the bowl with the rhubarb and give it all a good stir. Leave for about 15 minutes, stirring a few more times. You want the flour and sugar mixture to moisten and cling to the fruit. Set aside.

• Preheat the oven to 160°C fan. Butter a shallow 20cm square, 5cm deep loose-based cake tin and line it with baking parchment.

• For the cake, using a hand-held whisk, whisk the kefir, egg, egg yolk, sugar and vanilla in a small bowl. Sift the flour, bicarbonate of soda, baking powder and ¼ tsp salt into another bowl. (I would recommend sifting here.)

• Add the butter pieces to the flour mixture and mix using a hand-held electric mixer until the mixture looks like fine breadcrumbs. Stir in the nuts, then gradually beat in the kefir mixture until smooth.

• Spread the cake mixture into the prepared tin, then scatter over the rhubarb mixture, leaving the flour mixture behind. I use a measuring tablespoon to scoop out the biscuit mixture, as it helps to compact it, then use a finger to prise it out of the spoon on top of the cake. You will have about 20 cute semi-spheres.

Continued →

Continued...

For the cake

- 75g unsalted butter, at room temperature, cut into pieces, plus more for the tin

- 80ml kefir, or plain yogurt

- 1 large free-range egg, plus 1 egg yolk

- 100g caster sugar

- 1 tsp vanilla bean paste

- 100g plain flour

- ½ tsp bicarbonate of soda

- ½ tsp baking powder

- 50g ground almonds or hazelnuts

- Bake for 40–45 minutes until golden. Insert a skewer into the cake, avoiding the rhubarb: it should come away clean.

- Leave to cool for 10 minutes. My husband Joe insisted this would be great with custard, but I like it just as it is. Serve either warm or cold in most of life's situations.

· ·

- TIP • You can just bake this crumble topping separately as little cookies; they are insanely delicious. Equally, you can make the cake and rhubarb bits without topping it with the biscuity crumble. Or, instead of rhubarb, you can play around with other fruit according to the season. Apples would work so well in autumn, while, in high summer, firm nectarines could be used, or plums or cherries.

· ·

Emma Lewis, Curator and Writer

On Cake Batter

···

'Everyone likes licking the bowl out, and, when you're a kid, it's the point of baking, surely? I remember summer holidays when my best friend Katie and I wanted to bake; we couldn't have been more than ten. We weren't allowed to cook unsupervised at hers, but we were at mine, and so would make bowlfuls of sponge batter or buttercream (with Stork margarine and icing sugar) with no intention of them ever becoming cakes or adornments to them. We'd then sit in front of Nickelodeon and eat the whole lot until we felt sick.'

Big Baked Snail with Tangerines

I love this recipe so much. Partly for its versatility, as you can use any number of things to fill the snail if you don't fancy tangerine. The ricotta filling for baked apples (see page 225) works, as does the poppy seed and pecan paste from my last cookbook, *Summer Kitchens*. You can also soften 200g unsalted butter, mix it with 200g Demerara sugar, some salt and 2 tbsp ground cinnamon and make a giant cinnamon bun! But I do recommend trying this tangerine compote, it's so easy, and delicious. It does catch a little, in a good way, but does not scorch acridly.

For the dough

·· 10g fast action dried yeast (but a 7g sachet will work too, if that's what you have)

·· 200ml warm whole milk

·· 60g Demerara sugar

·· 2 eggs

·· 1 tsp vanilla extract

·· 400–420g plain flour, plus more to dust

·· sea salt

For the filling

·· 300g fruit from the Tangerine Compote (see overleaf)

For the glaze

·· 2 egg yolks

·· 2 tbsp milk

- To make the dough, mix the yeast with the warm milk and the sugar in a bowl. Leave for 10 minutes or so to make sure the yeast works: it should develop a kind of a frothy 'hat' as we call it in Ukraine. Now whisk in the eggs, vanilla and 1 tsp salt. Make sure the eggs have broken up properly.

- Now, if you want the dough to be more like a cinnamon bun, use a food mixer fitted with a dough hook to do all the mixing, but I like the gentle fluffy texture you get if you do everything by hand as described below.

- Sift in 400g of the flour. The dough will be sticky and wet, but only if you feel it's too wet to handle, add the other 20g of flour.

- Now wet your hands (it will help the dough not stick to them) and work the dough a little in the bowl, to bring it together. Then do a stretch and fold action (see page 274) for a few minutes. Your dough will look pretty rough still, but don't worry. Pat it down, cover and leave for about 1 hour somewhere warm to rise.

- QR CODE • *Scoop the dough out on to a well-floured surface. It will be sticky but floured hands make it easier to work with. Knead for about 5 minutes. The dough will be soft and airy, a real pleasure to work with. Finally, shape it into a smooth ball. Leave it on your lightly floured work surface covered with a tea towel for 10 minutes, as it will be easier to roll out once the gluten relaxes.*

- *Now make sure your work surface is very well floured and start rolling out the dough, aiming for a thin 40cm circular sheet, rotating it to stop it sticking.*

- *Dot the filling all over the dough and gently roll it up into a log shape. Cut this log in half lengthways so you have 2 long pieces of dough with exposed filling.*

- *Put a sheet of baking parchment over a flat baking sheet and dust it with some flour.*

- *Take the first piece of dough and twist it around itself into a snail shape, exposed filling-side facing upwards. Now wrap the other piece of dough around the snail and pinch the ends together to secure. You may need to even out the filling a little.*

- Cover and leave to prove for 30–45 minutes. Preheat the oven to 180°C fan.

- Mix the egg yolks and milk for the glaze, brush it all over the bread and bake for 30–40 minutes. Check on it halfway through; if some of it is becoming too dark (my oven definitely has hot spots!), cover those bits with foil.

- As soon as it's out of the oven, slip the bread gently off its paper on to a wire rack to cool down. Enjoy with unsweetened lemony tea, or a glass of dry white wine.

- TIP • To make a bread and butter pudding, in case you have half of this snail left over, do the following. Butter a pie dish generously (use 30g butter), then slice the bread-snail and layer it in the pie dish. Whisk 300ml whole milk, 150g double cream, 3 large eggs, a pinch of sea salt, 1 tsp vanilla extract and 50g Demerara sugar together in a bowl. Pour this evenly over the slices of bread and leave to soak for at least 30 minutes, or up to overnight in the fridge. Preheat the oven to 160°C fan. Before baking, sprinkle loads more Demerara over to create a crispy topping. Pour some hot water into a large roasting tray, put the pie dish into it and bake for 40 minutes. Now crank up the oven temperature to 200°C fan and bake for another 5–10 minutes. If you have any leftovers of *this*, slice, then fry them in butter over a high heat!

Tangerine Compote

We always have a lot of citrus in our house in winter, we are obsessed! Once a box of tangerines arrived and they were disappointingly pappy, kind of lifeless and not very good. I could not bring myself to chuck them away, so

I sliced them, cooked them in some sugar syrup… and they turned into something very delicious. So delicious that I now make it with tasty tangerines, too. I love using this to make the big baked snail on the previous page.

·· 12 tangerines (total weight about 1kg)

·· 700ml water

·· 200g sugar (I use Demerara)

·· 1 tbsp orange blossom water (optional)

• Slice the tangerines horizontally (parallel to their 'equators'), skins and all, into 5mm circles. Put them into a medium saucepan and cover with the measured water. Now don't skip this step: bring them to a simmer and cook for about 20 minutes over a medium heat.

• Add the sugar, give it all a good stir and simmer for another full hour, checking on it from time to time and stirring gently so as not to break up the tangerines too much. Add the orange blossom water, if using, at the very end.

• The syrup will reduce and the tangerine skins will become very soft. I lift out the tangerine bits and eat them with buttered toast, but the syrup itself can be used as a cordial, or a glaze. My husband uses it to make kombucha, too. But one of the main reasons I have this recipe here is so you can have a go at making the giant snail-shaped bun (see page 236). It's a delicious thing.

Stefa's Stone Fruit Cake

This is inspired by my friend Marianna Dushar's grandmother's cake recipe... with the addition of cardamom, which another friend Katrya Kaluzhna uses in her plum tart. The original recipe uses plums, but you can use most fruit here. I suddenly became allergic to stone fruit after my pregnancy with my first son, but after I had my second son nine years later, the allergy was gone... isn't that the strangest thing? So I now go to town and make up for the lost time. Whenever I can, I use all the stone fruit that I can get hold of, because I just love them all – apricots, plums, peaches, cherries – but you can pick any, or a mixture.

- 150g stone fruit (plums, apricots, cherries), or even sliced apples

- 100ml flavourless oil, plus more (optional) for the tin

- 20g unsalted butter, for the tin (optional)

- seeds from 4 cardamom pods

- 200g Demerara sugar, plus 1 tbsp

- 200g plain flour

- 2 scant tsp baking powder

- 2 eggs

- 150ml kefir or *ryazhanka* (see overleaf)

- 1 tsp vanilla extract

- sea salt

- If you are using stone fruit, cut the flesh in half along the seams, then twist and take out the stones. If your fruit is unripe, you may need to use a small knife to prise or cut the stone out; if that shreds one of the fruit halves into smaller pieces, it's not a big deal, you can still use them.

- Preheat the oven to 180°C fan. Line a 20cm cake tin with a circle of baking parchment, then either lightly oil it or butter it heavily. The butter will add richness and flavour, so it really is up to you which one you pick.

- Pound the cardamom seeds with the 1 tbsp of Demerara until well ground. Sprinkle over the base of the prepared tin.

- Mix the flour with the baking powder and sift them, if you have patience. Mix in 1 tsp salt.

- Whisk the eggs in a mixer, then gradually add the 200g of Demerara sugar and whisk until very pale and fluffy. Gradually add the kefir or *ryazhanka*, whisking on a slightly lower speed, then trickle in the 100ml of oil and add the vanilla. The mix might look grainy and split, but it will be all OK once you add the flour.

- Fold in the flour and baking powder with a spatula, making sure there are no dry pockets of flour. Place the fruit into the batter, then scrape it into the sugared-and-cardamomed tin, smoothing it over on top.

- Put it into the oven and cook for 45 minutes. Check by inserting a skewer, which should come out with no cake mixture stuck to it. But remember the fruit is wet, so it's OK for the skewer to come out moist. The cake will continue cooking for a bit when you take it out, so be careful not to dry it out.

Baked Milk Yogurt Jelly

In Ukraine we adore a baked milk yogurt. The good news is that you can now buy *ryazhanka* commercially, but it is also easy to make, especially if you have tried making regular yogurt before. Bring milk to a near-boil in a heavy-based casserole that has a lid and then slow cook, covered, in a low (150°C fan) oven overnight. The milk's sugars will naturally caramelise, giving you a bronze-hued crust on top and dulce de leche-tasting milk underneath. We then mix it with homemade sour cream or yogurt, and make it into yogurt, using a regular yogurt-making method. This pudding was made by Thom Eagle and me for a dinner we held at a restaurant called Little Duck The Picklery. It is delicate and pairs so well with Strawberries Macerated in Lime Tree Syrup (see page 229) in June, or ripe peaches in high summer, or a small amount of blackcurrant compote. You can add

vanilla if you like, but I think the flavour of that baked milk is so lovely that I wouldn't mess with it too much. It is worth getting a good-quality honey for this, but again, if you are using *ryazhanka*, pick one that doesn't have an overwhelmingly strong flavour.

You can also use kefir, but it is more sour than *ryazhanka*, so you may need to up the honey a little (and you can also most certainly add vanilla in this case). Sometimes, when I am short of time, I just use 200ml water glasses for this and serve the pudding straight out of the glasses, with some fruit on top. But if you yearn for a pudding with a bit of panache, make it in a fun jelly mould as in this picture (it's 1 litre in volume) if you are having a few friends over for dinner. There is something so decadent and fun about a big jelly.

···

- 3 gelatine leaves
- 100ml whole milk
- 100–120g runny, gently flavoured honey
- 400g *ryazhanka* (baked milk kefir), or regular kefir
- ½ tsp vanilla extract (optional)
- about ½ tbsp flavourless oil (optional)
- canned peaches, or Strawberries Macerated in Lime Tree Syrup (see page 229), or berry compote, or fresh fruit, to serve

• First soak the gelatine leaves in cold water in a small bowl. Follow the packet instructions, but please do hold your nerve and soak them for as long as the packet implores you to. They should become really soft and pliable.

• Heat the milk in a small pan until it starts to steam, then pour into a bowl. This should cool it enough to safely add your gelatine. Squeeze the water out of the gelatine and whisk it into the milk, making sure it dissolves. Now whisk in the honey until it also dissolves. Make sure the milk has cooled down to just warm, so the kefir doesn't split and make your jelly grainy, stir in the *ryazhanka* or kefir and add the vanilla if you really love vanilla (but taste the mixture first to decide). I prefer mine without vanilla.

• Now, if you are using six 200ml glasses, fill them halfway up. If you are using a flamboyant 1-litre jelly mould, oil it lightly with a brush. It should be well-oiled, especially in all the grooves, but not so much that the oil is pooling at the bottom. Pour in the mixture and let it set in the fridge. For the glasses, it shouldn't take longer than 3 hours; for a big mould, give it 4–5 hours, or leave it covered overnight and eat it within 2 days.

• If you are serving the jellies in glasses, spoon a little bit of fruit on top and serve. If you are using the big mould, take it out of the fridge. Fill a big bowl with hot water and put the jelly mould in, making sure the water doesn't trickle inside. It only needs 30 seconds or so, the heat will help the jelly to separate from the mould. You can then run the tip of a butter knife round the very edge of the jelly, to break the vacuum. Now lightly wet a serving plate; this allows for the jelly to be moved if you turn it out not bang in the centre. Put the plate over the mould and turn it out very gently, agitating it a bit. It might look like it won't separate, but hold your nerve and wait for 5 seconds or so. If it is indeed being stubborn,

put the mould back in the hot water for another 10 seconds and try again. When the jelly comes out, some of it may have melted and might pool around on the plate. I use kitchen paper to dab it off lightly and then pile lots of fruit around it to conceal the mess (fact). In the very unfortunate event that the jelly comes out and breaks (it has happened to me), just use a dessert spoon to plop chunks of it into each person's plate, call it 'deconstructed jelly' and (again) surround it with lots of attractive fruit.

- When I serve the big jelly for a bunch of close friends or family, I normally just give everyone a small plate and some spoons and then we all just… well, jiggle the jelly for fun first and then dive into it tipsily with our spoons.

Poached Peaches with Butterscotch Sauce, Nuts and Whipped Cream

This recipe started as a Bosnian dessert called *tufarhije*. You peel apples, poach them whole in sugar syrup, stuff them with a nut paste, then serve with whipped cream. Then I messed the poaching bit up, but had a jar of Navarrico peaches in syrup (I *love* canned peaches) and used them instead. I think peaches in syrup are so underrated, and you don't need the fancy ones if you can't find them, just use canned. Or if you have fresh peaches that might not be at their best, the method below makes them taste far better.

For the peaches

·· 1 litre water

·· 150g soft brown sugar

·· 700g not-too-ripe peaches
or
8–12 halves of Navarrico jarred peach halves in syrup

For the rest

·· 120g pecans or walnuts

·· 50g soft brown sugar

·· 1 tbsp salted butter

·· 150g double cream

·· 1 tbsp caster sugar (optional)

·· 1 tsp rose water, or to taste

- Preheat the oven to 180°C fan.

- For the peaches, if you're poaching them yourself, mix the measured water with the sugar in a saucepan and bring to a simmer. Pop the peaches in and cook for about 10 minutes; they will bob up, but if you cover the pot with a lid loosely, it will help them cook on the exposed sides. After 10 minutes, try and turn them so the exposed sides cook. Depending on size, they may be ready after 15 minutes. You want them to be tender and for the skins to easily peel off. Lift them out, let cool a little, then peel off the skins. The syrup can be reduced a bit further and used as a cordial. Separate the peach halves and discard the stones.

- Meanwhile, to toast the nuts, put them on a baking tray and pop into the hot oven. Roast for 8 minutes, checking halfway through. The nuts should be lovely and toasted. If they are when you take them out, remove them from the tray to stop them cooking. If they don't look or taste deliciously toasted, give them another 2 minutes in the oven.

- To make the sauce, heat the soft brown sugar and butter in a pan over a low heat until fully melted and starting to bubble, then whisk in half the cream until the sauce thickens a little. Throw in almost all the nuts and stir to coat.

- Whip the remaining cream into soft peaks with the caster sugar, if you like. Make sure not to overwhip. Add the rose water, starting with 1 scant tsp, then taste and see if you would like more. But a gentle amount is best, I think.

- To serve, put 2 peach halves on a plate, spoon over the sauce and dollop with the whipped cream. Sprinkle over the rest of the toasted nuts and serve.

Buckwheat and Rice Pudding Cake with Sour Cherries

The very first time I visited New York (and the US) to promote my first cookbook, my American publisher put me up in a wonderful hotel in Manhattan called the Martha Washington. It all felt so exciting, so glamorous, so sky-scrapery and so steamy, just like in the movies! I was living my childhood *Home Alone II* fantasy, but better, because it was a warm and sunny early autumn and I wasn't a child, I was a US-published author. So wild! The hotel restaurant served excellent pizzas and more. Once, they served a small, unassuming-looking buckwheat tart that tasted so unusual yet so familiar (as you may have gathered by now, my favourite kind of feeling). With nutty crisp pastry, soft rice pudding and sour cherries it was more than the sum of its parts. I have been playing with these flavours ever since. Here is a reincarnation of that recipe's flavours and textures in a *torta di riso* of sorts (because I hate faffing with individual tarts and love *torta di riso*).

....

For the rice pudding

·· 200g pudding rice, or arborio or vialone nano rice

·· 800ml whole milk

·· 300g double cream

·· 4 large eggs

·· 100–150g light brown sugar

....

For the buckwheat biscuit base

·· 75g cold unsalted butter, cut into small cubes, plus more for the tin

·· 75g buckwheat flour

·· 75g whole oat groats (whole oats, not oat flakes)

·· 75g light brown sugar

·· 1 tsp baking powder

·· pinch of sea salt

·· 1 tbsp runny honey

....

For the compote

·· 200g frozen sour cherries

·· 1 tbsp honey

• Butter a 23cm springform/loose-based tin (although I have used 20cm before and it was fine!) and line it with a disc of baking parchment.

• Mix all the dry biscuit ingredients together. Gently rub the butter cubes into the dry mix with your fingertips until there are no floury areas or lumps of butter. I will be honest, I find this step really annoying in recipes, mine always look like clumps rather than neat crumbs. But don't worry, if you tend to make clumps like me the mixture will still be delicious. Add the honey and bring the biscuit dough together.

• Sprinkle the biscuit mix evenly over the base of the prepared tin, then press it down with your hand. Encourage the biscuit mix into the corners and very slightly up the side of the tin. Chill in the fridge for 20 minutes or in the freezer for 5. Preheat the oven to 160°C fan.

• Bake the biscuit base for 15 minutes until a deep golden brown. Leave to cool (I take it outside).

• For the next step, if you have time at your disposal and don't want to be watching the milk, you can cook the rice, covered, in the oven at 180°C fan for 1 hour, instead of on the hob.

• Combine the rice, milk, cream and a pinch of salt in a large saucepan. Bring to the boil, then reduce the heat to its lowest and cook, uncovered, for 30 minutes, stirring every so often. You may need to stay nearby as milk tends to run away easily. By the end of cooking, when the liquid has almost evaporated from the saucepan, pay attention to the bottom, scraping so the rice doesn't burn and stick. When ready, the rice should still be fairly creamy looking, not too dry, but will start spitting like a volcano (so watch out). The rice grains will be soft if you taste them. Transfer the rice mixture into a big bowl if the pan you've been cooking it in is not very big. Leave to cool (again, I take it outside if I can). The rice should be at room temperature or just ever so slightly warm when you mix in the eggs.

• Preheat the oven to 170°C fan.

- Whisk the 4 eggs for around 5 minutes until creamy in colour and foamy. Gradually add spoonfuls of the light brown sugar, whisking as you do. Add the full 150g of sugar if you have a sweet tooth, otherwise keep it at 100g, as the biscuit base is sweet and I feel it's nice to have the rice just a little less so.

- The eggs and sugar will look very voluminous and foamy. Stir one-third of the egg mixture firmly into the warm, but not hot, rice pudding. Now add the rest and gently fold in, turning the bowl as you go.

- Pour into the cake tin and bake in the centre of the oven for 40–45 minutes until the top is a deep golden brown and there is a very gentle wobble in the centre. It will be custardy, but shouldn't be undercooked. Test by inserting a skewer in the very centre, it shouldn't be too wet, but it's OK for it to be a little bit moist. Please do be patient and leave it to cool and set, otherwise the middle might collapse.

- Gently warm the cherries and honey in a saucepan until they release their juice, then simmer until the juice begins to thicken slightly. Serve the cake with the compote. Keep any leftover cake in the fridge.

Peanut and Dulce de Leche Cake

Just like people went nuts for banana and sourdough breads in the UK coronavirus lockdown, in Ukraine there seems to have been a slight Japanese baked goods craze. My mum's friends started baking Hokkaido milk bread and making Japanese castella sponge cake. The latter is actually very similar to sponge cakes we make in Ukraine, but the steaming part is different and makes the sponge so soft! The peanut part comes from my mum updating a cake from her childhood with a distinctly

Soviet-cheer name: *ulybka* ('smile'). The original, sold in Soviet shops, had nothing to smile about, with its scattering of 10 peanuts, synthetic barberry syrup and dubious icing ingredients. And still everyone pined for it. My mum turned the memory of this cake into something else. This is an indulgent and moreish treat that hits all the spots for me. It's for a real peanut lover, mind, as instead of ten peanuts she scatters it with closer to one hundred.

For the sponge cake

· 140g unsalted butter, plus more, melted, for the tins

· 120g plain flour

· 120ml whole milk

· 8 eggs, separated

· 160g caster sugar

· 2 tsp vanilla extract

· fine sea salt

....

For the dulce de leche buttercream

· 150g roasted peanuts

· 150g salted butter, softened

· 280g cooked condensed milk (bought ready-caramelised, or homemade in the can), or dulce de leche

· sea salt flakes, to serve

- To roast the peanuts for the buttercream, if yours came unroasted, preheat the oven to 180°C fan. Put the peanuts on a baking tray and roast for 8–10 minutes. You may need to shake the tray a little halfway through. They should taste delicious and toasted. If you have a very hot oven, check them after the first 5 minutes. If you forget them and take them out and they look really dark, taste before you chuck them, as peanuts can go pretty damned dark before becoming acrid. If they have lots of skins on, you can put them inside a tea towel and rub them around a bit, but more often than not I just embrace the skins (too lazy).

- Reduce the oven temperature to 150°C fan. Put 2 large baking trays half-filled with water in the oven.

- QR CODE • *Line two 20cm, 8cm deep cake tins. If they have removable bases, line the insides (or wrap the outsides) of them tightly with foil, to cover the bottom seams and make them waterproof. Butter the bases and sides and line entirely with non-stick baking parchment, so the sponge doesn't stick to the foil or the tin.*

- *To make the sponge, measure the flour into a large bowl. Now chop the 140g butter, mix it with the milk in a small saucepan and heat it up until the butter has melted and the mixture is steaming and is almost too hot to touch. Watch it, though, and do not let it boil. (If you have a thermometer, it should read about 90°C.)*

- *Pour the hot milk mix over the flour and whisk. This cooks the starch in the flour and causes this sponge to be very soft (for days!). Let it cool down until just warm.*

- *Start whisking the egg whites in a separate bowl using electric beaters until fluffy. Now gradually add the sugar and ½ tsp salt, bit by bit, and keep whisking until you achieve soft-peak meringue: it shouldn't be too stiff and powdery. Divide in half.*

- *Whisk the vanilla into the flour mixture, then whisk in the egg yolks one by one, incorporating them properly each time. Put half this mixture into another bowl.*

- *Working with half the yolk mixture and half the meringue, add a large spoonful of the meringue to the yolks, and whisk it vigorously to loosen the batter up (this makes it easier to incorporate the rest of the meringue).*

Continued →

Continued...

- *Now, add the rest of the fluffy egg whites, in 3 confident batches, using a folding action and trying to incorporate the meringue without deflating the air too much, but making sure there are no pockets of meringue or flour in the mix. I just use my whisk manually, dragging it through the batter so it falls through the slits with each folding motion.*

- *Pour the mixture into one of the prepared tins, then tap it on a work surface to remove any large air bubbles.*

- Repeat with the remaining yolk and egg white mixes to make the second sponge.

- Put each tin into one of the trays filled with hot (not-quite-boiling) water in the oven and cook for 1 hour, or until a skewer comes out clean. This cooking method will both bake and steam the sponges at the same time.

- Put the sponges on a wire rack and let them cool down completely before taking them out of the tins. Don't be alarmed if their sides feel a little damp: the sponges will emerge from the oven puffed up, but will inevitably deflate somewhat. Again, that's OK as long as they don't look like pancakes (if they do, something went wrong either with the stiffness of the egg whites, the folding technique, or the oven temperature).

- For the cream, put the soft salted butter into a mixer bowl and start whisking it, adding the cooked condensed milk or dulce de leche as you go. Do not overwhisk it, or the mixture will split. If it does split (happened to me once), I would still use it: it will still be delicious and you can cover everything in peanuts so only the most perceptive will ever know.

- Make sure the sponges are completely cool before putting the buttercream on. Put a sponge on to a serving plate, spread half the buttercream in the middle and scatter with 2 tbsp of the peanuts. Then put the second cake on top, add the rest of the buttercream and sprinkle over the rest of the peanuts. The sides are OK left naked, or you can cover them with buttercream if you prefer. Scatter the cake with sea salt flakes, then serve.

Greta Zilyte, Cook and Pastry Chef

Coffee with Eggs

'My mum is a big coffee drinker. She has at least three cups a day and the usual accompaniment is a small treat, such as a slice of cake or a chocolate-glazed curd cheese bar (we're addicted to those in Lithuania). As a child, every time I saw her making coffee, I always felt enticed by the deep scent of roasted beans meeting the steaming hot water. I remember my first sips of coffee whitened with creamy milk when I was about 12 years old. Coffee grains stuck between my teeth and my heart beat a little faster. To accompany the coffee, I got into a habit of quickly whipping up a luscious little pudding called *gogol mogol* or *kogel mogel*. I would whip up egg yolks with sugar so hard that my arm started to ache. I knew it was ready when the yellow liquid turned into a voluminous fluffy cloud of joy.'

Serves 6

Greta's Lithuanian Buckwheat Cake

This cake was a game-changer for me. Now, I am not a person who would scrape cake batter from the bowl after finishing cake-making. My son does, my friends in the UK do, but it does not naturally entice me. I thought it was because my mum discouraged eating raw eggs, like Greta's mum, but I do clearly remember making a small hole in a raw egg and drinking it as a kid, so it couldn't have been that. Perhaps it was the raw flour that my mum thought was the culprit. Whatever it was, my fear

of raw batter was lifted after I tasted the batter for Greta's buckwheat cake: I couldn't stop licking the spoon. This is called *babka* in Lithuania and the recipe was generously given to me by Lithuanian-born London chef Greta Zilyte. It makes the perfect base for the spiced quince trifle or the cake inspired by tiramisu on the following pages. But honestly, this cake naked and unadorned is just the best tea cake ever. And it's gluten-free too, if you care.

- ·· 150g unsalted butter, softened, plus more for the tin

- ·· 150g Demerara sugar (or any brown sugar)

- ·· 3 eggs, lightly beaten

- ·· 150g buckwheat flour

- ·· 1 tsp baking powder

- ·· 60ml kefir

- Preheat the oven to 170°C fan.

- If you are using the cake on its own as a tea cake, use a 15cm round cake tin with a removable base. If you're planning to use it for the trifle or tiramisu cake (see pages 258 and 260), the cake benefits from being drier and crispier, so you can use a 20cm round cake tin. Butter the tin, then line with a circle of baking parchment, going slightly up the sides.

- I do recommend having the butter really soft, not half-heartedly soft, which I am often guilty of too. Do leave it somewhere to become so soft that you can poke your finger into it smoothly with no effort at all. Don't try to soften your butter in a microwave; that will just melt the outside and that's not what you want. If you did forget to leave it out and it's fridge-cold, slice it into thin slabs, then put those between 2 pieces of baking parchment and roll over with a rolling pin to flatten. You don't have to roll for ages, just flatten a couple of times, scrape the butter off the baking parchment into a bowl, and voilà! It should be sufficiently soft for our job here.

- Now, we need to cream the butter with the sugar until light and fluffy. I usually use an electric mixer to do this. Whisk the butter and sugar at high speed. Then gradually add the eggs, trickling them in and watching the mixer drag its viscous threads into the vortex. When all the eggs are in, the mixture will look sloppy and worryingly split. But, please, don't worry.

- Mix the flour with the baking powder. Sometimes, when I am rested and I feel up to it, I sift them together through a sieve a couple of times, aerating them and mixing them together properly. And sometimes, I just sprinkle the baking powder on top of the flour, give it a quick whirl with my finger and hope for the best.

- Fold them both gently through the wet mixture with a silicone spatula, if you have one, then brusquely fold in the kefir, making sure it is incorporated homogeneously enough. I know that mixing a wet ingredient into the cake after you added the flour may seem strange, but please, do it. Scrape the cake mixture into your prepared tin and smooth it out on top as best you can. OK… that's it! So easy. Time to put it in the oven.

- Bake it for 35 minutes and perform the skewer test; I use a chopstick and shove it in the thickest part of the cake, then if it comes out wet I put the cake back in the oven for another 5 minutes. Keep testing until the chopstick comes out fairly clean. I say *fairly* because remember, even when the cake comes out of the oven, it will still keep cooking.

- I like this as it is, with a cup of strong coffee in the morning. Greta loves it with plum compote or apricot jam and whipped cream in the middle. I think this cake is so good that I have used it in the following 2 recipes, to make a quince trifle or the tiramisu cake of dreams.

Quince Trifle

As you may have noticed, I am a big lover of turning one recipe into another and I also do not love shop-bought savoiardi biscuits, so I usually use Greta's Lithuanian Buckwheat Cake (see page 254) wherever a recipe calls for them. There's nothing wrong with using shop-bought if you love savoiardi biscuits or want to do a trifle quickly without bothering with the cake: please go ahead, using your judgement about how many you would need depending on the size of your bowl. But if, like me, you love the gentle flavour of buckwheat, or want to make a gluten-free trifle, this recipe is for you. As always, you can just use some sweetened frozen or fresh berries or any other poached fruit instead of the quince.

For the quince

·· 1 unwaxed lemon

·· 2 quince

·· 120g caster sugar

·· 1 litre water

For the custard

·· 8 egg yolks

·· 6 tbsp cornflour

·· 120g Demerara sugar

·· 500ml whole milk

·· 200g double cream

For the rest of the trifle

·· ½ Greta's Lithuanian Buckwheat Cake, ideally slightly stale (see page 254)

·· 250g double cream, whipped, with (optional) 1 tbsp icing sugar

·· handful of toasted flaked almonds (see page 182)

• Preheat the oven to 120°C fan.

• Using a vegetable peeler, take the zest off the lemon and put it into a large bowl. Juice the lemon and add the lemon juice to the zest. Now pick a non-reactive baking dish (ceramic, Pyrex or stainless steel). Peel the quince and put the peel to the side. Now cut the quince in half and then into quarters. Put each quarter on a stable side and cut off the cores. Toss the quince quarters in the bowl with the lemon juice. Add the cores to the quince peel. Arrange the quince cores and peels in the baking dish and cover them with a sheet of baking parchment. These will help produce the maximum quince-y flavour and also help tease out the deep colour.

• Put the caster sugar and measured water in a saucepan, set over a medium heat and cook, stirring, until the sugar dissolves. Simmer for 3 minutes, then remove from the heat.

• Arrange the quince quarters on top of the baking parchment in the dish and pour over the simple syrup. Now cook in the oven for about 4 hours, or until the quince are a beautiful copper colour.

• To make the custard, I always have a bowl with a fine strainer perched over it, just in case my custard splits and I need to strain it. Put the egg yolks, cornflour and Demerara sugar into a medium bowl. Heat the milk and cream over a medium heat. When it starts steaming, splash some of it into the egg yolks while whisking, then pour this mixture back into the cream and milk pan. Stir and cook over a medium-low heat until the custard thickens. Sometimes the custard takes its time and you can start to think it'll never work! But please be patient; I promise that even if it looks like it never will, it will – eventually – thicken.

• Slice the cake and put it in a large glass bowl. Then slice the quince and layer it on top. Add the custard and top with the whipped cream, either unsweetened or slightly sweetened, as you prefer. Top with the toasted flaked almonds.

Buckwheat Cake Tiramisu

My first ever restaurant job (at a bistro in Fulham) put me under the wing of a bunch of ex-Jamie Oliver Fifteen chefs: Aaron Craze, Richard Blackwell and Slim. The first two shared the head chef position and Slim was the sous chef. He made the best tiramisu I'd ever tried. I asked for the recipe and he gave it to me. It involved this cool technique I'd never tried before: pâté à bombe, to make the cream. It was the Fifteen restaurant tiramisu, he said. Fifteen sadly no longer exists, nor does the recipe Slim shared (I lost it), but I am attempting to recreate it here.

You can use this cream recipe and go with the more traditional savoiardi lady fingers, but I do implore you to try it with buckwheat sponge. Buckwheat and coffee is such a brilliant combination, and this cloud of a cream just makes for the most indulgent experience. It's a very good make-ahead pudding, as the cake benefits from being a couple of days old. The cream, by the way, makes a really wonderful no-churn ice cream. Simply scoop it into a tub and stick in the freezer, then thaw a little bit, scoop and serve!

·· 4 egg yolks

·· 150g caster sugar

·· 100ml water

·· 500g mascarpone

·· 300g double cream

·· 1 Greta's Lithuanian Buckwheat Cake, ideally a day old (see page 254)

·· 300ml strong coffee (espresso), cooled down

·· 4 tbsp Cognac, or other booze you like

·· cocoa powder, to dust

·· sea salt

• First you need to make pâté à bombe: egg yolks whisked into a foam with very hot sugar syrup. Trust me, I have a sugar syrup phobia, but I find this process very easy. In many recipes they say the sugar syrup must be 118°C, but I have made this plenty of times without a thermometer and it worked. So, this is what you do, it's such a cool process.

• Put the egg yolks into a food mixer bowl, or into a large bowl if you are using a hand mixer. Mix 125g of the sugar and the measured water in a pan and set it over a low heat. Heat it slowly at first so the sugar has a chance to dissolve. You can give it just one very gentle stir to help it along. Make sure not to swirl it around too much though, as the sugar can crystallise on the sides of the pan and ruin your syrup. Then just leave it alone and bring to the boil. It should boil quite hard for 3–4 minutes. The bubbles will look big and the syrup will look thicker.

• As soon as it starts boiling, start whisking those egg yolks on the highest speed. They will look paler and foamy. Once your sugar syrup has boiled for 4 minutes (or you have used a thermometer and it showed 118°C), start trickling the syrup on the wall of the mixing bowl as you whisk the egg yolks at a high speed. At first, even after all of the syrup has gone in, you might think that it will never work – the egg yolks just stay liquid – but give it a little time, just keep whisking for even up to 10 minutes and they will eventually become pale and voluminous. That's it, you've made your first pâté à bombe.

• Now put the mascarpone into a large bowl, add a good pinch of sea salt and give it a whisk. It will be firm at first but should slacken up slightly. Now add a big spoonful of the pâté à bombe and whisk it in quite energetically to further slacken the mascarpone. Keep adding the pâté à bombe spoonful after spoonful. You will end up with a billowing cream.

• Now separately whip the double cream with the remaining 25g of sugar. You need it to be at soft peak stage, but stop before you think you should as you will whisk it further when you add it to the mascarpone cream.

• Fold the whipped cream into the mascarpone and you are very nearly there! (For ice cream, at this stage transfer it to a 1.5-litre container, then freeze until firm.)

- Now cut your cake in half as if you are cutting a loaf of bread in half. Then flip it on the cut side and slice it into 1cm pieces. You don't want the cake pieces to be too thick as those won't be so nice to eat, but you also don't want it very thin, because then it will fall apart in the coffee mixture.

- Have a glass bowl or pie dish at the ready (I use a 2-litre one and it just about holds it all in). Mix the cooled coffee with the alcohol in a shallow bowl in which you can easily dip your pieces of cake. Now dip your pieces of cake into the boozy coffee, but be careful not to leave them in too long otherwise the cake will break. (If some pieces do break, don't stress, no one will notice or care.) Arrange one-third of the cake in a single layer in your chosen bowl or dish, then add one-third of the cream. Put another layer of cake in, then more cream, and finally add the rest of the cake on top and finish with the remaining cream. If some cake is left over, just eat it as a snack with a cup of tea.

- Leave the tiramisu in the fridge to let things absorb and set (a couple of hours is OK, overnight is great), then dust with cocoa powder. Enjoy whenever.

Self-Care Marbled Semolina Cake

My mum has been going to the same masseuse for the past 25 years. When I come to visit our small town in Ukraine, I also go to her every other day. Natasha, the masseuse, is a real ace of her craft. There is no stroking of the oil around the back languidly, she does a proper, bruise-inducing deep tissue massage. If you experienced it blind, you would think The Rock was pummelling you, not a glamorous tanned woman in her sixties. She really works it and has guns of steel to show for it. She does a full body thing for a whole two hours each session. It's the biggest act of self-care I allow myself annually. We often keep shtum, me in my dream-like pleasure-pain zone (when I usually write in my head, this recipe included). But sometimes we talk, about our families, her adult grandchildren and her love of baking. Natasha is

in such high demand with her work, she has no time to faff (although I think what is considered 'faff' in Ukraine and the UK are two different things), so the recipes need to be quick and effortless-ish as well as delicious. She bakes these speedy delights often, in huge quantities, and distributes the cakes around the *babushkas* in her building as well as her large extended family. A cocoa version of this recipe was revealed, and tasted, during one of our sessions when we were in a mood to chat. My mum once joked, 'Natasha, I want you to massage me until the very end.' They both started laughing hysterically, imagining themselves in another 25 years, 90-year-old women, Natasha crouched over my mum's back, bruising away still, feeding Mum cake in the interim. I am keeping everything crossed that this will happen.

·· 110ml sunflower oil or melted, cooled unsalted butter, plus more for the tin

·· 250ml kefir

·· 90g fine semolina

·· 100g soft brown sugar or honey

·· 1 tsp bicarbonate of soda

·· 1 egg, lightly beaten

·· 70g plain flour

·· 20g cocoa powder, or poppy seeds, or toasted and ground nuts

·· sea salt

·· custard or cream, to serve

• Prepare a 20cm cake tin with a removable base by buttering it at the bottom and around the sides. Line the bottom with a circle of baking parchment and the sides with a strip of parchment.

• Mix the kefir with the semolina in a large bowl. Add the sugar or honey and half the bicarbonate of soda. I don't want to research why, as I fear I will spoil the magic, but Natasha swears that adding half the bicarb at this stage makes a huge difference to the cake's final fluff factor. Leave this be for 30 minutes while you prep everything else and do some minimal faffing.

• Preheat the oven to 180°C fan.

• Now whisk the oil or melted butter and the egg into the semolina mixture. Mix the flour with the rest of the bicarbonate of soda and ½ tsp salt (I don't bother sifting, just stir it all together in a separate bowl). Fold this through the semolina mix thoroughly with a spatula.

• Now, take a cupful of the mixture out and put it back into the bowl where you mixed the flour just a moment ago. Mix in the cocoa, poppy seeds, nuts, or anything else you might enjoy. Swirl this mixture loosely through the main cake mixture, to achieve a marbled effect. Pour the batter into the prepared tin and bake for 30–40 minutes or until a skewer comes out clean from the thickest part of the cake.

• I would never normally serve cakes with cream on the side (it's such a British thing and remains alien to me, in spite of my otherwise successful assimilation), however... Natasha did mention that sometimes she makes a three-tiered cake using this recipe and uses crème pâtissière to bind them together. So I feel like serving this with custard or cream (or even yogurt) is completely justified.

Custard Pies

I love custard and I love custard slices even more. This recipe comes from my friend Anna Corak's Croatian mother-in-law Vesna Zadravec. It has one of the most interesting and light crème pâtissière recipes I've ever come across. It might feel counterintuitive to whisk egg whites into hot custard, but bear with me and trust Vesna's recipe please. It does make for a very light result and works so well with the puff pastry. The original dish, called *kremsnite*, actually looks like a custard slice, but I felt that getting the custard thick enough to set

has turned into a bit of a gamble, so I reimagined this *kremsnite*'s shape and turned it into a more forgiving, more approachable pudding. If you don't care about shape and form as much as what's 'on the inside', try this version. For flavouring, you can go with classic vanilla, but other extracts work so well to add interest. I tried coffee extract for a bunch of adults and chocolate extract for my chocolate-obsessed son and both versions were loved. And because these are individual puddings, you can even make a roulette of flavours for fun.

- 325g pack of puff pastry
- 100g icing sugar
- 3 large eggs, separated
- 600ml whole milk
- 70g caster sugar
- 50g cornflour
- 2 tsp vanilla extract, or coffee/almond/chocolate extract, or rose/orange blossom water (see recipe introduction)
- sea salt

- Preheat the oven to 180°C fan. Now, you can always dust the icing sugar on the *kremsnite* at the very end, but I personally dislike the dustiness of raw icing sugar. So what I do is this. I put the pastry sheet on a baking sheet lined with baking parchment. Then, I put 50g of the icing sugar into a fine sieve and I dust the raw pastry with sugar (you may not need the whole amount). This way the icing sugar will caramelise while the pastry bakes. Prick the pastry all over with a fork.

- Now take one of the bowls that you will serve this in and use it to cut out circles from the puff pastry. If you are using mismatched bowls, use each one to cut out an individual lid.

- Put the circles of pastry into the preheated oven and bake for 10–15 minutes. I am afraid this is the bit where you really have to pay attention and not get distracted. You do not want to burn the pastry and the sugar, if you are following this process. Also be mindful that your oven might have hot spots (mine does), so turn the tray around 180° halfway through cooking.

- Check the tops of the pastry circles look golden, shiny and laminated. If not, return them to the oven for another 5–10 minutes. You can use these on the same day, or keep them in an airtight container to be assembled the next day.

- To make the cream, whisk the egg whites and a pinch of sea salt first on their own to get them foamy, then gradually add the remaining 50g of icing sugar. Beat it all together until you get soft peaks that look glossy and not at all powdery. Set aside for a minute.

- Have a bowl and a fine sieve ready. Whisk 50ml of the milk with the egg yolks, caster sugar and cornflour in a bowl. Put the rest of the milk into a medium saucepan and bring to a near-boil. When it's hot, add some of the hot milk to the egg yolk mixture, whisking so the egg doesn't scramble. Then pour this back into the pan with the milk. Keep stirring the custard and cooking over a medium-low heat. At first it will all look pretty loose, but within a minute or so the mixture will thicken dramatically. It will look rough and lumpy for a while and then it smoothes out and thickens. You need to be patient here, and keep stirring all the time, perhaps reducing the heat, and you must not let the mixture bubble.

Cook for about 10 minutes to make sure to cook out the raw flour. You can dip a spoon in and taste: the custard should be thick and should not taste of flour when it's ready. Pour the custard into a large bowl and immediately do the next step.

- Fold the egg whites into the hot custard with gentle confidence, if that makes sense! Meaning: don't be too rough, so as to keep some of the volume, but also don't go so gently that the egg white doesn't incorporate properly. Add the vanilla extract or any of the other flavourings of choice. If you taste the custard now, it may seem just a little bit underwhelming (those were my thoughts the first time I tried it). But once you eat it with the buttery puff pastry, it really works, feels light and the flavour comes out more.

- When the custard is cool, pour it into 4 x 200ml bowls. You can put it in the fridge for at least 1 hour, or overnight. But it is also good eaten straight away. Just pop the pastry lid on top to serve!

Useful Recipes

New Cupboard Staples

Useful Recipes

It was 2009. The financial crisis had reached its climax and swine flu looked to be creeping into the UK. I remember watching the TV huddled on the sofa, wrapped in a goat's wool blanket, in a small flat by Alexandra Palace that I shared with Alexis, my first husband. I was extremely ill, probably with flu, but watching figures in Hazmat suits on the screen, plus the incessant redundancies at work, made me think hard about my life.

I was a junior reporter at a film industry magazine. Alexis wrote for *The Bookseller*, a publishing business weekly. Life was pretty hand-to-mouth, but luckily I had nothing to compare it to. Then, on one of the food channels, an advert for Leiths School of Food and Wine came up. I turned around to Alexis and croaked, 'Why am I not doing this?' He replied casually, 'I have no idea. You are obsessed with cooking.'

The next day I was back in the office. I remember this moment so clearly, perhaps because I have thought about it so many times since. I turned to my friend Caroline and told her about the Leiths advert, without voicing any ambitions. There must have been something in my voice. She was looking at her computer, typing, but calmly asked, 'Are you thinking of retraining?' It was so casual and easy, she made it seem so possible… it totally threw me.

I rang my mum the next day and announced that I had something important to tell her. She asked me to listen to her first. She'd had a dream, she said, about us being on a bus together. My mum got off the bus and felt terrified that she had left me behind… but then in the distance she saw my bus and me going up the hill. And she said it made her feel good and safe. I listened with my mouth agape and then told her that I would be quitting my job and getting a loan to finance a new, unexpected career path. I don't know if my mum's bus dream was a key catalyst for her here, but she implored me not to go to the bank. Yes, my parents had already paid for my school and university, but Mum says that I sounded so madly elated… They helped me and saved me from a long-lasting debt.

I enjoyed Leiths immensely, finished with flying colours and – despite my dreams to work at a food magazine – ended up in professional kitchens, first in restaurants for two years and then catering for many more. I experienced it all: eighteen-hour shifts, sleep deprivation, burnt limbs, chopping boxes and boxes of veg, working intense services, having to grow a thick skin fast, carrying heavy crates, grindingly low pay…

Years later, I found out from my cousin that my mum and aunt had secretly sobbed together after seeing the strips of oven burns tattooed on the tender side of my forearms. But I loved it. I loved it all. I burned out at some point and experienced darkness, but I learned so much. The practical stuff, the life stuff. I still recommend other people to put themselves through it if they want a career in food. Giving birth after experiencing restaurant life felt more do-able; my stamina had already been pushed to its limit!

In this chapter you will find some recipes and tricks I picked up in professional kitchens.

Dumpling Dough

I use this dough for all sorts of dumplings and sometimes for noodles, too. Eggs wouldn't actually be used in dumpling dough in Ukraine, Caucasus and Central Asia, but I add them, as I feel they help with elasticity. If you need to make this dough vegan, simply substitute the 3 large eggs with 190–200ml water.

·· 3 large eggs

·· 45–100ml water, or
as needed

·· 500g '00' or plain flour, plus
more to dust if needed

·· fine semolina or polenta,
to dust if needed (optional)

• You can make this in a food mixer fitted with the dough hook attachment and it is undeniably the easiest way. Just put the wet ingredients in the bowl, add the flour and start mixing: first slowly, then a little faster. If your machine is small and it feels like this amount of dough is too hard for it to handle, take half of it out and knead one half first, then the second. It will be firm and not necessarily silky-smooth just yet, so cover it and leave to rest for 10–15 minutes.

• QR CODE • *If you are doing it by hand, keep the following tips in mind and it will all work great. It is easier if you add the flour in stages, as, if you're working manually, you may not need it all. In a bowl, using a fork, whisk the eggs with 45ml of the water, then mix in half the flour, first using a fork, then add almost all of the rest of the flour and use your hand to scrunch the flour in. Just grab it and squish with your hand to make a rough dough. If you feel like it's way too dry (some large eggs can be not that large, I find), trickle in a little bit more water and swoosh the rough dough around to incorporate it. Turn it out on to a work surface, leaving any super-dry flakes of dough behind in the bowl. It will look shaggy. Leave it alone for 10 minutes, covered so it doesn't dry out, to allow it to relax.*

• *Now give it a quick knead. You shouldn't need too much flour, in fact I don't use any. But if your dough does feel sticky, flour the surface and your hands generously and keep adding flour, while you knead, until it stops sticking. If you are kneading by hand, do so for 2 minutes only at first, no need to overexert yourself.*

• *After the 2 minutes it will still look pretty wrinkly and rough, but just cover it up and leave it be for a further 10–15 minutes. This rest works miracles, just knead for a couple of minutes again and watch it become smooth as if by magic. It should feel firm and elastic.*

• Wrap the dough up tightly, so it doesn't dry out, and leave it for its final rest for at least 30 minutes or longer. This will relax the gluten and make it easier to roll it out. It will be OK overnight in the fridge, or in the freezer. Dough that has spent some time in the freezer might become a little softer and sometimes a little greyer, but it shouldn't cause too much trouble. To thaw frozen dough, I just take it out of the freezer and keep it overnight in the fridge, or in my kitchen for a few hours (this depends on how warm my kitchen is).

Easy Flatbreads

The technique for rolling these exists in many cultures, but I always connect them to chef Andrew Wong, whose book I recipe-tested at the beginning of my cooking career. His water-based dough was made with yeast, but I find the technique works with this dough too. This is a super-fun thing to teach your kids to do. Sasha, my elder son, has become the main maker of these in our house and we cook them at least once a week, usually when I forget to make or buy bread and we need something quick and carby to have with lunch. I use wholemeal flour to add nutrients, but you don't have to.

- 200ml kefir (or 100ml yogurt mixed with 100ml water)

- 10g honey, or sugar

- 4 tbsp olive oil

- 250g self-raising wholemeal flour, or plain flour mixed with 1 tsp baking powder, plus more to dust

- sea salt

- Put the kefir into a large bowl and whisk in the honey or sugar and half the olive oil with 1 tsp salt. Add the flour and stir first with a spoon and then get your hand in there and bring the dough together.

- Now take it out of the bowl and knead on a lightly floured surface for a minute or so. The dough won't be smooth straight away, but do not worry. Leave it covered for at least 5 minutes, or for as long as 30 minutes, if you have time.

- QR CODE • *Now divide it into 8 equal parts (roughly 50g each) and form each wedge into a rectangle.*

- *Roll each piece out over a lightly floured surface into a strip about 15 x 3cm. Brush with oil and roll it up like a Swiss roll.*

- *Stand it coil side up, squash it down with your palm, then roll out again into a 15cm circle. Repeat to form all 8 flatbreads.*

- Now heat a dry frying pan, add 1–2 flatbreads and cook for 2–3 minutes on each side over a medium-low heat. I pinch off a little bit to check it is cooked inside.

- I keep the cooked breads in a bowl covered with a plate, so they keep warm and steam a little, becoming softer as they do. Serve them with Lamb Cutlets in Kefir and Harissa Marinade, Saffron Broth with Chickpea and Rice Balls, or Lamb Shoulder with Herbs and Preserved Lemons (see pages 25, 37 and 171).

Tromsø's Seeded Rye Bread

This is another brilliant recipe from my Norwegian friend and excellent cook Hedvig Winsvold. I had never soaked seeds and nuts before putting them into bread before, and was so pleasantly surprised when I used this method in the recipe. They become plump and give the bread a beautiful texture and moisture. This loaf is extremely flavoursome as well as good for you and so I make it very often indeed.

For the pre-soak

- 200ml water
- 50g walnuts, or any other nuts you like
- 50g pumpkin seeds
- 50g sunflower seeds
- 10g sea salt

For the dough

- 15g fresh yeast or 7g fast action dried yeast
- 100ml kefir, yogurt or sour cream
- 50g black treacle, or other dark molasses
- 400g dark rye flour
- 50g rye flakes (optional)
- 50g mixed seeds, to finish the bread

- The night before, mix together the ingredients of the pre-soak, cover and leave in the kitchen overnight, or for a minimum of 12 hours. This plumps up the nuts and seeds and really adds to the texture of the bread. Some of the water will absorb into the nuts and seeds. Strain the rest of the water into a bowl that you have placed on your switched-on scales, squeezing the nuts and seeds over the sieve to extract as much water as possible. You will have roughly 50ml; add enough warm water to make it up to 200ml, or 250ml if you are using rye flakes.

- Add the yeast to this lukewarm water and give it a whisk. Add the kefir, black treacle and pre-soaked seeds and whisk again to combine. Then add the flour and rye flakes, if using, and mix well with a spatula. The mixture will be very sticky. I recommend having a bowl of water on the side to dip your spatula in, as the water helps the dough not stick too much. I eventually get in there with the best tool of all: a wet hand. Once the dough is well mixed, smooth it over – again with a wet hand – cover the bowl and leave to prove for 1 hour. The dough won't rise much, so don't be alarmed.

- Now to shape the bread, Again, the water trick will be your saviour here, wet hands will prevent the dough sticking to you and you don't want to use extra flour, as it will dry out the dough. In your hands, form the dough into a shape about the size of your tin. Roll the shape in the mixed seeds. Line a 1-litre bread tin with baking parchment, so it overhangs the edges, and place the shaped loaf into the tin. Leave, loosely covered, to prove for 1 hour. The bread should visibly rise, but do not expect it to double in size, we are dealing with 100 per cent rye flour here, so it will be heavier than regular bread.

- Preheat the oven to 200°C fan and bake for 1 hour, then take out of the tin and leave to cool on a wire rack. I recommend patience: try not to cut into the bread before it is fully cool, or even until the next day. I use this to make my Brown Shrimp, Mayo, Egg and Pickles on Rye (see page 30) but it's good with anything. Slathering it with butter and Tangerine Compote (see page 238) turns it into an almost-dessert.

- TIP • Use up any stale rye bread in Rye Bread and Apple *Sharlotka* with Spiced Custard (see page 226). Or, for a savoury use, try rye bread croutons. Cut the bread into cubes, toss it in oil, sprinkle over sea salt and bake until crisp, then use to top broths, stews, or eat as a delicious crunchy snack.

Mum's Ciabatta

My mum developed this recipe for me, so I could start making Chicken Cotoletta Sandwiches for myself and the kids (see page 119). If you want crusty ciabatta, add a tray with hot water to the bottom of the oven to create steam. The dough may be a little tricky to make the first time, as it's so wet. A dough scraper really helps. I have a very cheap plastic scraper that I've had for years, but it is worth investing if you can in a big metal one, which can be used for all sorts of things. It is very useful for cutting through dough, or for cleaning surfaces that have lots of muck or dry dough stuck to them! You will need two baking trays for this.

- ·· 350ml water
- ·· 7g sachet of fast action dried yeast
- ·· 10g sea salt
- ·· 7g caster sugar
- ·· 20ml olive oil
- ·· 450g strong white bread flour, or '00' flour, plus more to dust
- ·· fine semolina, to dust (optional)

- • Whisk the measured water, yeast, salt, sugar and oil together and mix in the flour with a spatula. The dough will look rather loose and paste-like, but do not panic. Wet your hand lightly and pat it down so it looks smooth rather than craggy. Cover the bowl tightly. If it's winter and your kitchen is cold, leave it in there overnight. If it is warm, put the bowl in the fridge for 8–12 hours or overnight. Because it's so easy to do (just mixing everything together with a spoon), I usually make my dough in the evening, once the kids are in bed. I then leave it overnight in my fridge and pick up the process the next day.

- • Next day, take the bowl out of the fridge and uncover it. The dough will look risen, but rather wet. This is how it should be.

- • Line 2 flat trays with baking parchment and dust them with flour or semolina.

- • QR CODE • *Wet your hands to prevent the dough sticking to them, and, keeping the dough in its bowl, loosen it from the bowl with your fingers. Now pull up the sides at points East, West, North, then South, one by one, folding them over themselves and letting drop, turning the bowl by 90° each time. Repeat until the dough becomes firmer. Cover the bowl, leave at room temperature and wait 30 minutes. Now repeat the stretching and folding process. Each time you will notice the dough seems a little bouncier. Repeat the 30-minute wait, then stretch and fold another 2 times. All in all, you should have done it 4 times. This is a good recipe to get on with when you have your taxes or lots of other boring admin to do. Or it's also a very good way to avoid doing all those things!*

- • *After all the stretching and folding and the final 30-minute rest, your dough will seem more 'together': smoother, bouncier, manageable. Dust a work surface very well with flour and pour the dough on to the floured surface.*

- • *Now dust the work surface and a dough cutter or knife with a little flour, and also lightly dust the top of the dough. Cut the dough into 6 equal parts. It will be very wet and wobbly. A dough cutter is very useful here. It will all be sticky, but do have faith. Make sure your work surface is well floured and shimmy the cut pieces of dough around with the dough scraper to bring them together, then lift them up and place, well spaced-out, on the lined, floured trays, any seams facing down.*

- • Dust very generously with semolina or flour, then cover loosely with a tea towel and leave them somewhere warm for 30 minutes. Preheat the oven to 220°C fan. Put 2 baking trays into the oven. If you want a crust on your ciabatta, add a

roasting tin half-filled with hot water to the bottom of your oven. Because I like the crust soft on my sandwiches, I don't bother.

- Now take the top hot baking tray out of the oven and (with some help if needed) transfer the baking parchment with 3 of your ciabattas on to it. Put it into the oven. Repeat with the lower hot baking tray.

- Bake for 15 minutes, then take the water tray out, if using, being careful not to splash yourself. Bake for another 15 minutes until the rolls look crusty and golden. If you tap the bases, they should sound hollow.

- Transfer the rolls to a wire rack to cool down. These are incredible with Chicken Cotoletta Sandwiches (see page 119), or indeed any other kind of sandwich.

Seeded Crispbreads

These are quick, easy and can be used as a savoury biscuit. We like them with cheese or dips and crunchy veg. Or you could add an extra 20g sugar and eat them as sweet biscuits. They become wonderfully crisp once they cool down. I once heard someone from the E5 Bakehouse talk about how amazing camelina seeds are on the Honey & Co podcast (listen to it while you make these, you won't regret it) and they are right. If you can find camelina seeds quite easily, do give them a go. Their other name, 'Gold of Pleasure', is correct when you know how to use them. Otherwise pumpkin and sunflower seeds work beautifully too.

- 270g plain flour, plus more to dust
- ¼ tsp sea salt
- 20g caster sugar
- 4 tbsp untoasted mixed seeds (see recipe introduction)
- 100ml water
- 100ml olive oil

- Mix all the dry ingredients together in a bowl. Heat the water with the oil in a saucepan and bring to a simmer, then take off the heat, pour it, hot, into the dry ingredients and mix well. You will have a wet, oily dough. Leave it in the bowl to rest and cool down for an hour or so, until it reaches room temperature. I sometimes take it outside in the garden to speed things along.

- Meanwhile, line 2 baking sheets with baking parchment and preheat the oven to 200°C fan.

- Dust a work surface with flour and cut the cooled dough in half. Roll out each piece of dough as thinly as you possibly can. You will have to dust the top of the dough as well as your rolling pin and have a certain lightness of touch, as if you press too hard the soft dough gets easily squashed and stuck to the work surface.

- If you can manage it, roll each piece of dough out into a 1–3mm-thick sheet (25–30cm in diameter) and cut it into 3cm-wide strips, then cut those into roughly 8cm lengths. Transfer the crackers to the prepared trays.

- Place the trays in the oven and bake for 10–15 minutes. Halfway through, swap the trays around, so they bake evenly. Check the crackers; they should be light golden brown and thoroughly dried out; they may need another 3–5 minutes.

- Transfer the crispbreads to a wire rack to cool down and crisp up.

A Very Good Vegetable Stock

If you make this stock, you will never feel the lack of meat in this book's broths, because it has so much flavour. You could double the quantity and freeze it, for almost-instant future lunches. The trick of soaking mushrooms and seaweed in cold water instead of hot was taught to me by my friend, Japanese cookbook writer and teacher Yuki Gomi. This step is optional, but if the dish you are using this stock for contains mushrooms, or if you just want a simple broth to go with noodles, I recommend you do it, for deeper umami flavours.

·· 50g dried porcini, wild mushrooms or shiitake (optional)

·· 50g dried kombu or dulse (optional)

·· 1 large onion, peeled and left whole

·· 2 carrots, scrubbed

·· 2 leeks (optional)

·· 1 parsnip, or parsley root, scrubbed, or ¼ celeriac, peeled

·· 2 celery sticks

·· 2 tbsp flavourless oil

·· 4 garlic cloves, peeled

·· a few thyme sprigs

• Put the mushrooms and kombu, if using, in a bowl, pour over 2 litres of cold water and leave to soak overnight. Take the mushrooms out, slice them, then return. The seaweed has done its work now and it can be composted, or just munch on it (it won't have masses of flavour, but it is good for you).

• Cut the vegetables, apart from the garlic, into 1cm pieces if you have time, or grate the hard vegetables on the coarse side of a box grater. If you use leeks, cut the green bits into large pieces and the white parts into small. You add the green parts when you add the water later.

• Heat the oil in a heavy-based pan and add the onion. Cook for about 10 minutes over a medium-low heat, stirring from time to time, until it softens and blushes a little here and there. Now, if you have time and patience, take the onion out and sauté the rest of the vegetables, apart from the green parts of the leeks and the garlic, in batches, again seeking out softness, sweetness and colour. Put all these sautéed vegetables in a large stockpot and add the garlic and thyme. Cook over a medium heat until you can detect the gentle, intoxicating waft of garlic.

• Pour the sliced mushrooms and their liquid, if using, into the pot, making sure you leave the gritty residue behind. Add the green parts of the leeks, if using, too. Cook for 40 minutes over a medium heat, then leave to cool.

• Now fish out the green parts of the leek. Your stock is ready and full of flavour.

Green Tops Paste

Use this as a spread on toasted bread, or stir it through potatoes and grains, or stuff into aubergines (when they are in season) before roasting. It's a versatile, beautiful thing. You do not have to use harissa or adjika if you don't have it, just add 1 tbsp each of good vinegar and honey instead.

- 200g nuts (walnuts are traditional, but just choose a nut that's definitely fresh and tastes good)
- 300g carrot tops, or other leafy vegetable tops (see overleaf)
- 100g dill or any other soft herb (this is a good use for the tired ones at the bottom of the fridge)
- 3 tbsp cider vinegar (or any vinegar you have), plus more if needed
- 3 garlic cloves, or to taste
- dash of pomegranate molasses
- 1 tbsp harissa or adjika (optional)
- a little extra virgin olive oil, or unrefined sunflower oil, if needed
- sea salt

- There is no need to toast the nuts here, though I know that feels like a real travesty. If you feel like your nuts are not quite at their best, give them the gentlest roasting in the oven (roughly 8 minutes at 180°C fan).

- If you can be bothered/are a purist/enjoy the sensation, please do go ahead and do all the grinding in a mortar and pestle. If you are short of time, chop through the nuts roughly. Put them in a food processor with the vegetable tops.

- All soft herbs apart from tarragon have pretty soft stems, so do not throw them away, use them in this recipe. Chop through the herb leaves and stalks roughly and add them to the vegetable top mixture.

- Add the vinegar, garlic, pomegranate molasses and harissa, if using, add 1 tsp salt and give it all a really good blitz. You should have a thickish paste. If it doesn't blend too easily, add some more vinegar or a few tablespoonfuls of oil. Make sure you taste it, it should be well seasoned. If it tastes underwhelming, it probably does not have enough salt, so just add a little more and blitz again.

- If you want to keep this paste for a while, pack it tightly into a jar and pour over unrefined sunflower oil or olive oil to seal.

- Traditionally, this paste is served with meat and polenta, but I do love it on toast as a healthy snack that will see you through an afternoon of work, or looking after a toddler.

- **TIP • This paste can be used pretty much as any pesto would. You can toss pasta through it, or use it to swirl into soups. Or cook a whole bunch of beans or chickpeas and stir the paste through while they are still hot. It would also be good stirred through some roasted beetroot, or used as a sauce for poached chicken for a kind of a Georgian *pkhali-satsivi* vibe.**

'I came across an Abkhazian
recipe called *acharkhal*.
All sorts of green tops
that you would normally
discard can be used'

By the Author

Green Tops Paste

'When we moved into our new home a couple of years ago, we immediately got rid of the lawn in the little garden at the back. Lawns do nothing for the environment or for us, and they look sterile to me. So we stuck in some wooden planks to mark up a vegetable patch.

One of the first things that I planted, having been told it was an encouragingly easy crop, was radishes. Very soon they sprung into action and spindly tender stems quickly turned into flamboyant outbursts of parakeet green. But that's all it was – a visual fanfare – underneath, the roots were dystrophic. All the Sun's and Earth's energy had been sucked up by the show of feathery leaves, or perhaps my soil was just wrong for radishes! I like radish leaves and they are great in salads, but, after a while, there were just too many of them and I started looking into different uses.

This is when I came across an Abkhazian recipe called *acharkhal* (see previous page). All sorts of green tops that you would normally discard can be used, such as those of carrot, kohlrabi and turnips as well as foraged herbs like young dandelions, nettles and wild garlic. Chard, spinach and beetroot tops would also work. So next time you have a gardening disaster like mine, don't throw the greens in the bin. *Acharkhal* is such a good recipe which will use them up, and, covered with oil, it will keep in the fridge for ages.'

Easy Honey and Caraway Kraut

I will admit, I can no longer be bothered to put lots of effort into bashing cabbage around to make kraut. I make this recipe instead, which requires very little effort. It was so easy to make that, when my mum stayed over during a grim winter month and we tested recipes for this book together, we would keep making batches of it incessantly, 'Just to make sure the recipe works'. During two weeks in particular, when we tested most of the cakes, come evening we would crave something very savoury and really simple for dinner. We would pile some kraut and shallots on to our plates, then add some toast and canned garfish or sardines. We'd balance the plates on our laps and watch a series set in Corfu. Perhaps this meal was suited better to a Nordic noir in its atmosphere, but it also went just fine with our dreams of sunshine, air filled with the heavy scents of Mediterranean herbs, waves rustling against the shore.

···

- 1.6 litres water

- 4 tbsp sea salt

- 2 tbsp honey

- 3kg white cabbage

- 350g carrots, or beetroot and a big knob of ginger

- 2 tbsp caraway seeds

- toast, canned fish and sliced shallots, to serve

- Clean a 3-litre jar with an eco-friendly detergent and hot water. This is the extent that I go to when prepping my jars for fermentation. Whatever you do, do not use aggressive chemicals around the place and implements you use when fermenting. Fermentation is life, so don't kill it.

- To make the brine, heat the measured water until it's hot enough to dissolve salt. Mix the salt through to dissolve, then let it cool to warm and whisk in the honey (warm water won't destroy honey's micronutrients).

- Trim the very end (usually dry) bit of the cabbage stalk. Slice the cabbage, including the core. I cut the core into thin slices, then across into matchsticks.

- Grate the carrots on the coarse side of a box grater. You can use beetroot if you fancy a pink kraut, in which case also add a big knob of roughly grated ginger, skin and all.

- Mix the sliced cabbage, carrots (or beetroot and ginger) and caraway together and pack it into the jar as tightly as you can. Then pour in the brine (it should be enough), poking at the cabbage with a fork or a chopstick to make sure all the brine makes it to the bottom. Even though we haven't punched the cabbage, it will still release its own juices. Cover with a lid and turn the jar on its head if you know it won't leak, otherwise just upend it a few times to make sure the brine is everywhere and there are no air pockets.

- Leave in your kitchen for 3–4 days, then taste it. When it is as sour as you'd like it to get, put it in the fridge or somewhere cool. It will keep in the fridge or a cool cellar for up to 5 months. Eat it with toast, canned fish and sliced shallots and dream of sunshine.

Fermented Mirepoix

A few years ago, I went to a restaurant near Bristol called The Ethicurean. After a mind-blowing meal, the chefs gave me a massive jar of their fermented mirepoix vegetables and this ferment is inspired by that very jar.

This is great used as a pickle, but I love cooking with it: fried in some oil, it makes the most fantastic base for a broth or a soup.

....

- ·· 1 small celeriac
  (total weight about 350g)

- ·· 2 large carrots
  (total weight about 200g)

- ·· 2 parsnips
  (total weight about 300g)

- ·· 2 large celery sticks
  and leaves (total weight
  about 150g)

- ·· 1 garlic bulb, cloves peeled

- ·· 10g sea salt

- ·· 500ml water

- Peel the celeriac, making sure you cut away all the grooves that may still be holding soil in them. For the carrots and parsnips, if organic, just scrub, don't peel. Now you can either chop all the vegetables and the garlic very small – another great knife skills opportunity – or use the coarse side of a box grater, though the latter will make for a sloppier result.

- Dissolve the salt in the measured water by heating it in a saucepan, then let the brine cool down. Put the vegetables into a jar (see the previous page for how to prepare the jar for fermentation) and pour over the brine. Close the lid and leave in the kitchen for a couple of days. Once you are happy with the flavour, keep the jar in your fridge for up to 3 months.

....

- **TIP** • **This is so versatile that it can be used as a pickle or even as part of the fixings when you are having a tortilla night. It can be used in a cheese toastie for a sour kick. Or you can also, of course, use it as a regular mirepoix/ soffritto. Fry some chopped onions in oil until golden and sweet, using the mirepoix brine to deglaze the pan if it gets dry. Add some of the mirepoix veg themselves and cook for a few minutes to soften, then use this as a base for a broth, borsch or stew.**

....

Quick Fermented Chilli Sauce

You can ferment vegetables that have been cooked! My mum blanches and presses aubergines before fermenting them, while Bessarabians cook onions and carrots and then stuff them into peppers with some cabbage, fermenting it all in brine for a delicious pickle. In this recipe we cook the chillies to remove their skins and also to make the process much faster. Instead of using brine, the cooked chillies are layered with salt and they release water to create their own brine. You need roughly five per cent by weight of salt to cooked pepper pulp.

· 5 large garlic cloves, peeled

· 800g red peppers

· 200g red or green chillies

· about 35g sea salt

· 1 tsp caster sugar (optional)

• Slice the garlic as finely as you can.

• Preheat the grill and grill the peppers and chillies for 5–10 minutes or until the skins look blistered. Your aim here is to be able to take the skins off and soften the flesh a little, but do not panic if you forget about them and they cook quite a bit. Put them into a bowl and cover with a solid cover that won't let the steam escape. (There are eco-friendly stretchable bowl caps on the market these days.)

• After about 5 minutes, the skins should be easy to peel off. When you open the large peppers, they may have some water in them, so pour that into the 400ml jar you will be using (prepare the jar for fermentation as on page 282). Discard the stalks and seeds and then chop the flesh into a rough pulp. Weigh the pulp: I had just over 700g here, so 5 per cent of salt came up to 35g. Add the salt to the pulp with the garlic and mix well. Put the peppers, chillies and garlic in the jar, finishing with a few slivers of garlic.

• Check the next day: the garlic slivers on top should be covered with brine and there should be no air pockets in the jar. If it isn't and there are, push everything down a bit with a fork and add a little water and the sugar, if using. Leave to ferment for 2 days in the kitchen. The brine should become bubbly, and, after 5 days, the garlic should taste pickled rather than raw.

• When ready to use, drain off the amount of peppers, chillies and garlic you want (keep the brine as seasoning for broths or stews) and blitz them into a spiky, sour condiment that is good to use on anything you would use a chilli sauce on.

Kefir Cheese

This is not dissimilar to labneh, though I find that freezing the kefir first and then draining it gradually is an effective way of making this cheese. It's so good eaten in the same way as any cream cheese would be: spread on toast, or even used in cake icing. Use the whey to make bread or dumpling dough, or use it to brine chicken.

·· 2 litres kefir

- Pour the kefir into a freezer-proof container, cover with a lid and freeze.
- Put the frozen kefir into a sieve lined with muslin over a bowl. (You may want to saw the block in half first, to make this easier.) As the kefir thaws, the whey will separate and drip through into the bowl, leaving its cheese in the sieve.

Serves 4–6

Kefir Cheese Dip
with Gherkins and Walnuts

This dip idea comes from Bulgaria. I love the idea of gherkins, walnuts and olives together; so good to dip bread or vegetables into. You can put all sorts of things on and into this cheese. A swirl of good olive oil and fried capers, rose harissa and roasted almonds, roast pepper purée and sumac… excitingly, endless possibilities.

·· 1 quantity Kefir Cheese (see above)

·· 1 garlic clove, crushed

·· 100g fermented gherkins, chopped

·· handful of dill and parsley leaves, chopped

·· 30g walnuts, lightly toasted

·· handful of olives

·· 1 tsp olive oil

·· sea salt

- Mix the cheese, garlic, gherkins, herbs and ½ tsp salt and spread it on a plate.
- Sprinkle over the walnuts and olives and drizzle with the oil. Eat with some crispbreads (see page 277 for homemade).

Crispy Pickled Shallots

There is a restaurant in Marylebone called Carousel, I have cooked recipes from my books there six times. Once I decided to put dumplings on the menu, both for the starter (*manti*) and for the broth (Azerbaijani *dyushbara*). I was serving 50 covers every night for six days, so we needed 500 dumplings every night! We had to make all 3,000 of them during Monday's prep. While I was busy practising this dumpling mindfulness with one of the chefs, another chef, Ruaridh Emslie, made these crispy shallots to accompany the dumplings. I thought the technique of pickling the sliced shallots in mild vinegar (he used rice vinegar) and then drying and shallow-frying them was genius. I highly recommend you make these and use them… in so many things! On top of dumplings, in stews, thick soups and sandwiches… or just grab a handful and stuff them into your mouth every time you pass the container. They are so brilliant. They are photographed on pages 55, 197 and 199.

- ·· 500g shallots or onions
- ·· 100ml rice vinegar, or another mild vinegar
- ·· 200ml vegetable oil
- ·· 50g brown rice flour (I've used white, wholemeal and even buckwheat before)
- ·· sea salt

- QR CODE • *Trim each end of the shallots or onions carefully, making sure to leave the roots intact, then score the skins lengthways and peel them off. Cut off a thin slice from the side of each so it is stable. Slice into fine-ish (2mm) slices, but not too fine, as you don't want them to burn instantly. The most important thing is to keep the slices the same size so they cook evenly.*

- Put them in a bowl and cover with the vinegar and a pinch of salt. You want them to pickle for 15–30 minutes. Then drain them; you can use the vinegar in dressings, don't chuck it.

- Heat the oil over a medium-low heat in a large frying pan. To drain the shallots or onions efficiently, have a tray covered in kitchen paper ready, or a fine sieve suspended over a bowl.

- QR CODE • *Pat the slices as dry as possible with kitchen paper, then put them in a bowl and run through the slices with your fingers to separate the rings a little.*

- *Flour the shallots or onions just before you are ready to fry. (If you leave them in the flour they will absorb it and become clumpy and wet.) So put the flour in the bowl of sliced shallots or onions and toss it about to coat, then shake off the excess flour. Throw a slice into the hot oil: if it sizzles straight away, you're ready to fry. Cook them in batches if necessary; they should be able to fit into the pan in a single layer, without overcrowding.*

- *Fry for about 3 minutes, but watch them. As soon as they are golden (as in the photo on page 199), take them out with tongs or a spider and drain them on the kitchen paper-lined tray or in the sieve. Remember they will continue cooking for a couple of seconds after you take them out, so don't cook them until they are too brown, or they will taste acrid.*

- Once cool, they keep well in an airtight container. If they do lose their crispiness after a while, just stuff them into a sausage sandwich.

Muhabbat's Xinjiang Sauce

I was meant to travel from Siberia to Tashkent in 2020, recreating my grandmother's journey in the 1950s. Alas, it was not meant to be. But the desire to explore more Central Asian recipes remained. Luckily my friend Rachel Evenden has been numerous times and this is her chef friend's famous dumpling sauce. Muhabbat and her family are Uyghurs living in Bishkek, Kyrgyzstan. Uyghurs are a Turkic ethnic group native to Xinjiang in North West China. Muhabbat is head chef at Naval Cafe, where, apart from this sauce, she also makes amazing *langman* noodles, *manti* and so much more. Don't skip through this: make it!

- 1 tsp each caraway seeds, fennel seeds and Sichuan pepper

- 1 tsp brown sugar or jaggery

- 4 garlic cloves

- small piece of ginger

- 4 tbsp chilli oil

- 1–2 tbsp Guilin-style chilli sauce

- 4 tbsp tamari or soy sauce

- 4 tbsp Chinese black vinegar, or another vinegar

- 2 spring onions, chopped

- Lightly toast the caraway and fennel seeds and Sichuan pepper in a dry frying pan until you can sense the warm aroma.

- Put them into a mortar and pestle with the sugar and roughly chopped garlic and ginger. Bash and grind into a paste.

- Mix with the rest of the ingredients and serve with dumplings.

Crispy Chicken Skin

I love crispy chicken skin. It's not often I have some that isn't used in a recipe, unless I'm making Chicken Cotoletta Sandwiches (see page 120 for a photo). I then collect them, freeze them flat and cook from frozen into crispy golden shards. They are amazing crumbled over pretty much anything. You can also eat them like a canapé with a mayonnaise dip or a mousse. But more often than not, I just scoff most of them as they are.

- 6 chicken breast skins

- Preheat the oven to 200°C fan.

- Put the skins on a large baking tray lined with foil and roast for 5–10 minutes until super-crispy.

Clarified Butter

I love clarified butter. It is very easy to make; all you are doing is heating butter up gently in a bain-marie until the milk solids and water separate from the butter fat. You are left with a tasty clear liquid which has a very high smoking point and a long shelf life. Essentially that's why people made it in hotter climates, to keep it for longer. This is the way I make mine; you can use a bowl instead of the top saucepan, but I find, because it heats up, it's good to have something with a handle for efficient (and safe) pouring-off at the end.

·· 500g unsalted butter

- QR CODE • *Find a medium saucepan and a smaller pan that will fit into it without touching its base. Put water into the bigger pan, then the butter into the smaller pan; you are essentially making a bain-marie. Cook over a medium heat for 20–30 minutes; watch the water in the bain-marie and top it up if it evaporates.*

- *About 8 minutes later, the milk solids and foam will rise to the top. Cook the butter until the solids come together and you can easily skim the mass off. (I collect them sometimes and add them to bread dough, but you can discard it.) At the end you will have all the clear butterfat on top and a few more milk solids at the bottom. Pour the clear liquid off into a bowl or a container, leaving the milk solids behind.*

Bulgarian Spice Mix (*Sharena Sol*)

Sharena sol means 'colourful salt' and it is indeed that, both in flavour and appearance. It is used to flavour many dishes, as you would use a Middle Eastern mix such as za'atar. You can use it in marinades for vegetables, meat and fish dishes. Or you can use it as finishing salt: it is excellent on eggs and in salad dressings. The mix in Bulgaria does not always contain salt, so you can omit it if you like to have better control of your seasoning.

·· 2 tbsp each toasted pumpkin seeds and dried summer savory

·· 1 tbsp each dried fenugreek leaves and dried oregano

·· ½ tsp each dried mint, hot paprika and sea salt

- Grind everything together in a mortar and pestle or a spice grinder. Keep in an airtight container. It's best used fresh because of the seeds, though it will keep for a couple of months.

Ingredients

Brown rice

We are obsessed by this stuff in my family. We make big batches of it and then use it in different recipes. We are often advised by public health bodies to use rice up very quickly, but as long as you chill it, we have found we can happily use it for the following 2–3 days, making anything from a simple egg-fried rice to Saffron Broth with Chickpea and Rice Balls to Rice Salad to Get Creative With (see pages 37 and 147). It really is a staple in our house and I recommend you try batch-cooking it, too; it makes weekday meals so much easier.

Buckwheat flour

As you may have noticed, I am made half of dill and half of buckwheat flour. In all seriousness, we used a lot of buckwheat groats when I was growing up, but buckwheat flour was something I only read about in old Ukrainian cookbooks, as it wasn't used at all in my family. I have started using it a lot in the UK and I love it! The flavour is superb and it works so well in cakes and biscuits. But if you can't find it, plain flour will work in most recipes where I call for buckwheat.

Kefir or *ryazhanka*

I use a lot of sour milk products, especially kefir and its beautiful cousin *ryazhanka*. To my delight, these have become easy to find in shops and online in the past few years. *Ryazhanka*, my favourite milk product, may also be sold as 'baked milk kefir' as this is exactly what it is. If you are deft with making kefir or yogurt, *ryazhanka* is very easy to make at home, too (the recipe is in my previous book, *Summer Kitchens*).

Olive oil

We use this a lot to add to cooked dishes (such as stews and beans) in the serving plate, as the Italians do. Also, it is one hundred per cent fine to fry things in olive oil. You may have heard it's bad for your health, but that's all lies. Please fry away in olive oil happily, even deep-frying is all good!

Salt

This is one of the most important ingredients and I buy sea salt flakes by the bucketful. I also have fine sea salt and use it to season pasta water, but for everything else it's sea salt flakes.

Season your food throughout cooking, a little bit at every stage, and taste, taste, taste. If you cook something that tastes bland, add a little more salt. Trust me, home cooks are often terrified of salt and use it too cautiously. It took working in a restaurant (Ottolenghi) for me to learn how to season properly.

I often tell you to add a generous pinch of salt when you cook onions. This is because it helps bring out the water from them, which helps them to cook without burning too easily (and also seasons them, of course).

A note on ovens

There's no getting away from it, ovens can be unpredictable. And it's almost certain that mine is a different temperature from yours, whatever the dial might say. So, for each recipe, I have tried to let you know what to look for in a dish when it's ready, as well as giving timings, so we will both get about the same results.

Shown on previous page: Clockwise from top left: Radish and Pomegranate Salad; A Small Herb and Sour Cherry Salad; Easy Crunchy Vegetable Salad-Pickle; Central Asian *Plov*; Sweet Water Salad

Suppliers

Belazu

For olive oil and rose/apricot harissa.
www.belazu.com

Bold Bean Co

For the best jarred beans and chickpeas.
www.boldbeanco.com

Clearspring

For the best unrefined (or any) sunflower oil,
soy sauce and miso paste.
www.clearspring.co.uk

Dorset Pastry

For the best, buttery-est puff pastry there is. It is well
worth the price, and you will never be able to use any
other unless you make it yourself.
www.dorsetpastry.com

Hodmedod's

Forever one of my favourite suppliers for all
things pulse, grain and flour.
www.hodmedods.co.uk

Ki Kefir

For the best organic kefir.
www.kikefir.com

Maldon Salt

I use fine sea salt for boiling water (for pasta),
but for everything else it's always Maldon.
www.maldonsalt.com

Natoora

For all the beautiful vegetables and winter tomatoes.
www.natoora.co.uk

Neal's Yard Dairy

For the best cheese.
www.nealsyarddairy.co.uk

Swaledale

For your sausages and beyond.
www.swaledale.co.uk

Super Ghee

They have fantastic stuff (including salted ghee,
roasted garlic-flavoured ghee and CBD ghee!)
if you feel too short of time to make your own.
www.superghee.co.uk

Vinegar Shed

For vinegars, garfish, anchovies, Taggiasca olives…
the whole cornucopia of the Mediterranean.
www.vinegarshed.com

Acknowledgements

Firstly, I would like to thank you, the reader, whether you have come here via my first three cookbooks or if this is your first. Thank you. Without you I wouldn't still be writing and publishers would not still be publishing. Your support is more invaluable than ever.

Thank you to Bloomsbury for this book opportunity and for letting me be me within it.

Sarah Greeno, this is the second book we have worked on and, as last time, I could not wish for a better designer (and person!) to turn my words and Joe's photos into such a beautiful book. You breathed space and lightness into my wordy manuscript.

Lucy Bannell, you are next level, one of a kind. It was a breeze to work with you, thank you for doing such expert and sensitive editing and so SO much more. I hope we get to do it again one day.

Rowan, it felt so reassuring to have your support throughout the whole process, thank you from the bottom of my heart. Lena, thank you for your brilliant suggestions, feedback and for keeping this whole ship afloat and organised.

Also many thanks to Joel Arcanjo, our Mercury among so many other things, to Laura Brodie in production, Ellen Williams in PR and Don Shanahan in marketing.

To my long-suffering husband, Joe Woodhouse. Thank you for shooting this book. What in a normal situation takes one solid week, I made you do for two and a half years. You had nowhere to run. But the book has such a serendipitous, natural feel to it, spanning seasons and homelands, it feels so special. I thank you, I'm sorry, I love you.

Dear Jo Yee, thank you for shooting and editing the videos for the QR codes in such a short time. You and your work are incredible. Oliver Smith, thank you for sorting out the technical gubbins during a crazily tough time at home.

They say it takes a village to raise a baby. It took a village to test the recipes for this book. So I thank EVERYONE. If I start doing names, I'm bound to miss someone. Thank you all.

Thank you to Ella Tarn for styling the cakes so beautifully, and to Alice Power and Holly O'Neill for the help with recipe development. Thank you Alissa Timoshkina and Tamzin for the help with the cover shoot. And thank you to everyone who kindly provided quotes for the back of the book.

Thank you Eliza Smith and Caroline Woodhouse for helping with Vilfik and general support.

Thank you to my best friend Caroline Parry, to Colin, Dot, Reggie, as always, for numerous acts of kindness and support. To Eleanor and Jimmy for pre-ordering one hundred books already (no wonder I'm so popular in Glasgow).

To all my brilliant neighbours, especially Parvin and Fatima for bringing delicious food and cakes over when Wilf was born and it was lockdown and I was trying to do it all and also write this book. Saviours.

Huge thanks to everyone who inspired me and were kind enough to let me use and reinterpret their recipes and also to everyone who supplied the heart-splitting vignettes. They added so much warmth and beauty to this book.

To everyone in Italy. To Natasha, Bobbie, Gabriella and Enza.

To my agents Ariella Feiner and Aoife Rice. I am so lucky to have been working with you all these years.

To Sash and Vilfik for being you and inspiring me to keep cooking and to keep connecting. To Sash also for all your feedback and for making me think about oniony apples (I know you are disappointed we couldn't call the book 'Oniony Apples').

And finally to my mum Olga. You are a genius, and the book wouldn't be the same without you. Thank you for helping me develop and test recipes, for reminding me of stories, and for sharing all those dark gloomy nights eating canned fish and honey kraut on toast in front of the telly after a hard day of work. I cannot wait for our well-deserved dream Greek island adventure as soon as we can.

QR Index

 Techniques Index Page

Online index of all Olia's videos for Home Food

 Walnut Esterhazy Torte

p182
Esterhazy Torte Piping Sponge

 Punched Potatoes and a Roast Chicken

p28
How To Make Punched Potatoes

 Dumplings over a Potato and Mushroom Stew

p193
How To Roll Puffy Dumplings

 Sardinian Ravioli with Ricotta, Greens and Saffron

p110
Sardinian Ravioli Method

 Rose Dumplings with Sweet Potato, Onion and Barberries

p196
How To Make Rose Dumplings

 Pumpkin and Orange Kolach

p164
Pumpkin and Orange Kolach

 Lazanky with Tomato Sauce p204 *and* Dark Greens and Noodles with Yogurt p213

Diamond Cutting Technique

 Fiadone

p169
Making Fiadone

 Bread for Eating

p215
Bread For Eating

Hedvig's Brown Butter,
Miso and Walnut Cake

p230

How To Make Brown Butter

Mum's Ciabatta

p274

How To Make Ciabatta

Big Baked Snail
with Tangerines

p236

Big Baked Snail

Crispy Pickled Shallots

p287

Crispy Shallots

Peanut and Dulce
de Leche Cake

p251

*How To Make Peanut and
Dulce de Leche Sponge*

Clarified Butter

p289

How To Make Clarified Butter

Dumpling Dough

p270

*How To Make Dumpling
and Pasta Method*

Easy Flatbreads

p271

How To Make Flatbread

Index

About the Author

Olia Hercules was born in Ukraine and has forged a career as a chef, food writer and cookery teacher in the UK. She is the author of the award-winning *Mamushka*, as well as the critically acclaimed *Kaukasis* and *Summer Kitchens*, which explores the people, landscape and recipes that continue to beckon her home. She lives in London with her husband Joe and sons Sasha and Wilf.

BLOOMSBURY PUBLISHING
Bloomsbury Publishing Plc
50 Bedford Square, London WC1B 3DP, UK
29 Earlsfort Terrace, Dublin 2, Ireland

BLOOMSBURY, BLOOMSBURY PUBLISHING
and the Diana logo are trademarks of Bloomsbury Publishing Plc

First published in Great Britain in 2022
Text © Olia Hercules 2022
Photographs © Joe Woodhouse 2022

A catalogue record for this book is available from the British Library.
ISBN: HB 978-1-4088-9910-6; eBook 978-1-5266-5081-8
2 4 6 8 10 9 7 5 3 1

Project Editor: Lucy Bannell
Designer: Sarah Greeno
Photographer: Joe Woodhouse
Food and Prop Stylist: Olia Hercules
Cover Design: David Mann
Cake Stylist: Ella Tarn
Indexer: Vanessa Bird
Printed in China by C&C Offset Printing Ltd.

MIX
Paper from
responsible sources
FSC® C008047
www.fsc.org

To find out more about our authors and books visit www.bloomsbury.com and sign up for our newsletters.